THE BRITISH NUCLEAR DETERRENT

The British Nuclear Deterrent

Peter Malone

CROOM HELM
London & Sydney

ST. MARTIN'S PRESS
New York

© 1984 Peter Malone
Croom Helm Ltd, Provident House, Burrell Row,
Beckenham, Kent BR3 1AT
Croom Helm Australia Pty Ltd, 28 Kembla St,
Fyshwick, ACT 2609, Australia
Croom Helm Australia Pty Ltd,
First Floor, 139 King Street,
Sydney, NSW 2001

British Library Cataloguing in Publication Data

Malone, Peter
    The British nuclear deterrent.
    1. Atomic weapons – History
    2. Great Britain – Military policy – History
    I. Title
    355.0335'41   UA647
    ISBN 0–7099–1790–2

All rights reserved. For information, write:
St. Martin's Press, Inc., 175 Fifth Avenue, New York, NY 10010
First published in the United States of America in 1984

Library of Congress Card Catalog Number: 84-40046

ISBN 0-312-10410-3

Typeset by Mayhew Typesetting, Bristol, England
Printed and bound in Great Britain

CONTENTS

FIGURES AND TABLES

Figures

Tables

PREFACE

Few issues so polarized British politics as did the decision of the Thatcher government to develop a new generation of the independent deterrent based on nuclear submarines and Trident II missiles. By 1982, the Labour, Liberal and Social Democratic parties had all vowed to cancel the Trident programme should fortune favour their cause at the next general election. Even Conservatives seemed restive. With Mrs Thatcher's recent electoral victory, the Trident issue has lost some of its urgency. But it will recur as defence spending comes under increasing scrutiny and the Trident programme will therefore remain vulnerable to cancellation for some years to come. This book is an effort to assess the logic and consequences of the Trident decision against the background of Britain's storied nuclear past, to consider how the several strands of British nuclear weapons policy contributed to a particular procurement decision. It also affords an opportunity to address more general questions about the political importance of military power in Western Europe.

If there is a bias to this study, it lies in the author's original conviction that Britain's nuclear weapons programme has been a rather striking success. After all, British governments have contrived to maintain a significant strategic nuclear capability — to remain, despite the protests of the French, the world's third nuclear power — without spending very much money and without cultivating a positive domestic consensus in support of independent deterrence. It is my personal view that the case for operationally independent British forces has never been stronger than it is today. If the Trident programme should be cancelled none the less, it may be because British governments have been rather too successful, too deft at securing independent deterrence on the cheap and avoiding contentious debate. Sacrifice, in short, may seem in hindsight to have been the missing condition for genuine consensus. People all too often equate value and price.

The reader will observe that while interview materials are cited in this study, sources are not disclosed. Interviews were conducted on a 'deep background' basis in Europe and the United States, with the understanding that comments would remain unattributed. In accordance with standard academic procedure, however, interviewees have been identified in a confidential annexe deposited with the Librarian of the Fletcher School of Law and Diplomacy.

P.M.
Boston, Massachusetts

To Pilar

ACKNOWLEDGEMENTS

This book, perhaps more than most, is a product of collective effort. My friend and thesis director, Dr Geoffrey Kemp, has been for some seven years now an intellectual guide, astute editor, constructive critic, necessary prod and generous advocate. He stuck by me long after I had drifted off to the Harvard Law School and he had assumed the Herculean task of overseeing Middle Eastern affairs at the National Security Council. This work could not have been completed — and might never have been undertaken — without him. My principal reader, Professor William E. Griffith of MIT, has been a warm friend and delightful companion as well as an invaluable critic and resource.

I wish to express my deepest appreciation to the International Security Studies Program of the Fletcher School of Law and Diplomacy for its financial support over the years. The Program funded part of my master's work and provided me with a generous research grant to conduct interviews in Europe in 1979. While I was in Europe, office facilities were made available by Drs Christoph Bertram and Gregory Treverton of the International Institute of Strategic Studies (IISS) in London; Dr Gregory Flynn of the Atlantic Institute of International Affairs in Paris; Dr Karl Kaiser of the German Society for Foreign Affairs in Bonn; and Dr Simon Lunn of the North Atlantic Assembly in Brussels. For their help and kindness, I am most grateful. Needless to say, I am especially beholden to the many American, British, French, German, Belgian and NATO officials who took time from busy schedules to respond to my questions and share their views.

The Center for Science and International Affairs at Harvard University provided me with a stipend, office facilities, staff support and just the right amount of intellectual diversion in 1979-80, while I worked on the first draft of my dissertation. The Rand Corporation offered me summer work in 1979 and 1980 and arranged for continuing typing support even after I had decided to move on to law school. I am most grateful to both institutions. A special measure of thanks is owed my friends and colleagues at the bar, Earle C. Cooley and Barbara L. Moore of Hale and Dorr, whose timely and generous intercession will always be remembered.

My parents have been since earliest days constant sources of support, affection and inspiration; my brothers and sisters, two of whom read

Acknowledgements

and critiqued drafts of this work, have been steady and very special friends. My wife, Pilar Bosch-Malone, has been both my closest companion and most demanding critic; she has managed to weather the trauma and tedium of my extended adolescence with love, humour and patience. It is to her that this book is dedicated.

1 THE TECHNICAL LEGACY

Britain was the first country to undertake atomic energy research and development for military purposes. In April 1940, the British government commissioned a group of scientists, later known as the Maud Committee,[1] to study the possibilities of manufacturing a 'uranium bomb' in wartime. The Committee's progress over the next fifteen months was monitored closely by Winston Churchill's scientific adviser and sometime political confidant, Lord Cherwell. When the group concluded that wartime weapons development was at once practical and necessary, the Prime Minister minuted the Chiefs of Staff:

> Although personally I am quite content with the existing explosives, I feel we must not stand in the path of improvement and I therefore think that action should be taken in the sense proposed by Lord Cherwell. I should be glad to know what the Chiefs of Staff think.[2]

Four days later, the Chiefs met with Churchill to urge 'immediate action with the maximum priority'.

After long and tortuous negotiations, Britain's wartime research and development programme was merged with the US Army's burgeoning Manhattan Project in 1943. The story of Britain's atomic efforts during the Second World War, therefore, belongs properly to a discussion of the genesis and evolution of the special nuclear relationship which obtains to this day between the United States and Britain. The object of this chapter is to outline briefly the technical development of the weapons and associated delivery vehicles which have comprised successive generations of Britain's 'independent deterrent'. This story begins properly in September 1945.

Two legacies of the war none the less merit consideration here. The first is political. The politicians, scientists and officials who had administered the Directorate for Tube Alloys, as Britain's wartime atomic energy programme was styled, and had staffed the joint Manhattan Project, shared a deep and unchallenged belief that Britain could and should develop and deploy nuclear weapons after the war. When the Labour government came to power just as the atomic era dawned in July 1945, none of their number was aware of Britain's intimate involvement in the development of the weapons soon to be dropped by American forces over Hiroshima and Nagasaki. The Ministers did not initially share but could not help but be influenced by the remarkably pervasive consensus which coloured knowledgeable official and technical circles.

The second legacy is technical.[3] By virtue of both their pioneering research at home and their later sojourn in the United States, the British were endowed with a substantial technical and material base from which to mount their post-war nuclear programme. Most important, secure access to uranium ore was available. Under the agreements governing Anglo–American co-operation, the two countries had procured existing uranium stores from around the world and had contracted future production jointly. The British had been instrumental in securing supplies for the wartime effort, particularly by inducing the Belgians to grant the allies exclusive access to the rich Congo mines over a ten-year period. Indeed, the Americans believed during and after the war that London had a special entrée to Belgian, Portuguese, South African and other Commonwealth sources. Nevertheless, London would have been at great pains to compete with the Americans, voracious and desperate for uranium, in the 'dollar hungry' post-war world. In the event, existing stockpiles coupled with contractual rights to Congo production were ample to fuel Britain's independent programme after the war.

Raw uranium must be 'separated' and enriched into fissionable U-235 or transformed into the man-made element plutonium if it is to be suitable for weapons purposes. The Manhattan Project endeavoured to produce each material by two different methods and British participation in, and hence knowledge of, these four processes varied. Electromagnetic U-235 separation, for example, was entirely a joint project and returning British scientists knew quite as much as their American colleagues. However, it appeared certain that electromagnetic separation would prove uneconomic in peacetime. The British had pioneered the second method of producing U-235, gaseous diffusion, but were familiar with only the earlier stages of construction of the Oak Ridge plants, which produced the U-235 used in the Hiroshima bomb. The Anglo–Canadian effort to produce plutonium in a heavy-water reactor at Chalk River was headed by an Englishman, Dr John Cockcroft, and British familiarity with this method was complete. The more promising graphite-moderated method of producing plutonium undertaken at Hanford, however, remained an exclusive American preserve throughout the war. Only Dr James Chadwick, head of the British Scientific

Mission, was permitted to visit Hanford.

The most delicate and closely held aspect of the wartime atomic effort was conducted at Los Alamos, where fissionable material produced at Oak Ridge or Hanford was tooled into working, air-deliverable bombs. Here British personnel participated quite extensively. Indeed, one of their number, the brilliant mathematician William Penney, was regarded by his American colleagues as indispensable. Margaret Gowing, the official historian of the United Kingdom Atomic Energy Authority (UKAEA), concludes that the returning British scientists and engineers 'knew among them most of what there was to know' about weapons fabrication.[4]

From this plateau, the British set out immediately after the defeat of Japan to develop nuclear weapons. A formal decision by Clement Attlee's government to build bombs was not taken until January 1947. The date of this decision – after the Iran crisis and after the unambiguous collapse of Anglo–American nuclear co-operation attending passage of the McMahon Act – would suggest that the determination to develop nuclear forces was in some sense a reaction to either a blossoming Soviet threat or American atomic isolation. Closer examination, however, reveals that decisions taken in late 1945 and early 1946 reflect an unmistakable military bias and indeed were informed by a political determination strangely immune to the drift of Britain's relations with either Moscow or Washington.

Sir John Anderson, formerly responsible for the Tube Alloys Directorate and now Chairman of the Advisory Committee on Atomic Energy, submitted a memorandum to the Cabinet in September 1945 calling for the formation of an Atomic Energy Research Establishment (AERE). Anderson had, in fact, submitted the same document to Churchill in June, but the Prime Minister had felt that decisions about the future of atomic energy in Britain should await the peace and deferred consideration of Anderson's proposal. Attlee's Cabinet approved the memorandum and vested ministerial authority in the Ministry of Supply, the agency responsible for developing weapons for the services. The Ministry surveyed locations appropriate for AERE's needs and a site at Harwell was eventually chosen.

Quite basic decisions confronted Anderson's Advisory Committee in late 1945. The British lacked the resources to mount a four-pronged programme as had the Americans. Which fissile material – plutonium or U-235 – should be produced and how? Officials and technical personnel who had remained in Britain during the war tended to favour building a U-235 gaseous diffusion separation plant because of Britain's long-standing familiarity with this process. Their colleagues, who had just returned from the United States, favoured plutonium production for entirely military reasons. Chadwick, in particular, was adamant — 'We must concentrate on making [plutonium] so as to produce atomic weapons as soon as possible'[5] — and his view prevailed. Heavy water was scarce, however, and thus when the Advisory Committee recommended construction of graphite reactors in early November 1945, the British embarked on the method of fissile material production with which they were least familiar.

A decision on how much plutonium and hence how many piles were necessary was clearly beyond the province of Anderson's Advisory Committee. Allocation of vast human, material and financial resources was at issue. The question was referred to a special subcommittee of the Cabinet, known as Gen-75[6] and chaired by the Prime Minister, on 18 December 1945. If, in view of military requirements, two or more plants were necessary, substantial economies could be achieved by simultaneous construction. The government, however, was concerned about the drain the project would place on vital export industries, particularly in the chemical engineering and heavy electrical sectors. Ministers agreed to build one pile immediately as 'a matter of the highest urgency and importance'.[7] A decision on the second pile was postponed until the Chiefs of Staff could state their requirements.

Attlee's reference to the Chiefs of Staff evinces the military nature of atomic energy policy at this juncture and afforded the Chiefs an opportunity to establish an overriding priority for weapons production. When, however, the Chiefs reported to the Prime Minister on New Year's Day 1946, their advice was vague and, for that reason, failed of effect. The military felt that Britain 'must be prepared for aggressors with widely dispersed industries and populations'. An atomic bomb stockpile 'in the order of hundreds rather than scores' appeared necessary for this purpose and consequently 'at least two' piles should be built.[8] The ambiguity of this recommendation has several explanations. First, British officers were remarkably ignorant about the effects of nuclear weapons; few details had been made available by their American colleagues at this point and British experts like Penney, who had observed the Nagasaki blast at first hand, were still at Los Alamos. Second, the chiefs were politically prohibited from specifying the Soviet Union as a likely enemy, although 'widely dispersed industries and populations' leaves little to the imagination.[9] Third, the international situation was unsettled and nuclear weapons were still the subject of both United Nations and Anglo–American negotiations.

Finally, it is possible that the Chiefs anticipated and were unwilling to address frankly an issue that was increasingly to plague atomic energy policy: could Britain produce enough weapons in time to meet and deter maturing threats and, if not, ought a military programme to be mounted at all? In any case, in the face of severe economic constraints and ambiguous military advice, Ministers took no action on the second pile. It was estimated that a single pile could produce only enough plutonium to fabricate 15-18 bombs annually from 1951 onwards.[10]

At this time the government authorized formation of a production organization under the leadership of an engineer, Christopher Hinton. This establishment was located at Risley, Lancashire, and charged with building a graphite reactor and chemical separation plant at Windscale. Simultaneously, John Cockcroft, who had administered the wartime Chalk River project, was named to head AERE at Harwell. Finally, Lord Portal, formerly Chief of the Air Staff, assumed the post of Controller of Atomic Energy within the Ministry of Supply. Portal was to oversee Cockcroft's and Hinton's establishments and was granted a highly unusual right of direct appeal to the Prime Minister on matters of atomic energy policy. This special access is comparable to the constitutional right of appeal to the Prime Minister enjoyed by British Chiefs of Staff and is indicative of the extraordinary importance Attlee attached to atomic energy issues. It is probable that by January 1946 even the 'inner circle' of the Labour government believed that a ministerial decision to build the bomb had already been taken.[11] When, in early 1946, reconsideration of the decision to concentrate on plutonium rather than U-235 production was urged in some quarters,[12] Chadwick argued: 'The decision has been taken to make bombs and therefore we must make plutonium.'[13] Design research on a low-separation gaseous diffusion plant was funded, but the primacy of plutonium production was maintained on the strength of this assumption.

The need to estabish an ordnance facility to fabricate weapons provided the occasion for a formal ministerial decision. Penney had returned from the American weapons trials at Bikini in 1946 and taken up his post as Chief Superintendent, Armaments Division, within the Ministry of Supply. At this time, Penney had no official contact with Britain's atomic energy programme; indeed he was closer to the American effort. In late 1946, he approached Portal with a plan for an atomic weapons fabrication establishment, which could be so isolated from the production and research organizations that it could credibly, albeit shamelessly, be described as a conventional weapons development effort. Lord Portal was apparently ill at ease with an anomaly of a full-scale programme in the absence of formal ministerial sanction and decided, after consultation with the Prime Minister, to seek a firm political mandate. Addressing himself to a small *ad hoc* Cabinet Committee, known as Gen-163[14] and again chaired by Attlee, Portal wrote: 'I submit that a decision is required about the development of atomic weapons in this country.'[15] In January 1947, Ministers authorized weapons development under highest priority conditions and approved Penney's plan for a highly secret agency to be known as the High Explosive Research Establishment (HERE).

With this decision the organizational framework for the development of the atomic bomb in Britain was established. Cockcroft with AERE at Harwell, Hinton at Risley and Penney at HERE, ultimately settled at Aldermaston, directed three allied agencies under the loose supervision of Lord Portal at the Ministry of Supply. Moreover, while in 1945–6 Britain's programme had a strong military flavour, now it enjoyed an unambiguous military mandate.

The decision to produce plutonium had been taken for military purposes but as 1948 approached plutonium production rates remained unrelated to specific strategic requirements. As the international situation darkened, Portal requested a 'review of the scale of atomic energy production in its relation to the requirements of defence'.[16] A subcommittee of the Chiefs of Staff undertook consideration of the requirements for deterring a Soviet nuclear threat which could be expected to emerge in 1957. The subcommittee was instructed to assume American involvement in a Western strategic offensive but not to assume that the United States would make any weapons available to the RAF in wartime. The subcommittee estimated that some 600 weapons were necessary and, in the absence of any information about American stockpiles, assumed that the USAF would provide 400, and the RAF the remaining 200, weapons. Windscale production was not sufficient to meet this requirement by 1957. In May 1947, two air-cooled piles had been substituted for the single water-cooled plant initially authorized in 1945, but this did not represent an increase in production rates. In 1948, for the first time, the military advanced a number and a date as targets. Ministers agreed at mid-year to construction of a third pile at Windscale and funded full-scale construction of a low-separation gaseous diffusion (LSD) plant and design research on a high-separation diffusion plant (HSD) at Capenhurst.

These decisions again reflected uneasy, and ultimately unsatisfactory, compromises between economic imperatives and strategic requirements. The sense of urgency prevented any reactor design innovations. When the third pile was cancelled in late 1949 in order to accommodate the Americans' desperate need for uranium, many at Harwell and Risley were relieved. Although negotiations with Washington collapsed yet again in early 1950, the third pile was not revived, and plutonium production remained insufficient to meet stipulated military requirements when Winston Churchill returned to power in October 1951.

Churchill, by all accounts, was both pleased and surprised to learn how far the atomic energy programme had advanced under the Labour government. The Prime Minister, who had chided Attlee for sloth, now went before the Commons and revealed what Labour had done in secrecy, affecting a parliamentarian's dismay that such vast sums had been expended without the House's approval. Final arrangements were made with the Australian government and, on 3 October 1952, 'Hurricane', the first British atomic weapons test, was conducted flawlessly aboard the frigate HMS *Plym* at Monte Bello.

The Attlee government also took steps to ensure that a strategic nuclear delivery vehicle would be available to carry Britain's atomic weapons. At no time was there doubt but that strategic nuclear strikes were the province of the RAF's Bomber Command. Alone among the services, the RAF maintained formal liaison with Aldermaston, and when the Navy expressed interest in Penney's operation, the Admiralty was curtly advised to attend to its own affairs. Similarly, there is no evidence of doubts, in any quarter, of Britain's capacity to build and maintain a first-rate bomber fleet. Aerospace technology was Britain's strength and, indeed, the V-bombers ultimately deployed by Britain in the late 1950s were the finest of their type and generation, vastly superior to counterpart Soviet aircraft and rather better than American medium bombers. Unfortunately, the force achieved full operational capability only after the marriage of thermonuclear weapons to ballistic missiles had undermined the survivability, and air defence improvements imperilled the penetrability, of high-altitude bombers.

At the close of the Second World War, the mainstay of Bomber Command was the veteran Lancaster. Production of an 'improved Lancaster', known as the Lincoln, had already commenced at war's end and in 1946 Lincolns entered the RAF's inventory in strength. With a range of 2,250 miles, the Lincoln could engage few Soviet targets, and its maximum speed of 290 m.p.h. and service ceiling of 22,000 feet compromised its utility against jet fighter defences.[17] Although some 450 Lincolns were built — some remained in service until 1955 — the Air

Staff knew that only a jet bomber could confront Soviet air defences. As 1946 began, however, only one jet-propelled aircraft, the Canberra light bomber, was under development, and it had been designed for a tactical rather than a strategic strike role.[18]

In the early post-war years, Attlee's government believed that there was little likelihood of war in the near future. In 1946, the Chiefs of Staff estimated that a credible Soviet nuclear threat to Britain would emerge no sooner than 1957 and the Defence Minister, probably in light of this estimate, issued new force planning guidance to the services. The planning guidance stipulated that the risk of major war in the next five years was to be regarded as negligible and would increase only gradually over the following five years.[19] With these directives, a distant target date for new aircraft development — 1957 — was set and the Air Ministry began to concentrate on highly sophisticated designs. There is no doubt as to the RAF's intentions — Bomber Command submitted a routine requisition for an 'atomic bomb', complete with weight and ballistics specifications, to the Ministry of Supply in mid-1946.[20] Simultaneously, work progressed on aircraft design needs and on New Year's Day 1947 specifications for three V-class bombers — the Valiant, Victor and Vulcan — were issued to the aircraft industry.

As anxiety about Soviet intentions increased over the next year, so too did concern within the Air Staff about the ten-year interim before the full complement of V-bombers would be available. In August, the RAF issued specifications for an 'insurance' jet bomber, styled the SA4.[21] Simultaneously, Valiant's design specifications were altered to accelerate development and, in April 1948, Vickers commenced work on a much simplified version of this aircraft. With Valiant development stepped up, there was little justification for the SA4 and, when the United States offered to make an interim aircraft available to the RAF in 1949, the SA4 programme was cancelled.[22] Seventy American B-29 bombers were transferred under the Military Assistance Program to Britain in 1950.[23] The B-29 was still the mainstay of the American Strategic Air Command (SAC) and, with a service ceiling of 35,000 feet, 400 m.p.h. air speed and a range of over 4,000 miles, compared very favourably with the RAF's vintage Lincolns. The United States had deployed B-29s on RAF bases in East Anglia in 1948, and by mid-1950 these aircraft had been reconfigured to carry atomic weapons.[24] There is no evidence that the RAF's 'Washingtons' were similarly modified[25] but this could easily have been undertaken covertly. In any case, the Soviet Union could never have been confident that these aircraft were not nuclear-capable.

Britain's first jet bomber to be equipped with nuclear weapons was the Canberra. Production orders were placed well before Canberra completed its first full flight trials in 1949 and squadron service commenced in early 1952.[26] It would appear that Mark I production atomic bombs, delivered to the RAF in November 1953,[27] were small enough to fit Canberra's bomb bay; in any case, the RAF let it be known in early 1954 that these aircraft, originally designed for conventional air strikes, were armed with nuclear warheads. With a top speed of some 540 m.p.h. and a service ceiling above 48,000 feet, only its limited range (2,100 miles) restricted Canberra's suitability in a strategic role. By deploying these aircraft with the nascent 2nd Tactical Air Force in Germany, however, targets within the Soviet Union could be credibly threatened and Canberra was explicitly earmarked for strategic missions. Over the next few years, the RAF procured approximately 650 Canberras; these aircraft probably accounted for three-quarters of Bomber Command's front-line strength until 1956,[28] and many remained in service in a reconnaissance role well into the 1970s. As the Canberra came on-line, Britain returned the borrowed 'Washingtons' to the United States. B-29 disposal was completed in 1954, an indication perhaps that 'Washingtons' were not in fact nuclear-capable and that Canberra's limited range did not concern the Air Staff greatly.

The RAF had initially hoped that the simplified version of the Valiant would enter service in 1953–4. In the event, the first squadron, No. 138, was not formed until late 1955[29] or perhaps later. Development and deployment of the Victors and Vulcans, in their various 'marks', took rather more time. Vulcan B-1s did not enter service in squadron strength until late 1957, and the first operational Victor squadron, No. 10, did not form up until spring 1958. Deliveries of Mark II Vulcans and Victors continued until late 1962. The target date of 1957 for full operational capability, established in 1947, had been missed by a quite considerable margin.

There can be little doubt that the delays which plagued V-bomber deployment resulted largely from the curious indifference of the Labour government towards offensive aircraft development. As early as 1946, the Joint Technical Warfare Committee of the Chiefs of Staff had recommended in a report to the Cabinet that high-performance bombers, as well as nuclear weapons, be developed under highest priority conditions.[30] The Cabinet accepted the Chiefs' report, but when Attlee directed in February 1947 that the atomic weapons programme be accorded overriding priority, he made no mention of bombers. Resources, particularly in the advanced electrical and metallurgical industries upon which the export trade depended critically, were extraordinarily scarce in post-war Britain, and any defence programme without a special claim could only languish. Bomber development enjoyed no special priority until 1949. At that point, Sir Henry Tizard, the government's chief adviser on weapons research and an increasingly vocal opponent of the favoured atomic weapons programme, focused attention upon the absurdity of maintaining differential priorities for the weapons and bomber programmes – the one was of little use without the other. In response, the Cabinet issued a new directive, establishing equal priorities for both the bomber and the weapons programmes. Only Harwell and Risley were accorded superior preference.

This prominence proved transient. The Russians detonated an atomic device in September 1949, and in June 1950 North Korean forces crossed the 38th parallel. Suddenly, war seemed imminent, and in the course of the Labour government's massive rearmament programme, the decision was taken, at Tizard's urging and with the reluctant consent of the Chiefs, to afford essentially defensive guided-missile research and development equal priority with Harwell, Risley and Aldermaston. This decision was informed by both the perceived immediacy of the threat – as a shift towards conventional defence it belied the growing emphasis upon nuclear deterrence in British strategic thinking – and, perhaps, by the knowledge acquired in recent negotiations with Washington that the American nuclear weapons stockpile was already quite substantial. In any event, the bombers were once again stripped of their priority and in practice fighter development took precedence. This ruling remained in effect throughout the closing months of Labour's administration. When Churchill returned to power in October 1951, he was forced to cut back the Korean rearmament effort. Fighter production, in particular, was sharply curtailed.

The doctrinal emphasis implicit in this decision surfaced in sharper focus in a global strategy paper drawn up by the Chiefs of Staff in late 1952. At that time, the Chiefs recommended, and the Conservative government extended, sustained 'super-priority' status to the V-bomber programme for the first time.[31] In their first six years of development, the V-bombers were accorded special preferences for no more than twelve months; they never enjoyed the overriding sense of urgency that informed and maintained the atomic weapons project.

The 180 V-bombers received by the RAF in the late 1950s were extraordinary aircraft. They could achieve transonic speeds at nearly 60,000 feet while carrying 21,000 lb of ordnance; their 4,000-mile range left no significant targets in the Soviet Union unthreatened. They compared favourably with the USAF's B-47 and outclassed the Soviet Badger medium bombers altogether. In the event, they were not 'atomic bombers', as their designers had intended ten years before; they carried thermonuclear weapons.

When the Conservatives came to power under Churchill in late 1951, the discrepancy between the Chiefs of Staff's request for a 200-strong atomic weapons stockpile and actual plutonium production capacity had not yet been reconciled. In his last months in office, Clement Attlee had authorized construction of a high-separation diffusion plant at Capenhurst. The government's objective in this decision was to increase the quality of fission weapons design by blending U-235 and plutonium; there is no evidence that serious consideration was given in political circles to thermonuclear development at this time. Enriched uranium from Capenhurst would not be available in quantity until 1956, however, and therefore when the Chiefs of Staff met in late 1952 to review Britain's global defence posture, they recommended that plutonium production be doubled within three years' time.

The Chiefs' recommendation came at a critical moment in the development of the atomic energy programme. The overriding objective of the early post-war years had been met successfully at Monte Bello; in this quest, the more challenging and attractive prospect of nuclear power had been set aside and now the engineers and physicists at Risley and Harwell argued forcefully for a substantial investment in power or dual-capable reactors – plants capable of producing both weapons-grade plutonium and electrical power. In Lord Cherwell, who had returned as Churchill's chief technical adviser with overall responsibility for the atomic energy programme, these individuals found a skilful advocate. At Cherwell's urging, the Chiefs agreed to a six-month delay in their production requirements.[32] This enabled Hinton to argue the attractions of dual-purpose pressurized gas-cooled reactors primarily on military grounds. The air-cooled reactors at Windscale were technically primitive, however favourably they compared with the Americans' facilities at Hanford and, if a brief delay was permissible, gas-cooled reactors could conserve scarce uranium and graphite. At the eleventh hour, Churchill proved reluctant to press ahead; he wanted an opportunity to negotiate with the newly elected American President, Dwight Eisenhower. After apprising the Prime Minister of the sorry state of Anglo–American relations on atomic energy, however, Cherwell secured his mandate: in early 1953, construction commenced on the Calder Hall reactors, the world's first successful nuclear power station.

Expansion of plutonium production facilities was paralleled by increased efficiencies in both Windscale's production efforts and Aldermaston's weapons fabrication procedures. In 1948, it had appeared that only a hundred weapons would be available to the RAF by 1956;[33] in that year the stockpile was estimated by the *Guardian* at 'at least a thousand'.[34] Moreover, weapons design took on an innovative character which has been a hallmark of Britain's programme ever since. In 1951, the Defence Research Policy Committee's Subcommittee on the Strategic Aspects of Atomic Energy produced a searching report on the potential utility of atomic weapons in tactical and counterforce missions.[35] As a consequence, the Chiefs of Staff issued guidelines on future weapons production, marrying designs to prospective missions. It is likely that, conscious of a comparative advantage over the Americans in 'small' weapons design,[36] the British began in the early 1950s to emphasize tactical mission requirements in the development of fission weapons. Early production at Aldermaston had in any case to be geared to the Canberra, a light tactical bomber temporarily devoted to strategic duties, and as the decade wore on, it became increasingly apparent that by the time the first Vulcans and Victors entered Bomber Command's inventory, hydrogen weapons would be available.

Very little is known about Britain's decision to develop thermonuclear weapons; unfortunately, Professor Gowing's official histories cover only the years 1939–52. It is clear that British scientists had returned from Los Alamos with a pale notion of a 'super bomb', but even initial research had of course to await completion of the atom bomb effort. The Strategic Aspects Subcommittee discussed hydrogen weapons in their 1951 report, and it is possible that the first official sanction for thermonuclear research came with the Chiefs' 1952 weapons design guidance. Certainly by that date theoretical work at Harwell and Aldermaston had raised hydrogen bomb development as a practical policy issue. Gowing notes that pessimism about Britain's capacity to produce such weapons grew as the year progressed. Penney, the country's foremost authority, doubted whether enough tritium could be produced or indeed whether the pool of scientific personnel in Britain was equal to the task. Even the perennially optimistic Cherwell told Churchill at the end of 1952 that hydrogen weapons were 'quite beyond our means'.[37] It seems likely that, despite this pessimism, research and development efforts commenced in 1952 with ministerial encouragement but without a specific mandate. Probably a formal Cabinet decision was not taken until 1954, when a decision about the standards, quantity and urgency of U-235 production at Capenhurst provided an occasion to sanction constitutionally the hitherto un-questioned direction of the research and production establishments.[38]

What is clear is that Britain's development efforts were remarkably successful. The first American thermonuclear test ('Mike'), conducted in November 1952, did not involve a 'bomb'; a 130,000 lb 'device', comprising an enormous refrigeration unit, was detonated. In the days preceding the test, Los Alamos personnel had happened upon the notion of employing the powder lithium deuteride, rather than pure tritium, as a fusion agent. Under bombardment from neutrons emitted by the triggering fission explosion, lithium deuteride would break apart into deuterium and lithium-6; neutron emission would further transform the lithium-6 into tritium which could then fuse with freed deuterium for a thermonuclear reaction. It was this discovery which ultimately made the transition from hydrogen 'devices' to hydrogen weapons practic-able. But for both the United States and the Soviet Union, the tran-sition took time; the United States apparently did not test an air-deliverable weapon until May 1956.[39] Just a year later, the RAF air-dropped three hydrogen weapons at fortnightly intervals over Christmas Island in the Pacific. In 1957, therefore, the gap between the British and American atomic energy programmes suddenly narrowed: Britain had trailed the United States in tests of fission weapons by seven years; of fusion 'devices' by more than four years; of engineered thermo-nuclear ordnance by merely twelve months.

By the late 1950s, thermonuclear weapons and sophisticated delivery vehicles were entering the RAF's inventory; the first generation of the independent deterrent was at hand. The immediate task then confronting British planners and politicians was to ensure its credibility in a rapidly changing strategic environment. When, in the mid-1950s, the Soviet Union began deploying nuclear-capable Badger medium bombers in quantity, the RAF had moved to secure the V-bomber's second-strike capability by adopting simple dispersal procedures and, in 1957, by dedicating Fighter Command aircraft to the defence of Bomber Command bases.[40] However, a far more serious threat to the bombers' survival developed as the Russians deployed intermediate-range ballistic missiles in increasing numbers. Interceptors could not defend bomber bases against missile attacks, and moreover the warning time available to Bomber Command was drastically reduced. The RAF's response to this threat was threefold. First, quite elaborate dispersal plans were adopted, where in the V-bombers with their weapons would be despatched in flights of four to scores of bases in Britain and around the world in times of crisis. Second, the V-bombers were fitted with powder cartridges which permitted a pilot to fire all four engines in just 33 seconds.[41] Finally, strategic warning capabilities were upgraded, principally through construction, in collaboration with the Americans, of a ballistic missile early warning station (BMEWS) at Fylingdales, Yorkshire. The RAF was confident of about four minutes' warning of an incoming ballistic missile attack and bomber crew scramble times were such that alerted aircraft would be airborne and at safety distance in just under two minutes.[42]

The Soviet Union coupled its deployment of ballistic missiles in the 1950s with development of the most extensive and diversified air defence system on earth. Thus even if, as appeared likely, a substantial portion of Britain's bombers would survive a Soviet first strike, they had still to confront and thwart in independent missions a network of interceptors and surface-to-air missiles (SAMs) designed to counter the vast resources of the American Strategic Air Command. Britain's initial response was to procure Mark II versions of the Victor and Vulcan bombers which were capable of higher altitudes and longer ranges. Extended range permitted the RAF to plan attack approaches which avoided significant air defence concentrations while it was hoped that the V-bombers could, by flying at higher altitudes, evade the lethal envelope of Soviet interceptors and SAMs. Simultaneously, a 'standoff' bomb, the Blue Steel I air-to-surface missile, was developed to relieve the RAF of the need to penetrate point defences clustered around high-value Soviet targets. These measures were seconded by development of progressively more sophisticated electronic counter-measures and by incorporation of limited defence suppression missions in RAF attack plans. As the decade wore on, however, it became clear that attrition of bombers flying high-altitude attack profiles would be unacceptable; this fact was brought home with clarity when, in 1960, Francis Gary Powers' U-2 surveillance aircraft was successfully attacked by a Soviet SAM while flying at upwards of 60,000 feet.

In 1963, the government announced that the V-bombers were being readied for low-level flight.[43] The Mark II Vulcans and Victors were modified slightly and equipped with a nuclear 'glide bomb' originally developed by Aldermaston for tactical missions. By 1964, it was publicly known that Bomber Command's war plans called for attack approaches below one thousand feet.[44]

Efforts to ensure the credibility of the V-bombers in the late 1950s were paralleled by development of second-generation strategic forces. Research and development commenced in 1955 on two strategic systems: the Avro-730 high-altitude supersonic bomber and Rolls-Royce's Blue Streak intermediate-range ballistic missile. By 1957, it was necessary to choose between them and in light of the actual or projected problems surrounding the V-bomber force, the choice naturally fell on Blue Streak.[45] Blue Streak, a liquid-fuelled missile, required fifteen minutes' warning for pre-launch preparation. The British could expect only four minutes' warning of ballistic missile attack and therefore, as Soviet IRBM accuracy improved, Blue Streak became vulnerable to a disarming first strike. In 1958, it was decided to deploy the missiles, at great expense, in hardened underground silos. By 1959, studies suggested that even when hardened, Blue Streak would still prove excessively vulnerable to a Soviet first strike. Consequently, Harold Macmillan's government began to search for an alternative.

In March 1960, Macmillan met President Eisenhower in Washington. In the course of wide-ranging discussions, the Prime Minister offered Eisenhower a site in Holy Loch, Scotland, as a forward base for the US Navy's new Polaris missile submarines (SSBNs). In exchange, or virtually so, Eisenhower offered the British an opportunity to purchase the USAF's Skybolt air-launched ballistic missiles or, perhaps later and as part of a broader alliance arrangement, the US Navy's Polaris sea-launched missiles (SLBMs). Quite probably, Macmillan could have secured Polaris on acceptable terms had he pressed the matter. For a variety of reasons, he did not. In this respect, it is noteworthy that in March 1960 neither USS *George Washington*, the first American SSBN/SLBM system, nor HMS *Dreadnought*, the first British nuclear submarine, had been fully tested.[46] Macmillan implies in his memoirs, as did government officials at the time, that Skybolt was seen as an interim weapon and that a consensus in favour of Polaris had emerged in Britain by 1960.[47] It was feared, apparently, that Polaris would not be available by the time the V-bomber force ceased to be credible as an independent deterrent. This analysis was reinforced by the biases of the services. Neither the Royal Navy, then planning a new generation of carriers, nor the RAF, deeply committed to its strategic role, were yet prepared for the transition to sea-based systems.[48] Finally, Eisenhower's desire for some broader NATO arrangement concerning Polaris contributed to, even if it did not cause, Britain's choice of Skybolt. On 13 April 1960, Defence Minister Harold Watkinson announced Blue Streak's cancellation to the House of Commons and, in subsequent debate, let it be known that Skybolt would be procured as a replacement.

Over the next two years, however, Skybolt steadily lost the support of civilian analysts brought into the Pentagon by John Kennedy's Secretary of Defense, Robert McNamara. The Kennedy administration became convinced that the missile would prove much less cost-effective than either of its competitors: the Minuteman ICBM or the Polaris SLBM. Having witnessed the strength of the Air Force's allies on Capitol Hill during his effort to cancel the B-70 bomber earlier in the year, moreover, McNamara was anxious to excise Skybolt funding from the fiscal 1964 budget before its presentation to Congress in January 1963. Thus, the time available for consultations with London was very limited. The Secretary's necessarily hasty decision came at a sensitive time for Macmillan's government and an extraordinary breakdown in transatlantic communication ensued. Each government awaited the other's move and, in consequence, the British did not request, nor did the Americans offer, Polaris. Public disclosure of Skybolt's fate in early December 1962 occasioned an exceptionally bitter crisis in Anglo-American relations. Kennedy met Macmillan at Nassau on 20-21 December and, in an atmosphere of high drama, agreed to transfer Polaris missiles to Britain.[49]

Almost immediately after the Nassau Conference, Britain's Polaris SSBN design and construction programme got under way. This effort was distinguished by both professionalism and urgency. The professionalism resulted from the Royal Navy's careful contingency planning and close co-operation with the US Navy. British observers had monitored Polaris's progress since 1955 and organizational plans for a British Polaris project had been approved by the Admiralty in June 1960. These plans were put into effect, and the Royal Navy's Polaris Executive established, on Christmas Eve 1962 — just four days after Macmillan's return from Nassau.[50] The urgency which coloured the programme reflected anxiety about a potential 'deterrent gap' in the late 1960s — fears which had justified the original decision to procure Skybolt as an interim weapons system. Morever, it has been argued that Ministers and Ministry of Defence personnel alike wished to confront a Labour government, should one be elected in 1964, with a *fait accompli*. The Labour Party, under Harold Wilson's leadership, was committed to 're-negotiating Nassau' and, it was generally believed, cancelling the Polaris SSBN construction programme. The Conservative government, in order to thwart Labour's policy, is said to have made contractual agreements so inflexible that compensation costs would exceed any potential savings from cancellation.[51] When the Wilson government took office in late 1964, it contented itself with cancellation of the fifth submarine originally budgeted by its predecessor.

Table 1.1: Development and Deployment of Polaris Submarines

HMS	Laid Down	Launched	Commissioned	First Patrol
Resolution	26 Feb. 1964	15 Sept. 1966	2 Oct. 1967	Jun. 1968
Renown	25 June 1964	25 Feb. 1967	15 Nov. 1968	Aug. 1969
Repulse	12 Mar. 1965	4 Nov. 1967	28 Sept. 1968	Jun. 1969
Revenge	19 May 1965	15 Mar. 1968	4 Dec. 1969	Sept. 1970

Source: Smart, *The Future of the British Nuclear Deterrent*, p. 25.

Among the reasons offered by Labour for proceeding with the Polaris programme was that it had largely 'passed the point of no return'.

The four submarines were developed and deployed expeditiously.[52] With a submerged displacement of 8,500 tons and measuring 425 feet in length, each vessel was designed to attain a maximum submerged speed of perhaps 30 knots. Each was powered by one British-designed N2 pressurized water reactor, fuelled by highly enriched uranium, driving steam turbines coupled to a single screw. The submarines were originally fitted out with an inertial navigation set and multiple communication systems. Very Low Frequency (VLF) transmitters were certainly constructed in the British Isles and there have been reports of others at Halifax, Nova Scotia, and Simonstown, South Africa.[53] It is likely that the VLF stations have been supported by secondary airborne communications systems similar to American Tacamo aircraft, operating out of the RAF base at Wyton. It is possible, as well, that arrangements were concluded affording British SSBNs access to American navigation and communications facilities. The vessels themselves were reputed to be 'quieter' and hence more secure from Soviet anti-submarine warfare (ASW) forces than their American counterparts.

Warhead development was equally successful. At the time of the Polaris Sales Agreement in 1963, the British were faced with an embarrassing variety of choices for missile procurement. The Americans had already deployed an 1,800-nautical-mile range SLBM, the A-2, which could carry a single-shot warhead; in production was the follow-on A-3 missile, which was capable of carrying multiple re-entry vehicles (MRV) for some 2,500 nautical miles; and, finally, the Poseidon C-3, another 2,500-nautical-mile range missile capable of carrying multiple independently targetable re-entry vehicles (MIRVs) was in development. With Skybolt fresh in mind, the British were unwilling to commit themselves to an American system whose deployment was not imminent and certain. Thus, they decided in favour of the A-3 and, like the Americans, deployed a 3 × 200–250KT MRV warhead configuration aboard the missiles. The nuclear warheads themselves presumably employed a small U-235 or mixed U-235-plutonium fission trigger and a lithium deuteride fusion agent reinforced with small quantities of tritium. Britain's Polaris re-entry system design differed slightly from its American counterpart. This was a result of a temporary breakdown in Anglo–American technical exchanges occasioned by American suspicions of the new Labour government's intentions in 1964–5.[54] A measure of Britain's relative prowess can be taken from France's difficulties with warhead miniaturization. The French did not succeed in mounting a purely thermonuclear warhead on a missile until 1975 and did not expect to deploy multiple re-entry vehicles until the mid-1980s.

Although the transition from Skybolt to Polaris in 1962 heralded the end of Bomber Command's traditional strategic role, the RAF had to plan for a continuing theatre and tactical nuclear role in Europe, the Middle and Far East. In 1957, just as the government cancelled the Avro-730 bomber, the Air Staff's Operational Requirements Branch issued specifications for a versatile strike and reconnaissance aircraft, known as the TSR-2, to replace the Canberras and Valiants. In view of Britain's East of Suez commitments, the specifications required a 1,000-mile combat radius, a 600-yard take-off capability, and a capacity to sustain Mach 2 speeds at high altitudes. On the other hand, penetration in the European theatre required a capability for transonic speeds at 'treetop' levels.[55] These demanding design specifications were in fact met in 1962–3, but costs had quadrupled over the original, perhaps understated, estimates. As talk of a 'deterrent gap' between the V-bombers and Polaris grew, the Macmillan and Home governments speculated on the TSR-2 as a strategic system, as it could, with aerial re-fuelling and high-low attack profiles, be expected to penetrate PVO Strany and engage targets in the Soviet Union.

Whatever hopes the RAF had entertained in this respect were shattered when the Labour government's Defence Minister, Denis Healey, cancelled the TSR-2 in 1965. Spiralling costs and declining export prospects made the plane appear decidedly uneconomical. TSR-2's East of Suez role was to be met by fifty American FB-111 fighter bombers ordered in 1965; its European role was to be filled in the first instance by American-produced Phantoms and refurbished Canberras and subsequently by the new Anglo–French Jaguar ground attack aircraft. Jaguar was developed as a nuclear-capable close support/strike aircraft capable of a 500-mile combat radius with an 8,000 lb ordnance load and a velocity of Mach 1.1 at sea level.[56] Squadron service commenced in 1973, releasing Phantoms for air defence missions. Finally, the Labour government announced in 1965 its intention of developing with France an advanced variable-geometry aircraft to replace the FB-111s as the RAF's mainstay strike asset for the 1970s.

These ambitious plans came to naught. In 1967, Anglo–French negotiations collapsed. In 1968, the Labour government decided to phase out Britain's military role East of Suez, and, its rationale gone, the order for FB-111s was cancelled. The RAF's mainstay strike asset for the 1970s proved to be the Vulcan B-2 medium bomber, an aircraft designed in the 1940s and developed in the 1950s. Ironically, the withdrawals East of Suez provided the RAF with what remained in 1980 the finest low-level strike and interdiction aircraft in Britain's inventory, the Buccaneer. Originally deployed aboard the Royal Navy's fleet carriers, Buccaneer became available to the RAF as the carriers began to leave service in the late 1960s. In 1968, the once fiercely independent Bomber Command was merged with Fighter Command to form RAF Strike Command, headquartered at High Wycombe. In 1969, as the third SSBN, HMS *Renown*, commenced its first patrol, Strike Command formally transferred responsibility for the strategic nuclear deterrent to the Royal Navy. Henceforth, the RAF's nuclear role was restricted to theatre and tactical support of the Atlantic Alliance, with Vulcan, Buccaneer and Jaguar aircraft. A second, naval, generation of the independent deterrent was in place, and a period of stability and refinement ensued.

When the Conservatives returned to power under Edward Heath in 1970, the most pressing nuclear issue confronting them concerned warhead modernization. The Wilson government had renewed Aldermaston's mandate to conduct nuclear weapons research as the Polaris MRV programme neared completion in 1968.[57] It is likely that initial design research on seaborne multiple independently targetable re-entry vehicle (MIRV) systems commenced at this time. In 1967-8, intelligence analysts on both sides of the Atlantic had concluded that the nascent Soviet anti-ballistic missile (ABM) system was configured for endoatmospheric interception.[58] Against such 'close-in' defences, only MIRV would suffice. Small, light penetration aids could not survive re-entry into the atmosphere. Thus, decoys would need to be exact replicas of the 'live' warheads in order to thwart Soviet interceptors. This was expensive, both because of the absolute costs of shielding the penetration aids and their absorption of payload capacity, and for a small force penetrating by 'leakage' hardly a cost-effective solution. Partly on the basis of this analysis, the US Navy's Poseidon-MIRV system had been developed and the British were similarly contemplating procurement of Poseidons in order to assure the effectiveness of their deterrent.

By 1969–70, analytical revision was under way in both London and Washington. It emerged that the earlier identification of Soviet ABMs was mistaken; the missiles were designed for exoatmospheric interception. Against these defences, a sophisticated combination of MRVs and small decoys were quite as efficient and substantially less expensive than MIRV. Wilson's leaked 'decision' to forgo Poseidon procurement came against the background of this re-interpretation; it was less a firm decision than a politically useful deferral of the nuclear issue until after the 1970 elections.

By the time Heath took office, the nature of Soviet technology had been clarified, but the number of interceptors the Russians intended to deploy remained unclear. In these circumstances, Poseidon might have been attractive simply because it would increase the total number of RVs. The ABM Treaty of 1972, however, limited Soviet active defence of urban areas to one hundred launchers. The argument for Poseidon retrofits lost much of its force and, in view of the ambivalence of American attitudes on this question,[59] the Conservative government decided to forgo missile purchases in favour of an effort to modernize Polaris front-end.

The Polaris Improvement Programme commenced in earnest under the Heath government in 1973 with the code-name 'Project Chevaline', although its antecedents could be traced to an Anglo–American research project known as 'Project Antelope' under way in the mid-1960s. A select and secret subcommittee of the Wilson Cabinet authorized continued development in the spring of 1974. Chevaline's objective was to ensure high-confidence penetration of exoatmospheric ballistic missile defences such as the Golosh system protecting Moscow. This was done by developing an extraordinarily sophisticated liquid-fuelled post-boost vehicle, or 'bus', capable of manoeuvring deep in space to confuse enemy radars as it began its descent towards earth.[60] At a given point still without the earth's atmosphere, the bus would release its load of 'live' re-entry vehicles together with an array of sophisticated penetration aids and decoys, further befuddling Soviet defences. The government never released the precise mix of live and dummy warheads. Speculation in the press tended to focus on Ian Smart's suggestion that the warhead comprised six 40KT re-entry vehicles of either the MRV or MIRV variety.[61] Senior British officials involved with the Chevaline programme, however, intimated that a smaller number of larger-yield warheads were to be deployed and that although the package had MIRV qualities, these arose 'quite as a by-product'.[62]

Chevaline was a remarkable technical achievement and engendered respect among American officials. There was, however, some concern that, while indisputably capable of performing its task, the new warhead may have been 'over-designed'. This sentiment was largely a consequence of Chevaline's very substantial costs – some £1,000 million.[63] There is no doubt but that there was a serious breakdown in cost management between early 1974, when the Wilson government authorized development with essentially unaccountable funds, and early 1977 when, at the insistence of the Ministry of Defence, a project management team from British Aerospace Dynamics (BAeD) was brought in to put Chevaline 'back on track'.[64] As a result, Chevaline almost certainly exceeded original cost estimates by about 100 per cent in real terms. Moreover, as with any programme involving frontier technologies, there were inevitable snags. After a very successful series of tests in the late 1970s, final trials in November 1980 at Cape Canaveral encountered problems. These were not, in themselves, serious, but they delayed deployment. Modifications to the *Resolution*-class submarines were necessary before Chevaline-armed Polaris missiles could be embarked and thus deployment had to be co-ordinated with SSBN refit schedules. Flight trial failures in 1980 were likely to result in delaying Chevaline full operational capability until the end of 1987.[65]

Chevaline was expected to ensure the effectiveness of Britain's deterrent into the 1990s. Nevertheless, replacement decisions with respect to the entire SSBN/SLBM system could not be postponed. While the United States was irrevocably committed to provide parts and maintenance facilities for Polaris missiles so long as they remained in Royal Navy service, Britain would have to fund infrastructure costs entirely once Polaris left US Navy service in the early 1980s. More important was the problem of submarine hull life. British SSBNs had been designed to operate for twenty years; thus HMS *Resolution*, originally deployed in 1967, should have been scheduled for withdrawal by 1987. The vessels had been scrupulously maintained, however, and could have served up to thirty years. But with a fleet of only four SSBNs – which could guarantee only one on-station in all circumstances – stretching operational life was risky. Loss of a single boat would undermine the efficacy of the independent deterrent. British officials believed that the Polaris force had to be withdrawn and replaced no later than the mid-1990s. Lead times were such that procurement decisions had to be taken by the early 1980s and, given budgetary pressures, the earlier they were taken, the better.

The RAF's venerable Vulcan B-2 bombers were also scheduled for withdrawal in the early 1980s. The switch to low-level strike profiles in the early 1960s had greatly increased airframe stress. Buccaneer, on the other hand, had stood the test of time rather better. Seemingly 'carved out of the solid', it continued to perform superbly in low-level flight. Vulcan and Buccaneer were to be replaced by the Tornado GR-1, a variable-geometry multirole combat aircraft which could achieve transonic speeds at 'tree-top' altitudes while carrying up to 16,000 lb of ordnance. The strike-version Tornado had been developed in concert with the Italians and West Germans and the latter would not be seen to procure a nuclear-capable aircraft of genuinely strategic range. Thus Tornado's operational radius when fully armed was only 860 miles[66] — insufficient to engage targets in the Soviet Union. As British officials contemplated the implications of Soviet intermediate-range missile deployments, and allied attention in the late 1970s began to focus on long-range theatre forces, they began to consider alternative means of retaining a deep-strike theatre nuclear capability after Vulcan left service.

By the simple process of mechanical decay, two technically demanding nuclear weapons procurement questions emerged on Britain's public agenda by 1980. By far the more important and emotive of these concerned the future of the independent deterrent, the physical repository of two generations of technical effort and political commitment. It is to the politics of independent deterrence that this study now turns.

Notes

1. The Maud Committee was chaired by Professor George Thomson and included James Chadwick and John Cockcroft. Its distinctive cryptonym derives from a telegram sent by Niels Bohr to Otto Frisch on the occasion of the German invasion of Denmark. The telegram closed with the words: 'Tell Cockcroft and Maud Ray Kent.' British Intelligence interpreted the last three words as an anagram for 'radium taken', fuelling fears of German progress on atomic energy. Years later it turned out that the message was intended for the Bohr children's former governess, Maud Ray, who lived in Kent. See Ronald Clark, *The Birth of the Bomb* (Horizon Press, New York, 1961), p. 41.

2. *Statements Relating to the Atomic Bomb* (HM Treasury, HMSO, London,

1945), excerpted in M. Gowing, *Independence and Deterrence* (St Martin's Press, New York, 1974), vol. I: *Policy Making*, Appendix 1, pp. 15–18. Professor Gowing is the official historian of the United Kingdom Atomic Energy Authority and enjoys unique access to still classified material. She has produced three volumes to date, covering the years 1939–52. The first, M. Gowing, *Britain and Atomic Energy 1939-45* (Macmillan, London, 1964), will be styled 'Gowing I' for simplicity here. The two *Independence and Deterrence 1945-52* volumes, *Policy Making* and *Policy Execution* will be called 'Gowing II' and 'Gowing III' respectively.

3. See, especially, Gowing II, pp. 10–12.

4. Ibid., p. 11.

5. Ibid., pp. 165–6.

6. The Attlee government's administrative approach to atomic energy issues can be baffling. 'Gen' stands for General Committee and is used to denote a non-permanent ministerial grouping. Membership often fluctuated on these committees. Gen-75, the usual group to meet on atomic issues, included senior Ministers: Attlee, Herbert Morrison (Lord President), Ernest Bevin (Foreign Secretary), Stafford Cripps (President of the Board of Trade), Arthur Greenwood (Lord Privy Seal), Hugh Dalton (Chancellor of the Exchequer), John Wilmot (Minister of Supply) and A.V. Alexander (Minister of Defence). See ibid., p. 21. On this occasion, Bevin and Alexander were not present. Ibid., p. 169.

7. Ibid., p. 168.

8. Ibid., pp. 169–70.

9. Even a year later, when the Chiefs circulated a report which identified the Soviet Union as Britain's only likely enemy, Attlee struck out this assertion. Again in June 1947, the Chiefs proposed that defence policy be based on the possibility of war with the Soviet Union and again Attlee and Bevin denied their proposition. Only in 1948 were the military permitted to assume a Soviet-Western powers conflict for planning purposes. Ibid., pp. 186–7.

10. Ibid., p. 172.

11. Ibid., p. 174.

12. Lord Portal was worried by reports of difficulties encountered by the Americans with the Hanford graphite reactors. Ibid., p. 176.

13. Ibid.

14. Gen-163 was a streamlined version of Gen-75. Dalton, Greenwood and Cripps were excluded. Ibid., p. 182n.

15. Ibid., p. 182.

16. Ibid., p. 214.

17. Alfred Goldberg, 'The Military Origins of the British Nuclear Deterrent', *International Affairs*, vol. 40, no. 4 (October 1964), p. 603.

18. *The Supply of Military Aircraft*, Cmd. 9388 (HMSO, London, 1955), p. 4.

19. Gowing II, pp. 186–7; Goldberg, 'The Military Origins', asserts that a Ten Year Rule, stipulating that the services should plan on the absence of major war for ten years, was imposed by the government in 1946. Gowing, however, has found no evidence of this and the evidence cited by Goldberg does not support his contention.

20. Gowing II, p. 20.

21. *The Supply of Military Aircraft*, p. 5.

22. Goldberg, 'The Military Origins', p. 608.

23. Ibid.

24. Gowing II, p. 311n.

25. Gowing states flatly that the RAF's B-29s 'did not carry atomic bombs'. Ibid., p. 235n.

26. Goldberg, 'The Military Origins', p. 610.

27. Gowing II, p. 235.

28. Goldberg, 'The Military Origins', pp. 610–11.

29. Ibid., p. 612.

30. See Gowing II, pp. 225–8, 234–5.

31. Ibid., p. 442.

32. Ibid., p. 447.

33. Ibid., pp. 216–17.

34. Quoted in A.J.R. Groom, *British Thinking about Nuclear Weapons* (Frances Pinter, London, 1974), p. 131. This estimate may be high. The British apparently still placed a premium on plutonium production as late as 1956, when they were optimizing plutonium rather than power output at Calder Hall. See Norman Moss, *Men Who Play God* (Victor Gollancz, London, 1968), p. 137. In a pamphlet – *Would Labour Give Up The Bomb?* (Daily Telegraph, London, 1964) – Leonard Beaton estimated the stockpile as of 1963 at 1,000–1,500 fission, and around 300 fusion, weapons. This figure has been widely accepted since. See, for example, Gowing II, p. 189n.

35. Gowing II, pp. 437–8.

36. Ibid., p. 441.

37. Ibid., pp. 438–9.

38. Anthony Eden states in his memoirs that the decision to produce hydrogen weapons was taken in 1952. See his *Full Circle* (Cassels, London, 1960), p. 368. Andrew Pierre – in his *Nuclear Politics* (Oxford University Press, London, 1972), p. 90 – asserts that a formal decision was taken in 1954 on the strength of research undertaken in 1952. The only evidence Pierre advances is a Cabinet paper circulated in 1954 by a junior Minister, Nigel Birch, which argued against development of thermonuclear weapons. A possible explanation for the discrepancy is that Churchill and his senior Ministers took the 1952 decision in secrecy.

39. M.W. Carter and A.A. Moghissi, 'Three Decades of Nuclear Testing', *Health Physics*, no. 33 (July 1971), pp. 60–71.

40. *Defence: Outline of Future Policy: 1957*, Cmnd. 124 (HMSO, London, 1957), p. 4.

41. Neville Brown, *Nuclear War* (Pall Mall Press, London, 1964), p. 37.

42. Ibid., p. 38.

43. *Statement on Defence: 1963*, Cmnd. 1936 (HMSO, London, 1963), p. 3.

44. See, for example, *The Sunday Times* (London), 9 and 16 February 1964. There was a widespread suspicion that the Conservative government's novel confidence in V-bomber penetrability may have been politically motivated.

45. *Defence: Outline of Future Policy: 1957*, p. 5.

46. John Simpson, 'The Anglo–American Nuclear Relationship', in Sixth Report from the Expenditure Committee, Session 1978-9, *The Future of the United Kingdom's Nuclear Weapons Policy* (HMSO, London, 1979), p. 232.

47. Harold Macmillan, *Pointing the Way, 1959-61* (Harper and Row, New York, 1972), p. 252.

48. See Chapter 3 for discussion of the role of the US Air Force and Navy in Britain's decision to procure Skybolt.

49. Perhaps the best brief account of the Skybolt crisis and the Nassau Conference is Henry Brandon's 'Skybolt: The Missile That Almost Split the West', *The Sunday Times* (London), 8 December 1963. See, for fuller accounts, Pierre, *Nuclear Politics*, pp. 215–43, and Richard Neustadt, *Alliance Politics* (Columbia University Press, New York, 1970).

50. John Simpson, 'The Polaris Executive: A Case Study of a Unified Hierarchy', *Public Administration*, no. 48 (Winter 1970), pp. 382–3.

51. Pierre, *Nuclear Politics*, p. 285. Professor Lawrence Freedman in his *Britain and Nuclear Weapons* (Macmillan, London, 1981), p. 32, argues that

cancellation remained a fiscally viable option when Labour came to power in late 1964.

52. Ian Smart, *The Future of the British Nuclear Deterrent: Technical, Economic and Strategic Issues* (Royal Institute of International Affairs, London, 1977), p. 25.

53. Ibid., p. 34.

54. Interviews.

55. C.J. Bartlett, *The Long Retreat* (Macmillan, London, 1972), p. 128. For detailed discussion of the TSR-2, see G. Williams, F. Gregory and J. Simpson, *Crisis in Procurement: A Case Study of the TSR-2* (Royal United Services Institute, London, 1969).

56. *Jane's All the World's Aircraft, 1978-79* (Jane's Publishing Co., London, 1979), p. 89.

57. Pierre, *Nuclear Politics*, p. 297.

58. Interviews.

59. See Chapter 3 for discussion of the Poseidon issue in Anglo–American relations in 1970-2.

60. See *The Times*, 25 January 1980, p. 1.

61. Smart, *The Future of the British Nuclear Deterrent*, p. 26.

62. Interviews.

63. *The Times*, 25 January 1980, p. 1.

64. *International Defense Review*, no. 3 (1981), p. 244.

65. P. Hennessy, 'Short Life for Stand-in Deterrent', *The Times*, 6 July 1981.

66. *Jane's All the World's Aircraft, 1978-9*, p. 86.

2 THE POLITICAL QUESTION

Technical obsolescence posed, by 1980, the quintessentially political question of replacement or renunciation of Britain's independent deterrent. At the simplest level, this potentially divisive issue was resolved with the advent of a Conservative government. Margaret Thatcher and her colleagues evinced an unequivocal determination to replace Polaris as and when necessary. The Cabinet appeared to enjoy the overwhelming support of the party on this question and the party commanded a comfortable majority in Commons. In the normal course of events, the views of the official Opposition — who as a matter of party policy opposed development of third-generation strategic forces — would have excited no more than academic interest.

Technical and political timetables do not always coincide, however, and procurement of major weapons systems often requires sustained political commitment. Prime Minister Thatcher felt bound to take a decision in 1980 about a weapons system which, if built, would not see service until the early to mid-1990s; her political mandate would expire no later than 1984. No successor to the Polaris force could be developed and deployed in a single government's lifetime. What was more important, capital investment schedules could not be accelerated in the hope of confronting future governments with a fiscal *fait accompli*; budgetary savings could still be achieved by cancelling development of third-generation strategic forces in 1984 or even in 1988. In these circumstances, it is necessary to look beyond the sentiments of the government of the day.

Domestic debate over the merits of independent deterrence first erupted in the wake of American hydrogen weapons tests in 1954 and quickened with Churchill's subsequent disclosure of Britain's own thermonuclear intentions. In one form or another, the controversy has continued ever since and, in its somewhat erratic course, a handful of persistent themes have emerged. The first of these concerns the structure of the political question itself. The original decisions committing Britain to her post-war pursuit of nuclear weaponry were, of course, taken in secrecy, in part because of Clement Attlee's anxiety about reactions within the Parliamentary Labour Party.[1] In the event, the Prime Minister's fears proved ill-founded; when, in 1952, Churchill revealed the extent of Labour's nuclear progress, no revolt raised its head along the Opposition's back benches. The party, like the country as a whole, affected indifference and Labour's leadership was able to espouse an essentially bipartisan defence policy until 1960.

From a national standpoint, however, the effects of Attlee's secrecy were enormous. By the time nuclear weapons policy came to public attention, a rich technical legacy had been amassed and a blossoming military capability was in place. Thus, the political question throughout the post-war era has been retention, rather than creation; abdication, rather than abstention. As Mrs Thatcher's Defence Secretary, Francis Pym, put it in 1980:

> The perspective in which we must view the national decision on our strategic forces is not whether that contribution is a good thing in the abstract but whether we should now plan to abandon it after making it and sustaining it without a break for a third of a century.[2]

In the domestic political setting, to renounce a strategic nuclear role was to break with decades-old assumptions while to renew it was to ally oneself with the inertial force of the past. The burden of proof thus lay with those who would effect a discontinuity, which is of no mean significance in an area so informed with risks and imponderables. On the international level, renunciation would invite the scrutiny of other powers and afford an occasion for collective re-evaluation of one's own political-military posture while renewal reassured allies and adversaries alike of the continuity of policy, presence and, perhaps, power. Again, in a country whose political classes combined a still deeply felt desire to influence the course of events with a grim recognition of national decline, the structure of the political choice has been very nearly a decisive substantive consideration.

Awareness of national decline accounts, in part, for the particular salience of a second theme in Britain's domestic debate: the nature of the relationship between nuclear weapons state status and international standing. Nuclear weapons afford their possessor an ultimate, awesome capacity for violence and, perhaps, a unique sense of national security. An argument that their possession is bereft of any political meaning is simply counter-intuitive. Rather, it is a question of emphasis. For a state in decline, capabilities which were once merely symptomatic of national standing can be seen as either increasingly significant elements of national power or increasingly embarrassing symbols of national pretension. So long as strategic forces were the exclusive preserve of the superpowers, British politics divided between those who accepted the former interpretation and defended the deterrent ever more zealously and those who believed it should be set aside in order to expedite the inevitable adjustment to a more modest, and hopefully more stable, equilibrium. The French test at Reggane thus radically altered the terms of the debate although this took time, in part because Labour leaders coupled their opposition to the independent deterrent with the smug assurance that French pretensions would soon collapse. There is a final, often overlooked, reason for the salience of this theme. In times of great technological flux, when military justifications were often seen as either absurd (if they posited the Alliance utility of British weapons) or disloyal (if they posited the national utility of the deterrent), political justifications were the last refuge of those who honestly believed that an independent deterrent was essential to the nation's security.

A third persistent theme has been economic scarcity and the consequent need for political choice among major defence roles. Coupled with sluggish economic growth, the alarming rise in the real costs of defence manpower and equipment compelled the British to retreat from a multidimensional, global military posture to a more specialized regional posture. Thus, governments have successively shed a large standing army (1957), independent strategic missile development (1960), independent tactical missile development (1962), completely indigenous military aircraft procurement (1965), a fully capable blue-water navy (1966), a pre-eminent military position East of Suez (1968), a major Mediterranean and a minor Far Eastern presence (1975). The perceived trade-off between conventional battle and peacekeeping capabilities and an independent deterrent gravely aggravated the politics of second-generation strategic force procurement. The possibility of a choice between independent deterrence and either general-purpose naval capabilities or the Rhine Army itself threatened to complicate the politics of third-generation force procurement.

The final and perhaps most consequential theme in British nuclear politics concerns the compatibility of Britain's defence posture with the political-military requirements of the Atlantic Alliance. Historically, Britain was and in some ways has remained the central conduit for the engagement of American power in the European balance; NATO was the offspring of Bevin's Atlantic and Continental initiatives. Not surprisingly, the resulting arrangement has suited British interests admirably: the Alliance has managed over thirty years to contain both Soviet power and West German potential, thus addressing London's two greatest security concerns. But the process has been costly and recognition of these sunk costs, as well as NATO's provenance and enduring utility, have profoundly affected the course of Britain's domestic nuclear debate.

Britain's role as a 'bridge' for American involvement in Europe has constrained military and diplomatic flexibility. Thus, Eden's commitment of the Rhine Army to the Continent in 1954 — in contravention of centuries of practice — vastly complicated economically unavoidable cutbacks in military manpower undertaken three years later. As a Continental commitment was seen as essentially irrevocable, cutbacks threatened politically popular extra-European roles and the nuclear force emerged as something of a scapegoat. The provision of British bases for American strategic forces similarly complicated the calculations of independent deterrence. It is likely that Attlee's calm acceptance of American B-29s in 1948 was premised upon his belief that Britain would be the second nuclear power. Once there, the aircraft could not be removed without imperilling the United States' commitment in Europe and, despite the permutations of the Labour Party, their immutable presence remained thereafter one of the most potent arguments for retention of independent strategic forces. But politics, and particularly the politics of fear, are not always rational; concerns generated by the United States' nuclear presence have periodically fuelled opposition to the independent deterrent. Finally, the perceived political utility of the deterrent has perhaps been compromised as well, because unlike de Gaulle, British governments have never felt that they enjoyed the luxury of challenging American commitment in the certainty that it would endure. French Gaullism was an irritant; British Gaullism could well have unravelled the whole structure of Atlantic defence. One consequence of this has been a peculiar sensitivity to allied and particularly American opinion in British deliberations. Ironically, another has been a desire for the military prerequisites, if not the political disposition, of independence. Having been the architects of American commitment, the British have been perhaps more conscious than any of their neighbours of the historical novelty and potential transience of that commitment. This insight, coupled with a history of military isolation and the pervasive pessimism about the future characteristic of Britain's political classes, has been the most important mainstay of the policy of independent deterrence despite decades of controversy.

Although debate has been continuous, its pitch and practical significance have varied more or less directly with procurement schedules. Thus, the controversy assumed national proportions as the Macmillan government moved towards a second generation of the independent deterrent. In its course, the Labour Party, seconded by many journals, commentators, academicians, officers and the small Liberal Party, came officially to oppose maintenance of national nuclear forces. This opposition, however, arose from an unusual confluence of events and was premised upon assumptions no longer tenable in the 1980s.

The politics of second-generation strategic force procurement were shaped in large measure by an anomalous constellation of five factors. The first of these was the Suez crisis of 1956. The Anglo–French invasion of Egypt occasioned political polarization over foreign policy questions unparalleled in Britain since the Boer War; its failure proved to be a watershed in British history. In the post-invasion malaise, Macmillan was moved to offer the independent deterrent as a mark of continuing greatness. The prominent role played by the United States in thwarting the invasion – by public protest, military obstruction, above all by economic pressure – naturally evoked a desire for political-military independence and the deterrent came to be seen in this light, as well. Military deficiencies evident in the operation's preparation and execution fuelled doubts about the direction and emphasis of the government's defence policy: the crisis had demonstrated the need for mobile, well equipped conventional forces; why then should conscription be abolished? The counter-argument that the crisis had shown quite brutally that economic vulnerability undermined political-military independence was not made as effectively as it might have been. The bitter disagreement between the political parties over Suez was the first crack in the post-war consensus which had set foreign and defence policy above the political fray; the precedent was of immense import to the nuclear debate. Above all, the crisis brought home with humiliating abruptness the change in British fortunes which, though wrought by the war, had heretofore been masked by diplomatic skill and political prestige. A period of national introspection ensued, wherein old roles, pretensions and capabilities were subjected to scrutiny. A cathartic event, Suez excised inhibitions and dramatized the need for critical examination of the assumptions of the past.

The extraordinary variety and pace of technical innovation further complicated nuclear politics in these years. The late 1950s saw the most rapid and revolutionary changes in nuclear weapons technologies. Solid- and liquid-fuelled ballistic missiles, nuclear-powered submarine launching systems, miniaturized thermonuclear warheads, surface-to-air missile defence systems, even ABM and MIRV were either in the research and development stage or undergoing deployment in this period. Cumulatively, they radically altered doctrinal expectations and severely inflated the costs of strategic systems. It happened that the British were developing second-generation forces in a highly unstable technical environment. The survivability and penetrability of the V-bombers came increasingly to be questioned. Moreover, there was a widespread impression that this remarkable technological pace would prove a permanent feature of the nuclear business, in which case independent deterrence was beyond the means of any medium power. This impression was reinforced when soaring costs and projected vulnerability forced the cancellation of the Blue Streak IRBM in 1960. For many who had favoured or opposed an independent deterrent in principle, the policy now appeared impractical.[3]

Technological developments materially contributed to a third anomalous factor in the debate: growing allied opposition. 'It was primarily the introduction of the missile, rather than the political overtones of European projects, that made American nuclear experts insistent on centralized command and control.'[4] The novel vulnerability of American cities attending Soviet ICBM deployment excited grave concern about the prospect of uncontrolled nuclear warfare; just as internally American investment in command and control capability escalated, externally American tolerance for autonomous nuclear decision-making centres declined. Coupled with political perceptions which found some resonance within the Labour Party, these views left Britons with the very distinct impression that the United States would welcome London's abdication of a strategic nuclear role. Self-evidently, American operational policy never took this course: Skybolt and then Polaris were offered to Britain on terms which preserved British independence. Nevertheless, these acts were seen as reluctant gestures towards a storied nuclear past and not accepted, as the Macmillan government would have wished, as evidence of American approval. Lack of enthusiasm across the Atlantic was mirrored by hostility across the Channel. The allies, and the Germans in particular, saw the 1957 Defence White Paper and the policy of independent deterrence as a scuttling of Britain's obligations to NATO and forward defence.[5] It was a difficult atmosphere in which both to defend the deterrent and support the Alliance. These factors in combination shook Tory confidence; coupled with the prospect of proliferation and the emergence of unilateralism, they shattered Labour's support altogether.

While the systemic implications of general nuclear proliferation and her responsibility as the 'first nth country' received considerable attention in Britain, proliferation as a domestic political issue essentially meant the prospect of West German acquisition of nuclear weapons.[6] Perhaps because victory obviated the immediate emotional need for reconciliation with post-war Germany, British attitudes towards West Germany were characterized by considerable distrust. It was of course the British who laid the diplomatic foundations for Bonn's entry into NATO, but this was done to assure American participation in European defence and was bitterly criticized by elements within the Labour Party. Indeed, one particularly astute Labour defence specialist originally welcomed the advent of thermonuclear weaponry because it 'destroyed the last case for German rearmament'.[7] Where conventional West German rearmament was suspect even within the confines of the London and Paris agreements, clearly a West German nuclear force was anathema. The Macmillan government was quite sensitive to this issue, despite its refusal to accept President Kennedy's argument that the maintenance of the independent deterrent 'might hasten the day when the Germans would demand nuclear weapons for themselves'.[8] Indeed, Macmillan was among the first to suggest a 'non-dissemination' treaty regime, characteristically as a device to foreclose West German options and pave the way for meaningful East–West arms control negotiations.[9] Within the Labour Party, however, where anti-German-ism throve, proliferation was a far more emotive issue. The American analyses which held that the *force de frappe*, itself inspired by Britain's example, would make West German nuclear forces inevitable, were widely embraced. Partly in response to this sentiment, the leadership put forward a proposal before the 1959 election for a Non-Nuclear Club,[10] under whose terms a Labour government would renounce nuclear weapons provided that all other states, except the superpowers, agreed to forgo weapons development. The Non-Nuclear Club evoked little support; the leadership's conditions made its realization very unlikely and, in substance, it was rather less radical than the Liberal Party's position. But it was the first break with the bipartisan nuclear weapons policy.

It was in this atmosphere of uncertainty that the 'unilateralist' challenge emerged and the 'multilateralist' compromise was forged. Initially espoused by an apolitical or at least extra-parliamentary movement known as the Campaign for Nuclear Disarmament (CND), unilateralism maintained that nuclear weapons were inherently im-moral; reliance upon their threatened use for one's security was there-fore ethically insupportable. A practical corollary held that stationing of such weapons invited nuclear attack. As a matter of principle, American weapons, based to a considerable extent in Britain in support of NATO's strategy of deterrence, were no more acceptable than British weapons. In consequence, unilateralism was practically indistinguishable from neutralism. So long as CND remained without the party-political structure, it was no more than an embarrassment to the labour movement, traditionally Britain's vehicle for social protest. As its creed attracted an alarming following among the unions' rank and file, the leadership became anxious and, partly for this reason, advanced the pre-electoral proposal for a Non-Nuclear Club. After Labour lost its third consecutive election — by a disconcertingly large margin — however, the unilateralist cause merged with an attempt by left-wing forces to seize control of the party and rid it of Hugh Gaitskell as leader.

It was Gaitskell who, with remarkable hubris, fired the first salvo in the war between left and right which ultimately drove Labour into opposition to the independent deterrent. In the wake of defeat in 1959, it was obvious to most that the political premisses of the party merited critical attention. Gaitskell, supported by a group of right-wing Labourites, concluded that the party must abandon its revolutionary pretensions; accordingly, he proposed that Clause Four of the 1911 party platform, which committed Labour to seek public ownership of all means of production, be suppressed. The contrary view, that Labour's failure to offer a clear radical alternative to the Conservatives accounted for its electoral weakness, proved more persuasive, and in November, at Blackpool, reform of Clause Four was rejected by a special party conference. In these circumstances, the nuclear issue could no longer be avoided. Unilateralist sentiment was widespread and the principal mainstay of consensus on defence policy — the imminent prospect of a general election — had vanished. Moreover, Gaitskell and most of his colleagues were convinced that Labour could not adopt an essentially neutralist position and survive as a mass party. Finally, both left and right reckoned that Gaitskell could not survive another defeat on an issue of principle. The left, in pursuit of much broader changes, raised its standard on the nuclear question and the leadership had little alternative but to join battle. In the March 1960 defence debates, Gaitskell made a remarkably ambiguous speech; in effect, he professed agnosticism on the merits of independent deterrence.[11] When in April, Blue Streak was cancelled, the leadership seized on this news as evidence of the practical impossibility of maintaining an independent deterrent. On these pragmatic grounds, Gaitskell was able to accommodate the primary demand of his principled opposition. The British deterrent would not be retained by a Labour government but British participation in NATO and NATO's dependence on the American deterrent would continue until multilateral negotiation could effect general disarmament.

Labour's new position was embodied in a document called *Foreign Policy and Defence*, published by the Labour Party and the Trade Unions Congress (TUC) in July 1960. The policy was debated and approved by the National Executive (17-4), the TUC General Council (18-5) and the Parliamentary Labour Party (99-15).[12] It proved unacceptable to Frank Cousins, leader of the powerful Transport and General Workers' Union and Gaitskell's principal antagonist. Tentative efforts at negotiations between Gaitskell and Cousins collapsed in personal antipathy; in any event, the former was unwilling to compromise over an issue touching Britain's membership in NATO. At the annual party conference at Scarborough, the official 'multilateralist' policy was rejected by approximately 300,000 votes and Cousins's resolution calling for 'A complete rejection of any defence policy based on the threat of the use of strategic or tactical nuclear weapons' was adopted.[13] Gaitskell contrived to view the vote as a demand for discussion rather than an expression of policy and pledged, in one of the great political speeches of the era, to 'fight and fight and fight again to save the party' he loved. So he did. Harold Wilson, who though apparently a multilateralist seemed sufficiently pliant to serve as the left's sunshine champion, bid for the Parliamentary Party leadership and failed. An intensive educational campaign was set afoot at the grassroots level and, at Blackpool in 1961, the party reversed itself and accepted the official policy by a margin of nearly 3,000,000 votes.

With the acquisition of Polaris, the heart went out of Britain's nuclear debate. The procurement issue had been settled and a superb second-strike force was to be built at extraordinarily reasonable prices. The flurry of controversy surrounding the general election of 1964 reflected somewhat intemperate Tory electioneering and not any willingness on Wilson's part to meet the nuclear issue squarely.[14] Wilson did not, of course, cancel the Polaris programme or 're-negotiate Nassau' as many had expected. Doubtless there were several reasons for this; one which is often overlooked is that Parliamentary Labour Party or TUC support for such a move, when independent deterrence no longer seemed impractical, was by no means certain. Moreover, the immediate usefulness of the deterrent as a diplomatic foil to the distasteful American plan for a Multilateral Force (MLF) suggested that renunciation of nuclear forces and prevention of West German access to the nuclear trigger might not be altogether compatible in practice.

In any case, after the undebated decision to proceed with Polaris, Labour policy statements came to focus on the third generation. The party pledged not to replace Polaris at the end of its operational life[15] and Labour governments went on to commit nearly £1,000 million to the Polaris Improvement Programme.

Multilateralist opposition to the independent deterrent responded to a specific political challenge to the post-war security system fashioned, in considerable measure, by the Attlee government. It was premised, both politically and intellectually, upon the assumptions that Britain's nuclear force was technically incredible as an independent deterrent, militarily inefficient as a contribution to the Alliance and politically unsettling as a spur to proliferation and a source of instability in Europe. Those assumptions, while never incontrovertible, were plausible in the atmosphere of the early 1960s. In their absence, the multilateralist position lost its rigour and became indistinguishable from simple appeasement of neutralist sentiments antithetical to the principles of the bulk of the Parliamentary Labour Party and unacceptable to the overwhelming majority of the British people. In the late 1970s, as decisions about the future of the deterrent neared, those assumptions seemed less and less supportable.

Britain's technical capacity to develop and sustain a credible deterrent could no longer be seriously questioned. The existing Polaris fleet was practically invulnerable to pre-emptive attack. In a decade of patrols, British submarines had never been detected or trailed by Sovet ASW forces.[16] The new Chevaline warhead developed by Aldermaston dispelled doubts about the force's capacity to penetrate existing or upgraded ABM defences in the 1980s. There was, of course, much less certainty about the strategic environment of the 1990s and beyond. With American–Soviet strategic arms control at a standstill and concern rising in Washington and perhaps Moscow over the survivability of land-based missiles, the prospect of a collapse in the ABM Treaty regime and a consequent expansion of Soviet ballistic missile defences could not be dismissed. Soviet perseverance in the arcane art of anti-submarine warfare could, moreover, eventually threaten the survivability of small SSBN fleets. But the technical environment was on balance far more stable than it had been in the years 1957–62. Uncertainties in the late 1970s did not approach the anguished scepticism which had tainted second-generation procurement decisions, when so sober a journal as *The Economist* had been led to conclude editorially: 'Without a shot being fired, technology and the small size of this island have made Britain – on its own – defenceless.'[17] Indeed, while the political credibility of the policy of independent deterrence was vigorously challenged – former Chief of the Defence Staff Field Marshall Lord Carver argued that circumstances in which it would be 'right' or 'responsible' for Britain to undertake nuclear strikes without American participation were simply inconceivable[18] – the technical credibility of that policy was never genuinely disputed.

There was, moreover, general agreement within the Atlantic Alliance that Britain's role as an independent strategic nuclear power geographically contiguous and politically linked to the European theatre contributed substantially to deterrence in an age of superpower parity.[19] The independent deterrent could no longer be characterized as a positive menace to the Alliance. While allied support could be expected to diminish if third-generation force procurement occasioned very substantial cuts in Britain's conventional contributions to NATO, such a trade-off did not appear unavoidable. Thus, while replacement of Polaris inspired general uneasiness about the related 'opportunity costs' and the implications for the conventional forces,[20] it could not colourably be portrayed as incompatible with allegiance to NATO. In contrast to the Macmillan years, there was no longer a perceived tension between the fundamental desire for military independence which has consistently informed British defence policy and the broad objective of Alliance cohesion. To the contrary, both strands of policy now argued for maintenance of independent strategic forces.[21]

Perceptions of the political import of Britain's position as a nuclear power had also evolved significantly since the early 1960s. Britain could no longer aspire to the global role qualitatively similar to those sustained by the United States and the Soviet Union. The status question underlying the Polaris replacement debate was whether Britain could long pretend to her present position as a major West European power alongside France and West Germany. The relevance of nuclear weapons to this question was difficult to deny in the prevailing atmosphere. If, as Denis Healey had once observed, a nation's political power in any particular sphere depends upon its ability to help a friend or hurt an enemy, then allied appreciation of Britain's nuclear posture afforded political influence. Economic decline had only highlighted the degree to which Britain's position in Europe and, indeed, the world, depended upon her military power and the political vantage point occupied by virtue of that power. As West German confidence in the efficacy of the American nuclear guarantee ebbed, British renunciation of nuclear weapons would quicken Franco–West German relations, perhaps to the detriment of the Alliance and very probably to the detriment of British interests. In any case, there was a growing recognition, in Conservative and Labour ranks alike, that the existing Anglo-West German-American triumvirate in NATO affairs could not long be sustained should Britain cease to be a nuclear power; in such circumstances, the stability of the Alliance could only suffer. Finally, there was an uneasy sense that British abdication might hasten the day when West Germany would set off on a national nuclear course. It was to this concern that Prime Minister Callaghan alluded upon his return from the Guadeloupe summit conference in January 1979:

> The decision on whether to proceed will have to be taken by the next government. Important decisions and issues of policy that will affect the whole future of Europe will have to be considered and I do not think that we should rush into an immediate decision without considering the political consequences of the possible acquisition of nuclear weapons by others.[22]

The proliferation argument in support of multilateralist opposition to the deterrent had thus come full circle: retention, rather than renunciation, now seemed the best hedge against a West German nuclear capability.

The practical foundations of official multilateralism had largely eroded by the late 1970s and a genuine unilateralist threat had yet to emerge. The Prime Minister's intriguing public evocation of the dangers of proliferation faithfully reflected the concerns of his Foreign Office advisers.[23] But it was also an astute opening bid for support for replacing the Polaris fleet. Decisions about the future of the independent deterrent were imminent and it would appear that Callaghan was beginning to prepare his party for a break with official policy. Had electoral defeat in 1979 not robbed him of authority, and his party of the discipline of governance, he might well have succeeded. Thus, it might be argued that, far from settling the political question of the deterrent's fate, the advent of the Conservatives broke the question wide open and shattered the prospects for consensus.

In 1978, Callaghan was forced to consider the politically difficult prospect of strategic force replacment decisions. The Prime Minister convened a small *ad hoc* committee of the Cabinet, comprising Chancellor of the Exchequer Denis Healey, Foreign Secretary David Owen and Defence Secretary Fred Mulley.[24] The committee met in conditions of exceptional secrecy to discuss both the Vulcan and Polaris succession issues. Studies on the technical and political implications of alternative options were prepared but no formal decisions were taken before the intervention of the May 1979 elections. It is clear neverthe-less that Callaghan, Owen and Healey all favoured replacing Polaris when the time came; it is also likely that a tentative consensus in favour of replacing Vulcan emerged. Apparently, only Mulley was agnostic: intellectually, he was disposed to abandon the deterrent, not least because of his intimate familiarity with the state and prospects of Britain's conventional force posture and perhaps because of his sensi-tivity to military ambivalence; institutionally, however, he was com-pelled to support replacement, particularly in view of the overwhelming consensus among Ministry of Defence civilians on this issue. The convic-tion of the other three leaders reflected not only the considerations discussed above, but also an instinctive unwillingness to bear the historic responsibility for discarding a potentially decisive military capability. It is said that Callaghan was haunted in these deliberations by the memory of Stanley Baldwin who, in a time of apparent security and real economic scarcity, had presided over disarmament only to see his country isolated on the brink of military disaster in 1940. With nuclear weapons, as Churchill had once argued, 'there will be no second chance. To abandon [the deterrent] now will be to abandon it for-ever'.[25] At the end of the day, Callaghan was simply unwilling to live with that responsibility.

To prepare the political ground for reversal of policy, the Prime Minister announced in February 1979 that a decision for or against replacement would have to be taken within two years. This broke with Labour's previous practice of suggesting that decisions need not be taken for five years or more and hence brought the issue squarely within the ambit of the election manifesto. At Callaghan's behest, new language was adopted in the 1979 manifesto:

> In 1974, we renounced any intentions of moving towards the pro-duction of a new generation of nuclear weapons or a successor to the Polaris nuclear force; we reiterate our belief that this is the best course for Britain. But many great issues affecting our allies and the world are involved, and a new round of strategic arms limitation negotiations will soon begin. We think it essential that there be full and informed debate about these issues in the country before any decision is taken.[26]

It is, of course, impossible to know whether Callaghan would or could have brought his party round to overt support for independent deterrence; defeat settled the issue by plunging Labour into ideological conflict strikingly reminiscent of the events of 1959–61. Championed by Tony Benn, left-wing activists had assiduously consolidated influence within the National Executive and the local constituencies during the 1970s. Now they argued that Callaghan's moderation had failed to offer a clear radical alternative to Margaret Thatcher's sweeping monetarism and was thus responsible for Labour's defeat. The times demanded dramatic solutions and just as the Tories had drifted to the right, it was argued that Labour must return to its socialist roots. The left began its campaign by challenging the method of selecting the party's leadership, seeking to shift the franchise from the traditionally moderate Parliamentary Party to the more militant party conference. The leadership struggle absorbed Labour's attentions throughout 1979, subsuming a range of substantive disputes over Britain's membership in the European Community, protectionism, nationalization and unilateral disarmament. NATO's year-end decision to deploy long-range theatre nuclear forces in Britain further seeded the gathering ideological storm within Labour's ranks. But the storm had not broken when, in January 1980, the Conservative government summoned the first formal debate on nuclear weapons policy to be held in the House of Commons in fifteen years.

Defence Secretary Pym's presentation of the government's case for third-generation forces appears to have been a determined bid for consensus. Pym eschewed discussion of such themes as political standing and military independence which, while comforting to Conservatives, were alien to multilateralist Labour thought. He set the military rationale for replacing Polaris firmly in an Alliance context:

> Public debate and learned discussion over the years has conjectured various possible themes of justification for British capability — political prestige, our status in the Alliance or a comparison with France. One hears sometimes the argument made out for the concept of a 'Fortress Britain' — some kind of insurance policy concept, should the United States go isolationist or the Alliance collapse. What weight there might be in such ideas I leave to others to assess. They all miss what is for me, and for this government, the main point — the decisive consideration. We think that Britain needs to be a nuclear power primarily because of what this contributes to NATO's strategy of deterrence and, through that, to our own national security.[27]

The government 'cast no shade of doubt' on American commitment.

But in a strategy of deterrence, 'what matters most is not what we think but what the Russians think'.

> In a crisis, Soviet leaders — perhaps beset by some pressures of turmoil in the Soviet empire, perhaps looking out upon a NATO Alliance passing through some temporary phase of internal difficulty — might conceivably misread American resolution. They might be tempted to gamble on United States hesitation.
>
> The nuclear decision, whether as a matter of retaliatory response or in any other circumstance, would, of course, be no less agonising for the United Kingdom than for the United States. But it would be a decision of a separate and independent power, and a power whose survival in freedom might be more directly and closely threatened by aggression in Europe than that of the United States. This is where the fact of having to face two decision-makers instead of one is of such significance.

Neither France nor West Germany could in practice make this contribution. 'If it is accepted that deterrence is helped by the existence of a second centre of nuclear decision-making in NATO — and our allies so believe — then we alone can provide it.' The government recognized 'that it would be gravely harmful if sustaining our nuclear contribution to the Alliance meant emasculating our non-nuclear contribution' and assured the House that it had no intention of running down conventional force strength. The government estimated that any successor to Polaris was liable to cost between £4,000 million and £5,000 million in 1979/80 sterling.[28] There did not appear to be 'any prospective alternative defence application of the same amount of resources that would bring Britain and NATO a bigger dividend in security than this one'.

As a bid for bipartisan support, Pym's speech met initially with considerable success. Labour's spokesman on defence matters, William Rodgers, confessed to a 'nagging feeling' that replacement 'would be a wise insurance policy for the next century'.[29] Fred Mulley, anxious about the costs and the state of the conventional forces, felt that 'it is at least arguable that that kind of money could be better spent in Alliance terms on conventional forces than on a replacement of Polaris'. But he conceded the existence of serious political arguments in favour of retention and acknowledged the military merit of multiple decision-making centres in deterrence.[30] The former Defence Minister concluded that he would await clarification of allied attitudes and arms control prospects before reaching any decision in principle. Labour's leadership displayed great conviction only when countering unilateralist tendencies, and similarly, the left reserved its fury for its own front bench, whose studied agnosticism they interpreted as low-profile support for the government's nuclear intentions. There was, on the whole, an air of vindication to the debate.

> In spite of strong opposition from the Labour Party, many hesitations in the Conservative Party, and strong American pressures not to embark on nuclear development, successive governments have stuck to the course of making sure that Britain had an effective independent deterrent . . . [Their] wisdom has been confirmed by events.[31]

The chimera of consensus did not endure. A Conservative government could hardly hope to effect a change in Labour's policy, particularly when the natural supporters of change had been discredited by defeat. Moreover, events contrived to exacerbate the politics of third-generation force procurement. The Soviet invasion of Afghanistan and the consequent deterioration of East–West relations occasioned widespread public concern with the dangers of nuclear war. Peace movements of varying ideological composition emerged across Europe. Nuclear anxieties were focused by the scheduled deployment of American cruise and Pershing II missiles in Britain and on the Continent and needlessly excited by irresponsible allusions to limited nuclear warfighting options by representatives of the Reagan administration. These comments suggested to some that the administration took a disquietingly sanguine view of nuclear conflict and helped to undermine European confidence in the sincerity of American arms control negotiating positions. As actual deployment of new theatre weapons was to take place only if an arms control solution could not be achieved, declining confidence in American good faith materially eroded political support for deployment at all. In Britain, the once moribund Campaign for Nuclear Disarmament flourished as converts to the cause of unilateralism increased and CND moved to spearhead growing and more broadly based opposition to American cruise missile deployments.

The rising tide of anti-nuclear sentiment informed ideological conflict within the Labour Party. Under a compromise electoral arrangement, Callaghan's mantle fell not to Healey, but to Michael Foot, an ambivalent unilateralist. Healey himself barely secured the deputy leadership in the face of a challenge by Tony Benn, a committed and increasingly vociferous unilateralist. The steady drift towards doctrinaire socialism and neutralism finally split the party in 1981 when four former Cabinet Ministers – Roy Jenkins, Shirley Williams, David Owen and William Rodgers – established the Social Democratic Party (SDP).[32] Two dozen others, vehement opponents of unilateralism all, followed. The moderates who remained, led by Healey, Peter Shore and Roy Hattersley, struggled in vain to stem the unilateralist tide. At the 1982 Labour Party conference, a motion calling for immediate abolition of British and American nuclear weapons bases in Britain finally secured a two-thirds majority and hence a presumptive right to inclusion in the manifesto as official party policy.[33]

The party conference's endorsement of unilateral disarmament did not command support among Labour's parliamentary representatives or its traditional constituencies. The British people, while dubious about the wisdom of American cruise missile deployment, were not neutralist; polls regularly registered strong support for both retention of American bases and maintenance of an independent deterrent.[34] A ministry determined actually to expel American forces and scrap the existing Polaris force would, in all likelihood, collapse. But a Labour or even a coalition government, coming to power while cancellation of Polaris's successor remained a fiscally attractive option, might well be vulnerable to unilateralist pressures and tempted to assuage leftist sentiments by abandoning modernization efforts. It may be that those fundamental concerns which had sustained the independent deterrent in the past would triumph none the less. For an island nation, utterly insupportable on the strength of domestic resources, isolation is not a viable option; Britain must be involved in the world to survive and involvement entails risk, the more so as nuclear weapons spread among the nations. For centuries, British governments have recognized that political independence can only be sustained by maintenance of a balance of power on the Continent and that effort entails great risk in the nuclear age. Indeed, it is difficult to imagine any British government assuming responsibility for abandonment of the independent deterrent. But the possibility could not be dismissed. It was therefore incumbent upon the Thatcher government to ensure that its successors, if tempted to appease unilateralist sentiment, could not plausibly argue that maintenance of a credible deterrent was beyond Britain's grasp or incompatible with the military efficiency and political cohesion of the Atlantic Alliance; to ensure, in other words that abandonment of the deterrent would be nothing more or less than appeasement. As a practical matter, this meant that the Conservatives were obliged to develop a technically unimpeachable successor to Polaris without occasioning substantial cutbacks in the conventional forces. This dilemma would be resolved, if at all, within the context of the Anglo-American special relationship.

Notes

1. Attlee was doubtless also concerned not to complicate UN negotiations, but this rationale for secrecy lost much of its force by 1947. In early 1948, the government acknowledged publicly its nuclear efforts in a manner designed to minimize attention. See Defence Minister Alexander's response to a parliamentary question on 12 May 1948, *Official Report* (Commons), vol. 450, col. 2117.

2. *Official Report* (Commons), vol. 977, 24 January 1980, col. 685.

3. After a cancellation of Blue Streak, Labour defence spokesman George Brown said: 'Those in the House, and the very many outside, who have always taken the view that the balance of argument was against an independent British deterrent will be glad if it has lapsed. I cannot take this view. I certainly could not applaud . . . the fact that Ministerial incompetence and blundering has destroyed a policy which, on balance, I thought was wise.' *Official Report* (Commons), vol. 622, 27 April 1960, cols. 232–44.

4. Alastair Buchan, 'Partners and Allies', *Foreign Affairs*, vol. 41, no. 4 (July 1963), p. 622.

5. It is British practice to issue annual 'White Papers' outlining current defence policy. The 1957 Paper was particularly notable for its announcement of the end of conscription by 1962; for its plan to reduce the Rhine Army from 77,000 to 30,000 men by 1961; for its somewhat stark restatement of the policy of nuclear deterrence and its corresponding emphasis upon nuclear weapons development. Although consistent with earlier statements of doctrine and force posture objectives, it was perceived in the wake of Suez as a novel departure. See, for fuller discussion, Chapter 4 below. Also see Lawrence W. Martin, 'The Market for Strategic Ideas in Britain: The "Sandys Era" ', *American Political Science Review*, vol. 61, no. 1 (Spring 1962), pp. 23–41.

6. 'The "nth country" problem in Great Britain means first of all the "German problem" ': Anthony Hartley, 'The British Bomb', *Survival*, no. 6 (July/August 1964), p. 175.

7. See R.H.S. Crossman in the *New Statesman*, 13 October 1955; quoted in A.J.R. Groom, *British Thinking about Nuclear Weapons* (Frances Pinter, London, 1974), p. 140.

8. Quoted in Arthur M. Schlesinger, Jr., *A Thousand Days* (Houghton Mifflin, Boston, 1965), p. 849.

9. Harold Macmillan, *At the End of the Day* (Harper and Row, New York, 1973), pp. 159–61.

10. *Disarmament and Nuclear War: The Next Step* (Transport House, London, 1959).

11. After assessing the advantages and disadvantages of the deterrent, Gaitskell concluded forcefully: 'These are matters of balance on which, frankly, I find it impossible to say that it is absolutely clear one way or the other. We have to weigh them up.' *Official Report* (Commons), vol. 618, 1 May 1960, col. 1138.

12. Groom, *British Thinking about Nuclear Weapons*, pp. 426–7.

13. Ibid., p. 436.

14. Wilson had succeeded Gaitskell as Leader of the Labour Party upon the latter's death in 1963.

15. The 1974 manifesto read: 'We have renounced any intention of moving toward a new generation of strategic nuclear weapons.' Quoted in P. Hennessey, 'Planning for a Future Nuclear Deterrent', *The Times*, 4 December 1979, p. 3.

16. House of Commons, Fourth Report from the Defence Committee, Session 1980–1, *Strategic Nuclear Weapons Policy* (HMSO, London, 1981), p. 80.

17. *The Economist*, 23 April 1960, p. 16.

18. *Official Report* (Lords), vol. 403, 18 December 1979, cols. 16, 28.

19. See, e.g., the Ottawa Declaration on Atlantic Relations, *Department of State Bulletin*, 19 June 1974. See also the discussion in Chapter 7 below.

20. See, e.g., *The Times*, 1 April 1980, p. 12. See also Chapter 6 below.

21. See Chapter 7 below for a discussion of the evolving military and political roles of the independent deterrent in the Alliance.

22. *Official Report* (Commons), vol. 960, 16 January 1979, col. 1501.

23. Interviews. Both British and French officials had been monitoring declining West German confidence in the efficacy of collective security arrangements with alarm and the French formally advised Callaghan's government in early 1979 that they felt abandonment of the deterrent would be highly destabilizing in Europe.

24. Interviews. See also Hennessey, 'Planning for a Future Nuclear Deterrent'.

25. *The Times* (London), 4 May 1963, p. 4.

26. Quoted in Hennessey, 'Planning for a Future Nuclear Deterrent'.

27. *Official Report* (Commons), vol. 977, 24 January 1980, col. 678.

28. Ibid., col. 682.

29. Ibid., col. 692.

30. Compare the orthodox multilateralist position as advanced by Labour's defence spokesman, George Brown, in 1963: 'the maintenance of more than one nuclear centre of power in the alliance with each retaining independence of action must destroy the alliance in the end and defeat any idea of interdependence'. Quoted in Hartley, 'The British Bomb', p. 177.

31. *Official Report* (Commons), vol. 977, 24 January 1980, col. 696 (Julian Amery).

32. See Ian Bradley, *Breaking the Mould? The Birth and Prospects of the Social Democratic Party* (Martin Robinson, London, 1982) for a detailed treatment of the origins of the SDP.

33. *New York Times*, 30 September 1982, p. 3.

34. See, e.g., the *Guardian*, 24 January 1983, p. 4.

3 THE AMERICAN CONNECTION

For nearly forty years, British governments of both parties have maintained the view that Britain must possess operationally independent strategic nuclear forces but that these should, as far as possible, result from Anglo-American technical co-operation. There is no evidence that any government has seen an inherent inconsistency in the simultaneous pursuit of these policy objectives. On the other hand, a number of political critics, foreign observers and academic analysts have felt that a policy of independent deterrence which depends in practice upon the timely provision of American hardware is, at best, paradoxical. Implicit in this criticism, however, are assumptions about the motives underlying British nuclear weapons policy and, as these colour our understanding of the special nuclear relationship, it is perhaps wise that they be addressed at the outset.

There is a view that London's nuclear efforts have, throughout most if not all of the post-war era, been driven primarily by considerations of prestige and international standing.[1] It is a credible argument, given the salience of discussion of the political significance of nuclear weapons in Britain's domestic debate over the years. If the assumption that prestige motives have been paramount is accepted, the increasing – and increasingly visible – technical dependence of Britain's forces on American assistance is evidence of policy failure. Procurement of American missile systems eroded the prestige attached to maintenance of an 'independent deterrent', particularly within Western Europe, and the strategic integration accompanying Anglo-American co-operation seemed to undermine the political independence attending nuclear weapons state status. Yet, as will be seen below, the British sought technological collaboration and integrated targeting assiduously throughout the post-war era. The decision to depend upon American-manufactured delivery vehicles was not taken *in extremis* after the Blue Streak project collapsed; well before Blue Streak represented a serious financial or political investment, the British had sought unsuccessfully to purchase first-generation American intermediate-range missiles. In this sense, the uneasy transition from Blue Streak to Polaris is evidence not of failure in Macmillan's nuclear weapons policy but of success, however clumsy, in the collaboration policy pursued by the Attlee, Churchill, Eden and Macmillan governments alike. Moreover, in

45

the larger question of policy motivation, the willingness of successive governments to trade off the prestige benefits of independent procurement for the technical and financial dividends of the American connection is the best measure of the primacy of security over political considerations in British nuclear weapons policy.

Alternatively, an argument is often advanced that the primary motivation driving the policy of independent deterrence has been London's desire to restore and sustain the 'special nuclear relationship' with Washington. As John Simpson put it, 'The United Kingdom nuclear deterrent has been, from its inception, directed toward creating a specific type of linkage with the United States.'[2] Again, given the importance attached to influencing American policy in both public discourse and private deliberations in Britain, this is by no means an outlandish thesis. Moreover, it is not necessarily inconsistent with the view that security considerations have been paramount in British decision-making. Nevertheless, it is, on balance, not much more satisfying than the 'prestige' thesis. No British government has been willing to sacrifice operational independence upon the altar of Anglo-American co-operation despite several opportunities and substantial diplomatic incentives to do so. Application of Occam's razor to Britain's tangled nuclear story suggests that the deterrent has been inspired, shaped and sustained primarily by security concerns, although successive governments have undoubtedly believed that maintenance of a credible national strategic capability, regardless of its technical provenance, affords political prestige. Similarly, the American connection has been primarily a mechanism for maximizing the effectiveness and minimizing the costs of that capability, although governments have unquestionably felt that nuclear co-operation, as the central strand of a complex bilateral relationship, yields political-military influence.

As a means for reducing costs and increasing efficiency, a continuing American connection was central to British procurement choices in the 1980s. Indeed, in certain circumstances, this relationship might have been a necessary condition for the development of third-generation forces at all. Moreover, the terms of nuclear co-operation with the United States — the degree of reciprocity and mutual dependence — were of considerable import to Anglo-American political relations generally and, therefore, to Britain's position within the Alliance. This chapter will examine the development and workings of the special nuclear relationship.

The Origins of Co-operation

An exchange of basic scientific data on atomic matters between the United States and Britain commenced with the arrival in Washington of Sir Henry Tizard, and his 'black box' of weapons-related secrets, in 1940.[3] Tizard's mission was to negotiate an agreement for the interchange of weapons design data and, rather as a sweetener, he released to the Americans detailed information on British breakthroughs in radar, fire control systems, underwater detection, aircraft gun turrets, jet engines and magnetrons. An agreement seemed mutually advantageous; from London's perspective, the United States was already a swelling overseas adjunct to the domestic armaments base and therefore technological advance in American industry was overwhelmingly in Britain's interests; from Washington's perspective, British information and know-how were immensely useful to the massive rearmament programme undertaken in the last year of peace. Indeed, one American characterized Tizard's 'black box' as the 'most valuable cargo ever brought to our shores'.[4] Pursuant to this agreement, basic atomic data were exchanged as part of a broader 'conventional' co-operation.

The Maud Committee's researches on atomic weapons were already under way at this time and as these developed so too did transatlantic communication. In August 1941, the Maud Committee recommended that weapons manufacture in wartime was feasible and the Tube Alloys Consultative Council, Britain's nuclear research and development organization, was established under Sir John Anderson's direction. The Maud Report itself was freely transferred to the United States within the framework of the Tizard agreement, apparently in the hope of stimulating American efforts. Indeed, the Report had recommended 'That the present collaboration with America should be continued and extended especially in the region of experimental work'.[5] If this was London's intention, transmission of the Report had the desired effect. Dr Vannevar Bush, Chairman of the National Defense Research Council, used it to secure President Franklin Roosevelt's support for a full-scale American atomic energy project. The President, struck by the origin as well as the import of Bush's data, wrote to Churchill on 11 October 1941 to suggest that the two countries' production 'efforts . . . be coordinated or even jointly conducted'.[6] Churchill, however, failed to respond for two months, and then only to avow his general willingness to co-operate in this area.

Observers have noted the irony that it was the Americans who first broached extensive atomic collaboration and the British who balked. Some have felt that in view of the long-term economic and strategic advantages of joint plant construction in the United States, British reticence may have reflected an unwillingness to compromise post-war prospects.[7] Although the British were precocious in their appreciation of the political significance of nuclear weapons, more straight-forward explanations are available for their behaviour in 1941. The monetary and opportunity costs of a weapons project were substantially under-estimated in London at this time. Moreover, the American project lagged well behind British efforts in pace and sophistication. Finally — and most important — Britain was at war and the United States was not. The spectre of German success haunted British personnel; their work was driven by 'the harrying spur of fear'.[8] In these circumstances, integration with a leaderless, somewhat leisurely peacetime project in the United States could hardly have seemed prudent. In 1941, short-term military requirements (construction of a weapon for 'this war') and long-term political-military objectives (development of an independent force for the post-war world) were simply indistinguishable.

By mid-1942, these interests were distinguishable. Not only had cost expectations soared, but the American project was expanding at an extraordinary pace in the wake of Pearl Harbor. In July 1942 the President had committed virtually unlimited funds to General Groves's Manhattan Project and there was now little doubt that, of the two Anglo-Saxon programmes, it was the United States which would achieve wartime success. It was now in Britain's interest to associate herself as rapidly as possible with the Americans in order to keep pace in this frontier technology and safeguard her post-war options. 'We now have a real contribution to make to a "merger",' wrote Anderson to the Prime Minister, 'Soon we shall have none.'[9] Churchill concurred and, on 5 August 1942, Anderson wrote to Bush to accept belatedly Roosevelt's generous offer. The Americans, however, were no longer interested. Groves, Bush and his deputy, Dr James Conant, were hard put to see what contribution the British could in practice make to *their* objective: rapid construction of a working bomb for wartime use. Moreover, noting that prevailing data exchanges had transgressed the limits common to other co-operative arrangements, they argued that nuclear interchanges should henceforth be governed by 'use in this war' criteria. The British believed that, given the fact that American plants were being constructed partially on the strength of British information, they were entitled to share in all aspects of the project. Bush and his colleagues, unmoved, prevailed on the President, and in late December 1942, the 'use in this war' principle was imposed, slowing technical exchanges to a trickle.[10]

In the aftermath of Roosevelt's decision, the British reconsidered the economics of atomic independence only to conclude once more that a national effort, while technically possible, would severely dislocate the war economy. It is possible that, had it proved necessary, London would have pushed on alone; it is certain that Churchill recognized that the threat of such a course, with all it would entail for Anglo–American armaments production, was an effective diplomatic lever, and he used it liberally to secure restoration of collaboration.[11] Two other factors contributed to the reversal of American policy. First, the President was personally quite well disposed to a joint undertaking with the British and certainly unwilling to see the nuclear issue poison allied relations. In late May 1943, he agreed in private talks with Churchill to resume collaboration, and, although he never informed his advisers of this commitment, his inclinations were well known.[12] Second, Bush and Conant, while opposed to any expansion of co-operation, were peculiarly concerned with Britain's commercial intentions. When, sensing this special anxiety, Churchill grandly disavowed any interest in nuclear power production data, the opposition of the President's advisers broke and the foundations of the Quebec Agreement was laid.

The Quebec Agreement of 19 August 1943 established the wartime collaboration regime. The two states agreed that

- neither state would use atomic weapons against the other;
- neither would use them against third parties except with the other's consent;
- neither would transfer relevant data to third parties except with the other's consent;
- transfer of commercially relevant data to Britain would be subject to presidential discretion;
- a Combined Policy Committee (CPC), including representatives from the United States, Britain and Canada, would be established to administer co-operation and allocate resources.

Full interchange of data on all aspects of the Manhattan Project was assured within the CPC, but working-level exchanges would proceed on a 'need to know' basis. Information specifically relating to design, construction and operation of large-scale plants was subject to *ad hoc* arrangements established by the CPC. In 1944, a Combined Development Trust (CDT) was set up to supervise collaborative acquisition and allocation of uranium ore.

After August 1943, British personnel joined the Manhattan Project in substantial numbers and worked on intimate terms with their American colleagues. The guidelines established at Quebec proved satisfactory and remained in force throughout the war. A second agreement – the Hyde Park *aide-mémoire* – was initialled by Roosevelt and Churchill in late 1944, committing the two countries, *inter alia*, to continued co-operation in industrial as well as military aspects of atomic energy after the war unless and until terminated by joint agreement. The President, however, apparently informed no one of this agreement, and the American copy was lost in his files for several years.[13] When, after his death, British officials first mentioned it within the CPC, the Americans present were stunned and embarassed.

Post-war British leaders could frequently refer to Britain's considerable, and long unrequited, contribution to the creation of the Hiroshima and Nagasaki bombs. That contribution is difficult to assess. General Groves felt that the British were 'helpful but not vital';[14] however, he confesses that, without London's constant encouragement and support, the Project might not have been so successful. Undoubtedly, the catalytic Maud Report, which galvanized American efforts and by laying the theoretical foundations gave the Manhattan Project something of a running start, was Britain's most important contribution. Margaret Gowing has convincingly argued that 'if it had not been for the brilliant scientific work done in Britain in the early part of the war . . . the Second World War would almost certainly have ended before an atomic bomb was dropped'.[15] As many as a million American casualties were expected to result from the scheduled invasion of the Japanese home islands; those who believe that nuclear weapons use provoked Japan's early surrender must take this as a measure of Britain's contribution.

The wartime nuclear relationship was but one aspect, however important, of an extraordinarily extensive system of bilateral co-operation. In combination, these links represented an unprecedented integration between sovereign states, and their dissolution was only natural once the wartime emergency had passed. Atomic energy was a somewhat special field in that the British had colourable legal and moral claims to access to the pool of technical data and resources they had helped to develop.[16] In the first months of peace, the Truman administration seemed prepared to recognize these claims. In November 1945, Truman, Attlee and Mackenzie King of Canada gathered in Washington to discuss plans for international control of atomic energy; the very composition of the meeting, as Attlee later pointed out to Truman, was indicative of a special trilateral relationship in things atomic.[17] At this conference, General Groves and Sir John Anderson met and rapidly agreed upon a framework for peacetime collaboration: '[f]ull and effective' interchange of basic scientific data was to continue; technical exchanges relating to the design, construction and operation of large-scale plants, 'desirable in principle', were to be regulated *ad hoc* within a revised, peacetime CPC; and co-operative acquisition and allocation of uranium ores were to continue within the CDT. The 'consent clause' of the Quebec Agreement, which was neither appropriate nor enforceable in the post-war environment, was revised to require 'consultation' about weapons use, and Britain was relieved of any restrictions upon the industrial application of atomic energy. The Groves–Anderson Memorandum was not ready in time for the leaders' signatures, so Attlee and Truman signed a simpler document calling for 'full and effective' co-operation and charging the CPC with the responsibility for recommending 'appropriate arrangements' for peacetime co-operation among the three powers.[18]

The Groves–Anderson Memorandum was not, in itself, a formal agreement; it was rather an agreed set of principles to guide the CPC's negotiation of a formal replacement for the Quebec and Hyde Park covenants. Difficulties over the form of agreement quickly emerged – a confidential Anglo-American agreement would conflict prima facie with Article 102 of the United Nations Charter while a public treaty would disrupt ongoing UN negotiations over atomic energy – and it soon became apparent that the Americans were quite prepared to acquiesce in the face of these procedural obstacles and forgo co-operation with the British altogether. In February 1946, London coupled a probing request for details about the Hanford reactors with disclosure of Britain's plans for Windscale.[19] The request was denied. By this point, the attitudes of American officials were hardening into overt opposition. The December 1945 CPC meetings had been cordial; the April 1946 sessions were frankly hostile, with Secretary of State James Byrnes denying any knowledge of the November accord.[20] With the collapse of the April CPC meeting, Anglo-American technical information exchanges ceased altogether.

What had happened in the interim was a startling politicization of atomic energy questions in the United States. American politicians such as Senators Hickenlooper, McMahon and Vandenburg recognized that atomic bombs were 'unconventional', portentous weapons, with revolutionary implications for diplomacy and war. An irresistible flood of opinion favoured retention of the United States' monopoly of 'the Secret'. The administration could not challenge this sentiment outright; it could only hope to channel it. As Congress began elaborating a legislature framework for atomic energy in early 1946, enlightened opinion in the administration had two overriding objectives: to secure legislative sanction for efforts towards international control and to wrest responsibility for atomic energy from the military. Success in these two objectives was costly in terms of executive flexibility; not only was the President's hitherto unchallenged right to transfer classified data severely restricted by the Atomic Energy ('McMahon') Act of 1946, but an aggressive Congressional Joint Committee on Atomic Energy (JCAE) was created to interpret the Act's provisions on a continuing basis. Article 10(A) of the new Act prohibited transfer of 'restricted data', a category comprising all information relating to the design, fabrication or utilization of atomic weapons, production facilities and power reactors, pending the establishment of an international legal regime in atomic energy matters.

In the political atmosphere of 1946, Britain's cause attracted few partisans in Washington. The administration apparently decided not to inform Congress of Roosevelt's wartime commitments[21] and, despite Senator McMahon's later suggestion to the contrary, it is unlikely that a forthright statement of the record would have decisively influenced events. Anglo-American relations were very unsettled at this point, and a special nuclear relationship with Britain would have threatened the interests of 'internationalists' and 'monopolists' alike. After a somewhat bitter exchange of letters between Attlee and Truman, the British moved to secure their share of accumulated uranium stocks and, with it, both the material base for independent deterrence and the principal incentive for the resumption of negotiations by the United States.

The first major effort to regularize Anglo-American atomic relations in the wake of the McMahon Act came in late 1947. By this point, co-operation between the two countries in defence and foreign policy was increasing, and this heightened the uneasy sense in Washington that solemn commitments had not been honoured. Congress had been informed at last of the wartime agreements and senators were very agitated about the consent clause of the still-lingering Quebec Agreement. Finally, and most important, a critical shortage in uranium was emerging.

'Without the stocks in Britain, without the Congo production allocated to Britain, the American production plants could operate at only a fraction of full capacity.'[22] In preparing for negotiations with the British, the administration was anxious to avoid an ugly Congressional connection between Marshall Plan aid and uranium supplies and, partly for this reason, was determined to minimize the one linkage which was politically unavoidable: technical information exchange and raw material co-operation. These were inextricably related: the CDT was organizationally a child of the CPC which was principally a vehicle for the interchange of data.

Negotiations commenced in Washington on 19 December 1947 and were concluded successfully on 7 January 1948. Nine areas of information exchange — known as the technical co-operation programme — were agreed and, in turn, the British gave up their rights to the 1948 and 1949 Congo ore production and permitted the Americans conditional access to uranium stores in Britain. A *modus vivendi* was accepted which formally abrogated the Quebec and Hyde Park agreements. Throughout the negotiations, Acting Secretary of State Robert Lovett and the Chairman of the Atomic Energy Commission, David Lilienthal, stressed the point that the modest information arrangements were but a beginning, that 'new areas of cooperation would be added'[23] in time. It was in this spirit that the British accepted the *modus vivendi*. Nevertheless, it must be said that London had little flexibility in the matter; obstinacy over uranium could quite possibly have led to a termination or severe reduction of American economic assistance.

The technical co-operation programme, meagre as it was, did not survive the year. By mid-1948, it became apparent to Commissioner Lewis Strauss of the AEC and his numerous allies in the Department of Defense and Congress that not only did the British seriously intend to develop weapons, but that they were overwhelmingly likely to succeed. That this should have alarmed American opinion is evidence of the tenacity of what one British official called 'an ill-defined and almost unconscious feeling that atomic energy is and should remain an American monopoly'.[24] In the ensuing furore, a British request for information on plutonium metallurgy was denied, in direct contravention of the *modus vivendi*, and new instructions were issued to American representatives on the Combined Policy Committee requiring them to refuse any requests for information of primarily military significance. Not only was this turn of events absurd in light of American legislation — the legal sanction for any bilateral co-operation lay in the preamble to the McMahon Act which spoke of 'common defense and security' while the Act itself prohibited absolutely any transfer of industrial information — but it was applied unevenly. Interchange of chemical separation data continued, despite its enormous military significance, largely because the British had more to offer in this field.[25]

Ironically, the *modus vivendi* collapsed just as the quickening intimacy of military contacts had led the British Chiefs of Staff to propose far broader collaborative arrangements to their American colleagues. The RAF and USAF had jointly undertaken the relief of Berlin and co-operation between the two countries' services was in general excellent. American B-29s had been deployed to East Anglia, inaugurating a strategic relationship which has continued throughout the post-war era, and the old Grand Alliance was emerging as the centrepiece of a wider Atlantic security system. Joint planning was, however, compromised by American inability to discuss nuclear weapons and, indeed, atomic isolationism was becoming increasing anomalous. It was in explicit recognition of this state of affairs that representatives of the concerned executive agencies met in January 1949 at Princeton to consider the prospects for a 'fresh start' with Britain.[26] It must be recalled that a new approach to London was ultimately unavoidable as the *modus vivendi*'s raw material provisions lapsed at the end of the year, but it is still fair to say that a genuine effort was made in 1949 to harmonize American nuclear and foreign policies.

At Princeton, a laborious process of consensus-building commenced; its object was to secure support for a comprehensive Anglo–American agreement, but at no time were the British apprised of its provisions.[27] After fragile executive agreement was reached, the President summoned Congressional leaders to Blair House and there, supported by General Eisenhower, Dean Acheson and David Lilienthal, ably presented a case for extensive collaboration. Eisenhower, in particular, was effective, bitterly attacking Congressional isolationism and acknowledging the centrality of the Anglo–American alliance to American war plans.[28] Finally, in September, against the background of the Soviet atomic test, American representatives presented a proposal for the complete integration of the national programmes. All fissionable material production, all raw materials, all weapons fabrication facilities and all finished weapons stockpiles should, as far as possible, be situated in the United States or Canada. Only those projects on which substantial investment had been made — in effect, the first two Windscale piles — were to remain in Britain. Weapons assembly should take place in the United

States given the overwhelming efficiencies achieved by American fabrication techniques. In return, Britain should second her scientists and engineers to the new Manhattan Project, and British fissionable material would be tooled into weapons at Los Alamos. Complete interchange of information would resume. A stock of weapons could be stored in Britain for use in agreed war plans. The overarching theme to the proposal was the pursuit of maximum efficiency in the allocation of resources for the common defence.[29]

At face value, the American plan entailed a complete subordination of Britain's national effort and British negotiators expected it would prove unacceptable in London.[30] No provision was made, for example, for civil use of atomic energy in Britain, something no great industrial power could tolerate. There was, however, much to commend certain aspects of the plan, and, with mutual flexibility, the outline of an acceptable agreement could emerge. The British recognized that no agreement was possible that prevented full utilization of American reactor capacity, and they were therefore willing to suspend construction of the third pile at Windscale.[31] This action proved in the event to be a blessing. Correspondingly, they insisted that the low-separation plant under construction at Capenhurst continue, because the LSD would not impose a drain on uranium resources and was essential to civil power production. To this the Americans seemed agreeable. The proposals for joint weapons fabrication had merit: the United States had spent three years and $100 million developing processes which cut weapons assembly times by a factor of 20 while increasing weapons reliability tenfold.[32] The British were on the threshold of a major investment in potentially obsolescent fabrication facilities at Aldermaston. Similarly, reliance on American highly enriched uranium was financially appealing given the great expense of HSD construction at Capenhurst. Initially, the Chief of Staff insisted that a 'buttons to bombs' surge capability be retained in a series of prototype plants; this was, however, an expensive and wasteful option. Eventually, London was prepared to accept a plan under which Windscale plutonium mixed with Oak Ridge U-235 would be machined into weapons at Los Alamos, tested in common facilities, and returned to British possession. Two caveats were imposed. First Britain must be free to pursue 'any new processes' of weapons manufacture so long as they did not interfere with the secondment of personnel to the United States. Second, Ministers agreed that as 'a condition precedent' to further negotiations, Washington must tender formal assurances about Britain's right to a supply of weapons which would be constitutionally immune from subsequent Congressional interference.[33]

By the time the British Ambassador delivered the British proposals to the Secretary of State, the fragile American consensus had unravelled. Days before, executive unity had collapsed when Secretary of Defense Louis Johnson had 'pitched it all out'.[34] The JCAE, unreconciled to co-operation, challenged Truman, and although the President appears to have felt that an executive agreement with Britain was within his prerogative, he was unwilling to risk bipartisan support for the weapons programme by insisting on a collaborative scheme 'opposed by strong elements in Congress'.[35] The *coup de grâce* came in February 1950 with the arrest of Klaus Fuchs, a member of the British team at Los Alamos and later at Harwell, for espionage.

American conduct of these negotiations has rightly been criticized; in the event, the United States took British uranium and gave little or nothing in return. It is important, however, to recognize that significant evolution in American thinking did take place in these years. In 1949, for the first time, informed political opinion accepted, however reluctantly, the reality of the British programme, and nuclear co-operation could be presented, not as a crude trade of a 'hunk of uranium for a hunk of "secrets" ',[36] but as the centrepiece of a living alliance. Significant support for collaboration surfaced within the administration and might perhaps have eventually prevailed over 'the tyranny of a tiny minority'[37] in Congress had successive security scandals not poisoned the atmosphere. Even after Fuchs, the Defense Department remained impressed with the efficiency of British plutonium production and, during the Korean emergency, developed a plan which recognized London's right to absolute control over a weapons supply.[38] Whatever the initial prospects for success in this endeavour, they were hopelessly compromised by the flight of Burgess and Maclean to Moscow. Finally, the American scientific community, persuaded of the impossibility of an international regime and daunted by the conceptual problems of thermonuclear development, came to support co-operation with their British colleagues.

The British too have been criticized – not least by Professor Gowing – for allowing themselves to be trifled with by the Americans in the early post-war years.[39] This is perhaps unfair. London had nothing to lose by trying, after all. Professor Gowing's principal concern with forgone opportunities for co-operation in Western Europe seems misplaced and unduly influenced by the presumed lessons of Britain's painful international adjustment in the 1960s. France, the only possible Continental partner, had an insignificant programme, technically light years behind Britain's. It was moreover dominated by a Communist who, with the support of his scientific colleagues, adamantly opposed military development.[40] Collaborative opportunities within the Commonwealth were, with the exception of Canada, hardly more promising. In their negotiations with Washington, the British showed admirable judgement. More aggressive exploitation of American uranium dependence could have imperilled Bevin's delicate efforts to entangle American and European destinies and was, for that reason, never seriously considered in London.

It has been suggested that it was only after they had learned of the Soviet atomic test and the extent of American stockpiles that the British were ready to consider such complete integration with the United States.[41] This may in fact have been the case. Certainly, these events helped bring home the reality of Britain's post-war position. It is interesting none the less to speculate about Britain's likely response had the United States offered, in 1945, to continue with an integrated Manhattan Project which would supply her with a stock of weapons under national control while permitting her liberty to pursue industrial power production at home. This would have been a very tempting offer, and might have been accepted. Of course, no such offer was made, and indeed between 1946 and 1949, close integration was not even a remote possibility. In 1949, London was on the verge of major capital investments in Aldermaston, Windscale and Capenhurst; Lord Sherfield has testified to the salience of cost considerations in Britain's deliberations.[42] When a cost-saving arrangement with the United States was no longer possible, Britain went ahead with Aldermaston's development and HSD construction at Capenhurst. These were the last major capital expenditures on atomic energy production for purely military purposes in Britain. Once spent, there was no point in integrating *weapons* production *per se*, which may explain in part why such integration was not considered later. After the early 1950s delivery technology was the high-cost aspect of deterrence, and the British were quite willing to depend upon American-produced delivery vehicles. In this sense, the 1949 negotiations set British motives in stark relief: independent deterrence was 'about' a national store of weapons; Anglo–American co-operation was 'about' reducing costs and increasing efficiency.

In 1952, the British detonated their first atomic bomb at Monte Bello, Australia; no American observers were present. Thereafter a slow return to collaboration commenced. Progress was delayed somewhat by the confluence of the McCarthy period in the United States and espionage revelations in Britain.[43] Prime Minister Churchill met with President Eisenhower in 1953 and secured the President's promise to seek amendments in the McMahon Act. A new Atomic Energy Act was signed into law in 1954 which permitted transfer of data concerning the external characteristics of nuclear weapons — size, shape, weight, yield and effects.[44] The United States and Britain agreed to co-operate within the terms of this Act in a bilateral agreement signed on 15 June 1955.

The great breakthough came ironically in the wake of the Suez campaign and the tremendous rift in Anglo–American relations which attended that crisis. Macmillan and Eisenhower met twice in 1957. In their first meeting, at Bermuda in March, the two leaders agreed to deployment of Thor missiles, under 'dual key' controls, in England; Eisenhower considered this 'by far the most successful international conference' he had attended since the war.[45] Meeting a second time in October at Washington, the President agreed to seek revisions in the Atomic Energy Act so as to facilitate scientific co-operation among 'Great Britain, the United States and other friendly powers'.[46] Three reasons for the President's commitment suggest themselves. First, in May 1957, the British had air-dropped an operational thermonuclear bomb at Christmas Island — just months after the first operational hydrogen weapons had entered American inventories. A remarkable technical achievement, the Christmas Island tests heralded potential advantages for the United States in a new co-operative arrangement. Second, the Soviet Union launched the Sputnik satellite, which threw into question assumptions of American technical superiority and incidentally cast new significance upon Britain's willingness to base American missiles. Finally, Suez itself clearly engendered instinctive efforts on both sides of the Atlantic to repair the break in Anglo–American relations. Perhaps it also suggested to Washington the dangers of British independence. The amendments adopted by Congress did not encourage co-operation with 'other friendly powers', but, in the 1958 Agreement, they met London's most optimistic expectations.

The Mechanics of Co-operation

The *Agreement for Co-operation on the Uses of Atomic Energy for Mutual Defence Purposes of July 3, 1958*[47] restored nuclear collaboration to its central position in the special relationship and has governed atomic relations between the two countries ever since. The Agreement itself comprises three substantive articles. Article I expresses the general intention of the parties to co-operate within the terms of the accord so long as the communicating party 'determines that such cooperation will promote . . . its defense and security'. Article II, divided into two paragraphs, regulates technical exchanges. Article II(A) stipulates that data will be transferred if it is 'jointly determined' that such a transfer is useful for the development of mutual defence plans; the training of military personnel; the evaluation of an adversary's nuclear capability; the development of delivery vehicles; or the design and operation of military reactors. The first three areas of co-operation had been sanctioned in the 1955 Agreement. Article II(B) permits the transfer of data if 'the communicating Party determines that such information is necessary to improve the recipient's atomic weapons design, development and fabrication capabilities'. Article III authorized a one-time transfer of an American nuclear submarine propulsion plant to Britain as well as a ten-year supply of enriched uranium fuel. Article III was amended in 1959 to provide for the continuing transfer of non-nuclear components of atomic weapons and 'special nuclear materials'.[48]

The arrangement embodied in this treaty is permissive; the two countries agree to consider each other's requests for information. In the United States, a prospective transfer must be approved on the political level within the Departments of Energy and Defense. In Britain, release of information requires the approval of the Chief Scientific Adviser to the Ministry of Defence. The provisions relating to weapon design information are strict in that it must be clear to the communicating party that a particular item is currently usable by the recipient. It is intended to consider here how the agreement has operated over time and how its provisions relate to other areas of co-operation in the special relationship.

Information Exchange

There can be little doubt that both countries derived substantial benefit from the resumption of technical exchanges after 1958. The United States had surged far ahead in engineering and weapons assembly techniques, and American procedures were rapidly emulated at Aldermaston, then in the course of building up the hydrogen weapons stockpile. American officials are said to have been 'amazed' at the breadth of British expertise: 'in certain areas British scientists and engineers were further advanced and had information of considerable value to the United States'.[49] Eisenhower administration spokesmen in Congressional hearings said that the United States would learn new techniques wherever the British had solved a problem differently, or receive important confirmation wherever they had independently adopted the same solution as had the Americans. Financial savings in the American weapons programme were expected to result, as co-operation would facilitate 'conservation of scarce talents and resources in both nations'.[50]

In the late 1950s and early 1960s, collaboration was evidently intimate and quite reciprocal. Aldermaston was, for example, deeply involved in the development of multiple-warhead technology. It would appear that there was only one serious disruption in the technical exchange system. The accession of Harold Wilson's government in 1964 raised doubts in Washington about Britain's nuclear intentions. The decision was apparently taken at the political level to restrict interchange between the two American laboratories and Aldermaston, then collaborating in the development of the A-3 MRV warhead, until after the promised 're-negotiation' of the Nassau Agreement.[51] It is not clear how long this hiatus endured although the flow of information probably resumed after Wilson confirmed Britain's order for A-3 missiles in mid-1965. By September, when the British conducted a thermonuclear test at Nevada, full interchange had undoubtedly been restored but, in the interim, design decisions had been taken in the absence of American information. In consequence, the British A-3 re-entry system differed slightly from the American model.

With time, it is likely that the relationship became quite one-sided. For one thing, the benefits the United States could derive from independent British development — new ideas where British and American techniques had diverged and corroboration where they had converged — necessarily declined after 1958. Moreover, the scale of the respective national programmes differed by orders of magnitude. As one British official put it in 1979:

> The United States has two laboratories and we have one; they spend five times as much as we do on these establishments; they have conducted some 870 tests — how many of which were really necessary, I wouldn't say — and we have conducted 30. That gives, I think, a fair indication of the 'hardware balance', although in the idea end of the business, the relationship is rather more equal.[52]

The structure of the Agreement makes access to American data conditional upon Aldermaston's development programmes, and this undoubtedly influenced Labour's decision to continue with nuclear weapons research and development after 1968. It may also have influenced the decision to proceed with the Polaris Improvement Programme after 1973. In any case, these decisions ensured virtually unbroken British access to American weapons design technology. By 1980, the laboratories were on familiar and comfortable terms with each other, and neither side would have welcomed termination of the relationship. The Pentagon had a special reason for favouring continued collaboration. Bitter competition prevailed between the two American laboratories, Los Alamos and Livermore, who often had different bureaucratic and Congressional sponsors.[53] Over the years, Aldermaston had emerged as a handy source of independent judgement, immune from the temptations of the budgetary cycle.[54]

Materials Exchange

The May 1959 Amendment to Article III of the 1958 Mutual Defence Agreement authorizes the transfer of non-nuclear weapons components and 'special nuclear materials' as may be agreed between the two countries. Apparently, the original intent behind the Amendment was to permit American-enriched uranium to be exchanged for British plutonium. Congress was informed that:

> This will benefit the U.K. by eliminating the need for that country to expend large sums of money for the construction and operation of expensive diffusion plant. The United States will benefit by obtaining needed plutonium for its small weapons program.[55]

This statement is somewhat misleading. In 1959, the Capenhurst high-diffusion plant was complete and operating at full capacity. It is possible that additional plant was necessary in order to fuel the hydrogen weapons build-up or that quality control problems had emerged at Capenhurst. What is more likely is that the administration was simply overstating its case, perhaps in order to obscure the fact that these 'swap' arrangements were primarily intended to meet American needs. British plutonium production was quite substantial, with the two military piles at Windscale seconded by a string of dual-purpose reactors at Calder Hall and Chapel Cross, and the United States was then engaged in a massive build-up of small weapons. Between 1958 and 1964, an estimated seven thousand fission warheads were deployed in Europe, doubtless imposing a heavy strain on American resources. It is possible that Britain actually fabricated a number of these weapons and transferred them for American deployment in Europe. Certainly by

1959 the British had very considerable experience in the design and assembly of small fission weapons.

No figures for the quantities involved in this exchange were released, although the exchange ratio – 1.76 grams of U-235 for each gram of Pu-239 –[56] was disclosed. One consequence of the Agreement was the cessation of production of enriched uranium for military purposes in Britain.

> We have now reached a point where supplies of fissile materials already available or assured will be sufficient to maintain our independent nuclear deterrent and to meet all defence requirements for the foreseeable future.[57]

The Capenhurst facility was placed upon a minimal production basis such that full production could be resumed within a year of a decision to do so. Other 'special nuclear materials' have in all probability been exchanged under these arrangements. The British apparently employed American-produced zirconium, for the cladding of reactor fuel elements, and hafnium, for neutron absorption, in their nuclear submarine propulsion plants. It is possible, but less likely, that United States-sourced polonium was used as an initiatory neutron generator in British warheads.[58] If this were the case, the element must have been made available on a continuing basis, given its short half-life. It is also probable that the British relied upon the United States for tritium, used as a secondary fusion agent in hydrogen warheads to reduce the yield requirements of the triggering fission device and increase the probabilities of thermonuclear reaction. Finally, of course, a ten-year supply of submarine reactor fuel was assured under Article III of the 1958 Agreement.

In 1969–70 the materials exchange regime was renegotiated. At that time, Article III as amended was segregated into two components. Under the first, the 1958 Agreement for a ten-year supply of submarine propulsion-grade uranium was renewed for a further ten years.[59] Under the second, the 1959 Agreement for special nuclear materials exchange was renewed for only five years.[60] Subsequently it was renewed for a further five years. Some observers inferred from the decision to split these two provisions that the United States' political interest in continuing weapons-grade transfers was declining. This does not appear to have been the case. In the context of a domestic quarrel between the Atomic Energy Commission and the Joint Committee, the two provisions were apparently segregated to accommodate the latter's interpretation of the strictures of the Non-Proliferation Treaty of 1968. Both provisions were to expire in 1979 and in November President Carter recommended Congressional approval of further extensions.[61] Change did occur in the materials exchange relationship, but for technical rather than political reasons.

In 1976, it was announced that construction of a tritium production facility was under way at Chapel Cross.[62] The plant was expected to be operational in 1980. This substance has a short half-life — 12.3 years — and therefore the tritium emplaced in the Polaris hydrogen warheads in 1968 had in any case to be replaced by 1980. This was presumably done in the context of the Polaris Improvement Programme. Project Chevaline apparently employed domestically produced enriched uranium as well; characteristically, this evidence of independence was revealed in an interview granted by Defence Secretary Pym to a French daily.[63] Moreover, the Ministry of Defence proposed in late 1979 construction of a new uranium enrichment facility at Capenhurst. Ground was to be broken in late 1980, and the new plant was expected to be operational by the middle of the decade. This effort was to be funded entirely by the Ministry of Defence and divorced from the Anglo-West German–Dutch co-operative effort to produce low-enriched uranium for civil purposes. A contract was placed with British Nuclear Fuels Ltd in 1980 for production of submarine-grade U-235.[64] While it may be that the British were concerned for political reasons to demonstrate their independence or that doubts about the American connection were growing, it is more probable that impending American shortages forced Britain to plan for self-reliance. The United States was on the threshold of a major expansion of warhead production — for the MX, the C-4, the D-5, the Pershing IIXR, SLCM, ALCM and GLCM — as well as a continuing expansion of nuclear-propelled naval forces. These developments were expected to strain severely already scarce fissible material production capabilities[65] and to diminish American capacity to supply British weapons and propulsion needs beyond the mid-1980s. British dependence on American materials assistance was expected to decline, and, although the United States agreed in 1980 to continue to furnish propulsion — and weapons-grade uranium, the British in turn agreed to transfer plutonium and perhaps other special nuclear materials as well to the United States.[66]

Delivery Vehicle Co-operation

Anglo-American co-operation with respect to strategic nuclear delivery vehicles — which emerged in the early 1960s as the most visible aspect of the special relationship — has had a rather complex history. Apparently, co-operative research and development of delivery technology were at one time viewed by American administrations as 'conventional' and hence beyond the ambit of the McMahon Act. Outright transfer of manufactured systems, conversely, was seen to conflict with the Act and was held to be illegal until after the 1957 amendments and the 1959 Anglo-American Agreement governing exchanges of non-nuclear components of atomic weapons.

Collaborative research and development commenced with Tizard's mission to Washington and the September 1940 agreement to exchange classified weapons design data. This agreement endured within incident for the duration of the war and while conventional information exchanges languished briefly in the post-war period, they revived much earlier than did the atomic connection. In December 1946, the USAF and the RAF concluded an accord to continue their wartime collaboration in staff methods, tactics, equipment and research. Thus, a framework existed for co-operation in the development of first-generation nuclear delivery vehicles — the American B-47s and B-52s and the British Valiants, Victors and Vulcans — but technical exchanges in this field were of little import. Britain had a qualitative advantage in medium bomber technology and as the V-bombers were more effective and less costly than the B-47, there was never any question of procuring American systems. Concurrently with the air forces' agreement, the American State–War–Navy Coordinating Committee issued a directive stipulating that

> all classified military information, including the United States order of battle, and all information about combined research and development to which the United Kingdom had contributed or was contributing and United States research and development projects could be released to the United Kingdom.[67]

This directive was quite broad in scope, covering manufacturing details as well as general technical information on weapons programmes.

The 1946 arrangements excluded guided-missile technology, an item quite closely held by both governments at this time. An agreement to collaborate in this area was not achieved until February 1950.[68] It is ironic that the foundations for American provision of delivery vehicles were laid just as the last major attempt to secure integrated weapons production had collapsed in the wake of the Fuchs betrayal. It has become apparent that a 'plethora of unpublished agreements' were concluded at this time, some of which — notably the so-called Burns-Templar Agreement — remained in force thirty years later, under whose terms technical military secrets were exchanged. The United States secured design data on British Chobham tank armour under these agreements in the mid-1970s.[69] Guided-missile technology was regarded as primarily defensive in Britain at this time and achieved high priority only during the Korean emergency. Thus, although the Chiefs of Staff recognized the crucial significance of strategic delivery systems in their review of strategy in 1952, it was the V-bomber programme which benefited, and missile development lost its brief prominence among defence priorities. This may explain why British strategic ballistic missile development got under way 'three years after' the American effort.[70]

In 1954, Duncan Sandys, then Minister of Supply, concluded an agreement with Eisenhower's Secretary of Defense, Charles Wilson, wherein Britain was to concentrate upon basic research while the United States emphasized engineering development and manufacture.[71] Perhaps this agreement galvanized British research efforts, but it was prima facie dangerously similar to the structure of wartime atomic weapons collaboration. The British could contriubte ideas but the United States would finance them and retain control of the product. It appears that the British first enquired into the prospects of purchasing first-generation American missiles at this time. A second attempt was made in 1956 and a third in January 1957.[72] None of these *démarches* was successful; the Americans were anxious to discuss dual-key IRBM deployments such as the Thor agreement but uneasy at best about transferring manufactured missiles for ultimate deployment under British control. British officials let it be known in later years that successive commitments to the Blue Streak IRBM programme were made only after it was clear that American missiles would not be available on terms consistent with the requirement for operational independence.[73]

The Blue Streak programme itself benefited from substantial American technical assistance. Within the ambit of the 1950 and 1954 agreements, Rolls-Royce entered into a licensing arrangement with the Rocketdyne Division of North American Aviation, securing access to engineering details on the Navaho-Atlas power plant as well as sensitive inertial guidance technology. It is said that American development assistance 'lopped five years and £400 million off the original estimates' for Blue Streak.[74] In 1956, President Eisenhower employed a legal technicality in the Atomic Energy Act of 1954 in order to transfer blueprints on the USS *Nautilus* nuclear propulsion plant to Britain. This decision was taken over the passionate objections of both the Joint Committee and the Atomic Energy Commission but with the full support of the US Navy, which was anxious to acquire conventional naval data from the British. Such mainstays of modern aircraft carriers as the steam catapult and the angled flight deck were pioneered by the Royal Navy and rapidly emulated by the US Navy in this period.[75]

Unable to procure American systems on acceptable terms, the British pressed ahead with Blue Streak at home. Wtih time, the weapons system acquired domestic political significance, not only because of the progressive commitment of funds but because of the Macmillan government's overly hearty defence of the missile's prospects. Unquestionably, the government was loath to abandon Blue Streak in the prevailing political environment, but it none the less did so within less than a year of the agreement which made an American replacement available. This is not a bad record by modern weapons acquisition standards. The weapon chosen to succeed Blue Streak was, however, a mistake which resulted in large measure from the structure and content of Anglo-American collaboration in delivery technology and the impact these had on the parochial biases of British services. Initially, the British may have conceived of Thor as a replacement, and Macmillan implied at the time and later that the Thors in Britain might ultimately have reverted to sole national control.[76] The strategic logic which doomed Blue Streak similarly undermined the attractiveness of Thor, however. As the Chiefs of Staff had concluded that only a mobile launch platform would meet Britain's future needs, the choice lay between Skybolt and Polaris in 1960.

British officers had monitored both programmes closely since 1955, and therefore Britain enjoyed identical access to information about each system. The relationships between the respective services differed in kind, however, and this conditioned the flow of information. Perhaps because of their common experience as junior services struggling for survival, and certainly as a consequence of their operational co-operation during the Second World War, the air forces enjoyed extraordinarily intimate relations. By 1960, they willingly made common cause in budgetary battles in Washington and Whitehall.[77] Eager to secure an ally for the procurement politics of the next administration, the USAF sang the praises of Skybolt to the British. This praise fell, of course, on receptive ears among the RAF command hierarchy, who had no desire to lose control of the deterrent. Moreover, Skybolt was an airman's dream, combining the high technology of the missile age with a continuing role for bombers and pilots. It was also, however, a systems analyst's nightmare, as it combined the bomber's disadvantages of vulnerability and slow response with the mobile missile's disadvantages of low payload and unimpressive accuracy. Conversely, the Navy was in 1960 deliberately underselling its Polaris programme.[78] A much more competitive relationship prevailed between the navies throughout the post-war era; indeed, it is instructive to recall the contrast between close RAF–USAF wartime co-operation and the navies' correct relations based upon regional sphere of influence: Admiral King fiercely opposed introduction of the British fleet into the Pacific in 1945. Admiral Rickover and his colleagues consistently advised the British to avoid Polaris in the years before 1960. This advice was heartily welcomed by the Admiralty who, eyeing a new generation of carriers, had no interest in donating the equipment budget to things nuclear. The Royal Navy has been rightly criticized for adopting a hostile attitude towards independent deterrence on principle rather than recognizing that, if the government favoured such a policy, Polaris was the best available system.[79] This unfortunate attitude would probably not have been tenable had the US Navy openly challenged the pessimistic appraisals of Polaris propagated by the two air forces and silently seconded by the Royal Navy.

After the cancellation of Skybolt in 1962, the navies adjusted to reality, and an intimate co-operation developed between the Special Projects Office in the United States and the Polaris Executive in Britain.[80] Indeed, the extremely favourable financial terms on which the British received Polaris in 1963 has been ascribed in part to this relationship.[81] Moreover, the US Navy took a leaf from the Air Force's book and endeavoured to enlist Royal Navy support in their budgetary politics. At the US Navy's suggestion, the Polaris Sales Agreement was drafted so as to give Britain a presumptive right to follow-on systems. The Navy hoped that London would forgo Polaris in favour of the nascent Poseidon system.[82]

As the Polaris fleet became operational in 1969–70, debate erupted in London about the wisdom of moving on to Poseidon and multiple independently targetable re-entry vehicles (MIRV). American Defense Secretary Melvin Laird reportedly offered Poseidon to the new Conservative government in 1970.[83] As we have seen, revised intelligence estimates removed the urgency and ultimately the rationale for procuring Poseidon. Nevertheless, a constellation of interests favoured an approach to Washington and learned to their dismay that the United

States was no longer anxious to sell. There was a view in the Ministry of Defence that Britain ought to strive for a more constant flow of expenditure on strategic forces so as to avoid both the fiscal difficulties and political pitfalls of budgetary peaks and troughs. Assuming that procurement of Poseidon would ultimately be necessary, these officials argued that it was better to spend money in the early 1970s. Additionally, a fierce bureaucratic battle between Aldermaston and the Navy seems to have developed. The weapons establishment favoured MIRV development both as a hedge against Soviet ABM improvements and as an exercise for the American connection. The Navy, anxious to preserve its conventional budget, opposed both procurement of Poseidon and construction of the fifth SSBN Labour had cancelled in 1964.

Against this background, Prime Minister Heath journeyed to Washington in 1972. It is apparent that the British were given the impression during this visit that while, if asked, the President would agree to a transfer of Poseidon, he preferred not to be asked. The Nixon administration took the view that, in light of the ABM Treaty, Britain did not need Poseidon, and this view was confirmed by the confused signals emanating from the bureaucratic battleground in Whitehall. Moreover, it appears that Dr Kissinger was anxious about Russian sensibilities in the SALT process. Finally, the administration was uneasy about the Joint Committee's reaction to a transfer of such current technology to Britain. Washington appears to have preferred that a Poseidon agreement be postponed and London readily accepted this preference. But the experience left many in Whitehall anxious about the future of Anglo-American strategic co-operation.

Britain's dependence in the nuclear relationship never lacked for critics. On the one hand, it was feared that Washington would someday prove unwilling to provide a replacement for the Polaris missiles. This would drive up the cost of independent deterrence and, perhaps, undermine political support for the policy. On the other hand, the availability of American technology and the attending restrictions on information exchanges seemed to complicate the prospects for Anglo-French collaboration.[84] It was also felt that purchase of American missiles somehow compromised the independence, and hence the *raison d'être*, of the deterrent.[85] This latter criticism, at least, was groundless. The supply relationship was a matter of money. The technology transferred was fully within Britain's grasp and could, at great cost, have been replicated in Britain.[86] Once deployed upon British boats, American missiles were entirely subject to British control. Termination of resupply and servicing arrangements could not impinge upon the operational independence of the deterrent, as domestic servicing facilities could be in place well before the military effectiveness of the missile would be affected.

Other strands of the special relationship raised potentially more serious questions about the operational independence of British forces. Although Britain maintained national command, control and communication (C^3) links with its Polaris forces, its resources for monitoring Soviet threats to the fleet were closely integrated with, and thus dependent upon, American assets. Moreover, Britain apparently relied completely upon the United States for satellite and aerial surveillance of the Soviet Union. An analysis of the extent and context of Britain's dependence upon American strategic intelligence resources is therefore critical to an appreciation of the operational reality of independent deterrence. It is also relevant to an understanding of both the Thatcher government's decision to purchase Trident missiles and the Carter and Reagan administrations' willingness to sell them.

The Intelligence Relationship

Anglo–American strategic intelligence arrangements were an aspect of a broader intelligence relationship — a relationship quite as unique and 'special' as the nuclear connection. The British had cultivated Colonel William Donovan during the Second World War and through both their example and their bureaucratic assistance, they were instrumental in effecting the centralization of American external intelligence activities. The close relationship established during the war survived both the dissolution of Donovan's Office of Strategic Services (OSS) and the general decline of Anglo–American intimacy in the immediate postwar period. In 1946, the American State–War–Navy Coordinating Committee issued a directive making 'available to the British all classified and military intelligence with the sole exception of atomic energy intelligence'.[87]

The advent of the Cold War led to the establishment in 1947 of the Central Intelligence Agency (CIA) and the National Security Agency (NSA) in the United States. In many instances, individuals prominent in wartime intelligence activities returned to staff those organizations and collaboration with the British was simply natural. Between NSA and Britain's Government Communications Headquarters (GCHQ), located at Cheltenham, an extraordinarily close relationship developed in the arcane arts of cryptography, signals and electronic intelligence. NSA and GCHQ quite literally divided the world into spheres of responsibility for interception and co-operated intimately in code-breaking and analysis efforts. Permanent British liaison staff settled in at NSA's headquarters at Fort Meade, Maryland, and Americans were ensconced at Cheltenham. An overt manifestation of this relationship was the jointly managed Foreign Broadcast Information Service. NSA–GCHQ links were replicated in collaborative arrangements between electronic and signals intelligence units of the individual armed services. For example, the two navies, backed by NSA and GCHQ, co-ordinated with Canada and Australia in a world-wide surveillance network to track shipping.[88] A series of detailed, secret agreements allocated rights and responsibilities between the two countries.[89]

Similar unpublished 'understandings' were executed in the late 1940s and early 1950s between the CIA and Britain's Secret Intelligence Service (SIS). Each service was prohibited from operating without consent in the other's sovereign territories,[90] while implicit 'turf arrangements' circumscribed operations within the services' respective spheres of influence.[91] Very little authoritative information is, of course, available with respect to covert human intelligence collection and political intervention operations. It is apparent, none the less, that collection efforts were sometimes jointly developed and exploited — most notably, perhaps, with Colonel Penkovskii — or undertaken by one service with the other's informed forbearance. It is also clear that several political interventions in the early post-war years — e.g. Italy (1948), Albania (1950), Iran (1953) — were jointly mounted enterprises and the two services co-ordinated their cultivation and management of 'resistance' networks in Eastern Europe during the heyday of the Cold War. The relationship was never trouble-free — for one thing, SIS's principal liaison officer in Washington in the late 1940s, Kim Philby, turned out to be a Soviet agent — and the two services were known to compete regularly[92] and, occasionally, very roughly indeed. But they remained on far more intimate terms with each other than with any third-country organization. Raw clandestine reports from CIA and SIS assets were apparently traded with some regularity to assist analysis and 'an informal liaison exchange system on the analytical level' flourished.[93]

The McMahon Act segregated 'atomic energy intelligence' from other forms of intelligence, and accordingly mandated the exception in the otherwise extraordinarily broad exchange authorized by the State–War–Navy Coordinating Committee's 1946 directive on Anglo-American co-operation.[94] It is not clear what fell into this anomalous category. Clearly detection of testing did: Congressional sanction had been necessary to facilitate collaborative efforts to monitor the Soviet

Union's atomic testing programme in 1949[95] and the Act itself was amended in 1950 to authorize intelligence co-operation. A treaty was signed to this effect in 1950 and its general provisions were subsequently incorporated into the 1955 and 1958 Anglo–American nuclear agreements. In 1950, too, USAF B-29s began operating out of East Anglia armed with atomic weapons and a primitive target list — light years removed from the complex Single Integrated Operational Plan (SIOP) of the post-McNamara era — was drawn up at this time.[96] It would seem then that collaborative reconnaissance of the Soviet target set and order of battle commenced around 1950. Both the USAF and the RAF overflew Eastern Europe and the Soviet Union at this time and it is overwhelmingly likely that information garnered in these efforts was exchanged.

In 1955, the CIA began operating its specialized U-2 surveillance aircraft out of Britain. It has been reported that the U-2 programme was, from the outset, a joint Anglo–American operation.[97] It is said that the programme was undertaken on a joint basis to maximize basing and overflight privileges and the arrangements allegedly permitted either the American President or the British Prime Minister to order overflights; RAF personnel seconded to SIS service, as well as USAF officers transferred to CIA's payroll, piloted the aircraft and up to one-fifth of all overflights of Soviet territory in the 1950s are said to have been undertaken by British pilots.

Whether or not British pilots regularly flew missions, there would seem to have been substantial British involvement in the U-2 programme and, very probably, coresponding rights to initiate overflights of targets of particular interest to Britain. An SR-71 based in California overflew the South Atlantic during the Falklands campaign in 1982 and American officials at the time suggested that they were merely honouring long-standing commitments. U-2s were certainly operated on a permanent basis out of Britain — a Thames TV camera crew filmed one landing at the USAF base at Mindenhall in 1980[98] — flying, on average, five missions per week.[99] Occasionally, U-2s operated out of RAF bases on Cyprus both to survey the Middle East and, after the loss of CIA 'listening posts' in Iran in 1979, to monitor telemetry signals from Soviet missile tests.[100] Again, this strand of the special relationship has not always operated smoothly. During the 1973 Middle East War, the Heath government forbade or, at least, successfully discouraged U-2 overflights of the battlefield from British bases in Cyprus or Britain.

Throughout the war we were given to understand, in the many

indirect ways available to a government as close to us as Britain's, that it would be appreciated in London if we did not use British bases either for the airlift [of supplies to Israel] or for intelligence collection in the Middle East. There was never a formal refusal on the airlift because it had been made plain that we should not ask. Our occasional overflights of the combat zone by SR-71 high altitude reconnaissance – essential for our decision-making process – had therefore to originate in the United States, adding to our expenses and reducing their effectiveness.[101]

Other accounts suggest that Heath formally vetoed surveillance operations, prompting both Kissinger's well publicized charge that the allies were acting 'as if the alliance does not exist' and a dramatic severance of the secure line linking SIS's communications centre in Whitehall with CIA headquarters in Langley, Virginia.[102] In any event, the rift was rapidly repaired.

The various American satellite reconnaissance programmes were bureaucratic as well as technical offspring of the original U-2 effort. American intelligence satellites, like the U-2s and SR-71s, collected varied visual images and/or intercepted communications. British governments routinely declined comment on the extent or nature of British participation in these undertakings.[103] It is apparent, none the less, that participation was substantial. Britain hosted a plethora of satellite tracking stations and communications facilities. Arguably, some were irreplaceable. For example, the array of tracking dishes at Menwith Hill were reportedly the only facilities capable of monitoring satellites hovering in the northerly 'Molniya orbit' over the Soviet Union.[104] Many were, at least ostensibly, staffed by British personnel. A GCHQ station at Morwenstow, in Cornwall, provided ground links for the RHYOLITE satellite system while RAF Oakhanger was actually identified in Congressional testimony as a control facility for American military satellites.[105] USAF aircraft, operating out of British bases, recovered film capsules ejected over the Atlantic. It may be that some American satellites employed British technology and it is quite likely that GCHQ participated extensively in analysis efforts.

The United States regularly transferred highly sensitive strategic intelligence products to Britain.[106] These transfers occurred within the context of a strategic intelligence relationship in which the United States had substantial interests and exposure. The sheer scale of the United States intelligence presence in Britain – let alone the likelihood that at least some facilities were jointly operated – suggests a relationship not of stark dependence but of broad interdependence. That impression is strengthened by the fact that strategic intelligence exchanges were part of a larger intelligence relationship which, if only because of GCHQ's efforts, remained 'quite reciprocal'.[107] The British could therefore reasonably rely on continued access to American strategic intelligence facilities -- whether or not they chose to replace Polaris with another American system -- and the intelligence relationship, in turn, made it very likely that the Americans would remain willing to transfer strategic nuclear delivery vehicles to Britain. In the absence of extraordinary circumstances, the United States was most unlikely to upset a pattern of co-operation which continued to pay it well.

The precise circumstances for which British strategic forces had to be optimized -- employment in the absence of the American -- would be nothing if not extraordinary. However durable the strategic intelligence relationship might be in peacetime, the costs and benefits of unilateral termination might look very different to Washington in war when, *ex hypothesi*, the British seemed about to employ nuclear weapons and the Americans did not care to do so. The United States might willingly suffer some degradation in its own capacity to monitor the Soviet Union if by so doing it could prevent an unwanted and dangerous escalation of conflict. This insight had direct relevance to the Thatcher government's procurement decisions. A sudden denial of access to American strategic intelligence might modestly degrade the effectiveness of an SLBM attack -- certain 'time-urgent' targets could not be engaged confidently -- and it might also moderately increase the vulnerability of the SSBN force to Soviet attack. But the bulk of Britain's national target list could still be engaged -- cities, factories, rail links and base complexes do not move -- and ballistic missile defences are not tactically mobile. Conventional air defences, on the other hand, are extremely mobile. Cruise missiles rely on computerized terrain maps derived from aerial reconnaissance for guidance and approach their targets over tactically selected routes at extremely low altitudes. They are very vulnerable to concentrated air defences. If, under the pressures of war, the United States denied access to strategic intelligence collection assets, the effectiveness of the independent deterrent could be severely degraded. Even if the British maintained terrain maps for very large numbers of attack approaches -- an expensive option -- selection among them would nevertheless be blind and the confidence of British governments would necessarily decline. This was one reason, among many, that cruise missiles were not an attractive option for third-generation strategic forces.

Collaborative strategic targeting was the realm where the two most important and 'special' Anglo–American relationships – nuclear and intelligence collaboration – commingled. The need arose with the deployment of American B-29s in 1948 and their subsequent arming with nuclear weapons. But despite the intimacy of military relations, discussion of nuclear weapons was prohibited under the McMahon Act. Limited information about the scale of American weapons production was released in the course of the 1949 negotiations, but it was not until Churchill's visit to Washington in 1952 that the British received a full briefing on the Air Force's strategic air plan.[108] By 1954, the RAF was beginning to equip its Canberra bombers with atomic weaponry and Churchill had assured Eisenhower that the RAF would be prepared to carry American weapons in a bombing offensive. Co-operation between SAC and Bomber Command was crippled by American inability to discuss atomic ordnance. Eisenhower proposed a new Atomic Energy Act and in 1955 the British and Americans executed an agreement permitting transfers of information on the external characteristics and effects of nuclear weapons. It is likely that informal co-ordination of targeting plans began around this time. However, the formal 'integration for operational purposes' of British and American forces apparently did not take place until 1958.[109]

There is no obvious reason why this integration had to await the 1957 amendments to the Atomic Energy Act; it could have been accommodated within the terms of the 1954 Act. It may be that formal liaison between SAC and Bomber Command had not been considered necessary while the bulk of SAC's resources were deployed in Britain and the V-bombers had not yet been deployed in force. In any case, it would be quite wrong to see integration as a British concession. The fact is that it was the British who had assiduously pursued targeting co-operation throughout the post-war era.[110] The British believed targeting integration was in their interest: 'the way to be consulted is to make consultation necessary and this Britain had managed'.[111]

The Future of Strategic Co-operation

In the wake of the Nassau Agreement and indeed for many years thereafter, an assumption prevailed in the literature that the special nuclear relationship between the United States and Britain would not endure beyond the life of the Polaris fleet. Essentially three arguments sustained this assumption. The first held that, with Britain's accelerating international decline, the political framework for strategic co-operation would erode. The second contended that an emergent arms control relationship between the superpowers made American technical support for Britain's nuclear pretensions a negotiating obstacle at best and a threat to systemic stability at worst. The third contended that independent British forces were incompatible with either the United States' military interest in centralized command and control of strategic forces or her political interest in an integrated West European community comprising Britain and intimately linked with the United States in an Atlantic partnership of equals. These arguments have proved fallacious; in 1980, the United States agreed once again to assist British efforts to sustain an operationally independent capability to engage targets in the Soviet Union. The failure of these analyses to predict events accurately results, it is contended here, from a misconception of the impact of British decline upon political relations between Washington and London and a misunderstanding of the costs and benefits of any American decision to foreclose strategic co-operation.

The sources of the Anglo-American 'special relationship' are myriad and disputed. Some scholars argue that history, language and ultimately simple sentiment are the prime factors in the Alliance. In this view, a sentimental predisposition to sympathize with each other's point of view endows the Anglo-American relationship with a 'propensity to repair' unique in the annals of alliances. Other observers contend that cold calculation of national interests accounts for the alliance and its tenacity; challenges — Dunkirk, Berlin, Korea, Sputnik — have driven the two countries together. This controversy is a little artificial: cultural, historical, geographical and ideological influences shape perceptions of national interest. The two governments have tended to take complementary views of international affairs. Washington is simply more confident with Britain than with any other power that, as an American official put it 'disagreements reflect honest differences in our tactical appreciation of a situation'. As Coral Bell has observed, 'The strength of the "special relationship" is that it is not a construction but a capacity — a capacity to see the elements of common interest in whatever international storms the times may bring.'[112]

For much of the post-war era, the Anglo-American alliance was characterized by two features: each country was the other's most powerful, as well as its closest, ally. On the broadest level, the former condition no longer prevailed in 1980. Many believed that Britain's decline would rob the alliance of its peculiar intimacy as well as its global political significance. It did not, for a variety of reasons. First, while Britain had certainly declined, those powers which had gained relatively were not politically at liberty to assume the role of the United States' first lieutenant. This was the case with Japan and West Germany, whose historical circumstances severely inhibited both national will and external political tolerance for prominent political-military presences. Periodic efforts by the Carter administration to coax West Germany into a leadership role, as, for example, with the theatre nuclear force issue, proved chastening in this respect. France suffered from no lack of will, but had neither the measure of American trust nor the desire to acquire it necessary to supplant Britain's privileged position. In these circumstances, 'Britain . . . persisted in emerging, on balance and over the long term, as the "most available ally".'[113]

The second reason is at once geographical and ideological. Britain's decline was most marked beyond Europe's shore; the 'special relationship' has been, historically, an essentially European phenomenon. The greatest challenges to the Alliance have been extra-European in origin. Suez heads a list which includes disputes over Palestine, China, Indo-China, the Middle East and the Indian subcontinent. Most of these troubles involved perceived American challenges to eroding British positions. Thus, although British withdrawal removed a sense of common endeavour, it also excised a source of conflict. Conversely, as Anglo–American political competition outside Europe declined, London remained, for historical and ideological reasons, Washington's most sympathetic and perhaps most capable ally in the global competition with Moscow. Within Europe, much was made of contrasting British and American attitudes towards political integration. Indeed, London's equivocal European credentials left her a poor, if willing, advocate for American economic interests. Consequently, economically minded administrations often looked to Bonn for diplomatic assistance. But, on the central question of Soviet power in Europe, its nature and implications, British and American views remained strikingly compatible. Historically, culturally and geographically peripheral to the Continent, Britain, like the United States, was neither peculiarly vulnerable to Soviet political pressures nor possessed of powerful constituencies predisposed to favour Soviet policy preferences. The same could not be said of West Germany or France.

The third reason for the retention of a peculiar intimacy in Anglo–American relations was functional: Britain's decline was least marked in the area of defence. The 'special relationship' always had a heavy bias towards national security affairs, and the most striking change in British fortunes lay in other areas — in particular, the economy.

Consider the differential between the change in Britain's economic position *vis-à-vis* West Germany and the change in each country's defence posture. In 1959, the two countries had virtually equivalent gross national products; in 1979, West Germany's economy was twice the size of Britain's. Yet the two states in that year made roughly equivalent contributions to the Alliance. One consequence of this was that for many national security bureaucracies in Washington, their counterparts in London remained their most important partners. This was obviously true of the nuclear weapons establishments and the intelligence community but was also the case with the NATO-related offices, the Navy and the Air Force. Thus, while few in Washington would have identified Britain as the United States' most important ally, few doubted that she remained the closest and perhaps the most influential.

In this context of continuing intimacy, the political choice posed to the United States by British pursuit of third-generation forces involved a calculation of costs and benefits. In the various collaborative arrangements discussed above, Britain was clearly the net beneficiary; she was not, however, the sole beneficiary. It was apparent that the relationship remained sufficiently reciprocal for the United States to derive some advantages from co-operation with Britain. Moreover, British decline had robbed the question of *relative* advantages of political significance. In the 1940s and even the 1950s, there was a competitive tension which contributed materially to the breakdown of atomic collaboration. Indeed, it may be that the evident change in Britain's status after Suez facilitated the resumption of nuclear co-operation. In 1980, when Britain's postion in world affairs was no longer even remotely analogous to that of the United States the balance of benefits was, politically, a moot issue; what mattered was that the absolute benefits accruing to the United States were still significant.

Moreover, the political costs attending unilateral American severance of the nuclear relationship were liable to be severe. Contemplation of these costs strongly influenced President Kennedy's decision at Nassau in 1962. The British Ambassador, David Ormsby-Gore, argued to Kennedy at the time that

the very same people who would criticize him for providing us with another weapon would be the first to point out that America had let her closest ally down if he did not provide us with such a weapon. 'You can never trust the Americans,' they would cry and in the latter circumstances they would be sure of a vast and receptive audience in Britain too.[114]

Ironically, the progress of superpower arms control efforts since 1962, rather than undermining American willingness to continue the special relationship, raised the political costs associated with its dissolution. The inclusion of a non-circumvention/non-transfer clause in the draft SALT II Treaty evoked grave suspicions in Europe, and the Carter administration went to great lengths to ensure that the treaty's *travaux préparatoire* clearly supported the right of the United States to continue collaboration with the British. American severance of the relationship would have been widely interpreted in Europe as a sacrifice of the interests of an exceptionally close ally in order to placate Russian preferences. This observation led one British official to argue that 'irrespective of the ambiguities of the non-circumvention/non-transfer clause, SALT, if anything, increases the changes of American assistance'.

Awareness of both the enduring benefits of the bilateral co-operative relationship with the British and the political consequences of terminating it led President Kennedy to sanction the Polaris transfer, despite the prevailing opinion within his administration that independent British forces conflicted with broader American political-military interests. Nearly twenty years later an identical calculus would, in all probability, have sufficed to ensure President Carter's approval in principle of an analogous transfer. Kennedy's decision was controversial; Carter's was not. After Prime Minister Thatcher's visit in December 1979, the White House issued a communiqué which read in part:

> The President and the Prime Minister agreed on the importance of maintaining a credible British strategic deterrent force and U.S.-U.K. strategic cooperation. The leaders agreed that their governments should continue their discussions of the most appropriate means of achieving these objectives for the future.[115]

No dissent, indeed no public discussion whatsoever, attended this announcement. What distinguished 1962 from 1980 was the unarticulated recognition that independent British forces were militarily useful in an era of strategic parity and politically essential in a time of growing West German power.

Notes

1. This view is represented in its least sophisticated variant by American journalism — see, e.g., *Time*, 21 July 1980, p. 36 — and in its most sophisticated, by American scholarship — see Andrew Pierre, *Nuclear Politics* (Oxford University Press, London, 1972). It is shared by a number of prominent British scholars. See, e.g., Michael Howard's review of Gowing's *Independence and Deterrence* volumes in *The Sunday Times* (London), 8 December 1974. Howard acknowledges that Britain's development of the bomb was 'an astounding technical achievement' but considers the enterprise a 'rather tragic story' largely because 'it did not establish Britain as a first class power'.

2. Simpson, 'The Anglo-American Nuclear Relationship' in House of Commons, Sixth Report from the Expenditure Committee, Session 1978-9, *The Future of the United Kingdom's Nuclear Weapons Policy* (HMSO, London, 1979), p. 224.

3. Vannevar Bush, *Modern Arms and Free Men* (Simon and Schuster, New York, 1949), p. 39.

4. J.P. Baxter III, *Scientists against Time* (Little, Brown, Boston, 1946), p. 142.

5. Gowing I, p. 91.

6. Ibid., p. 123. After the war, British leaders would imply, incorrectly, that Anglo–American co-operation dated to Roosevelt's *démarche* of October 1941. See Churchill's statement of 6 August 1945 in Gowing II, p. 16. Also see Attlee's telegram to Truman of 6 June 1946. Ibid., pp. 126-7.

7. Pierre, *Nuclear Politics*, pp. 26-9.

8. Ronald Clark, *The Birth of the Bomb* (Horizon Press, New York, 1961), p. 41.

9. Gowing I, p. 137.

10. Pierre, *Nuclear Politics*, p. 37.

11. Gowing I, p. 42.

12. Pierre, *Nuclear Politics*, p. 42.

13. Leslie R. Groves, *Now It Can Be Told: The Story of the Manhattan Project* (Harper and Row, New York, 1962), p. 402.

14. Ibid., pp. 456-8.

15. Gowing II, p. 1.

16. Lord Sherfield, who, as Sir Roger Makins, played a central role in the post-war negotiations, has argued that the Quebec and Hyde Park agreements 'were, on a strict interpretation, valid for the war period only, and they therefore provided a rather weak basis for the claim that collaboration and exchange of information should be continued in time of peace'. See Lord Sherfield, 'Britain's Nuclear Story, 1945-52', *The Round Table*, no. 258 (April 1975), p. 194.

17. Gowing II, p. 129.

18. Ibid., p. 76.

19. Ibid., p. 98.

20. Ibid., p. 100.

21. Congressional leaders none the less had some idea of the wartime arrangements. The British statements of 6 August 1945 were attached to Senator Mc-Mahon's April 1946 report on the redrafted Atomic Energy Bill. On more than one occasion, legislators requested, but did not receive, details about Britain's involvement from the administration. Ibid., p. 108.

22. Richard G. Hewlett and Oscar E. Anderson, *A History of the United States Atomic Energy Commission*, vol. I, *The New World 1939-46* (Pennsylvania State University Press, University Park, 1962), p. 276.

23. Richard G. Hewlett and Francis Duncan, *A History of the United States*

Atomic Energy Commission, vol. II, *Atomic Shield 1947–52* (Pennsylvania State University Press, University Park, 1969), p. 281.

24. Gowing II, p. 289.

25. Ibid., p. 262.

26. Hewlett and Duncan, *Atomic Shield*, p. 296.

27. Gowing II, p. 295.

28. David E. Lilienthal, *Journals*, vol. II (Harper and Row, New York, 1964), p. 565.

29. Hewlett and Duncan, *Atomic Shield*, p. 301; Gowing II, pp. 282–5.

30. Hewlett and Duncan, *Atomic Shield*, p. 306.

31. Gowing II, p. 285.

32. Ibid., p. 297.

33. Ibid., p. 297.

34. Lilienthal, *Journals*, p. 615.

35. Harry S. Truman, *Years of Trial and Hope* (Signet Books, New York, 1956), p. 304.

36. Lilienthal, *Journals*, p. 565.

37. Ibid.

38. Gowing II, p. 301.

39. Ibid., pp. 319–21.

40. See Laurence Scheinman, *Atomic Energy Policy in France under the Fourth Republic* (Princeton University Press, Princeton, 1965).

41. Gowing II, p. 319.

42. Sherfield, 'Britain's Nuclear Story', p. 196.

43. Thomas E. Murray, *Nuclear Policy for War and Peace* (World Publishing, Cleveland, 1960), p. 166.

44. Pierre, *Nuclear Politics*, p.139.

45. Dwight D. Eisenhower, *Waging Peace, 1956–61* (Doubleday, New York, 1965), p. 124.

46. 'Declaration of Common Purpose of 25 October 1957', reprinted in Ian MacDonald (ed.), *Anglo-American Relations* (St Martin's Press, New York, 1974), pp. 138–42.

47. Cmnd. 537 (HMSO, London, 1958).

48. *Amendment to the Agreement between the Government of the United Kingdom of Great Britain and Northern Ireland and the Government of the United States of America for Co-operation on the Uses of Atomic Energy for Mutual Defence Purposes of July 3, 1958*, Cmnd. 859 (HMSO, London, 1959).

49. Pierre, *Nuclear Politics*, pp. 143–4.

50. US Congress, *Report of the Joint Committee on Atomic Energy*, HR 2299, 85th Cong., 1st Sess., 1958, Appendix 2, p. 19.

51. Interview.

52. Interview.

53. See, e.g., Walter Pincus, 'U.S. Scientists Make Rapid Advances in Nuclear Warhead Technologies', *Washington Post*, 22 October 1979, p. 3.

54. Interview.

55. *Report of the Joint Committee on Atomic Energy*, HR 672, 86th Cong., 1st Sess., 1958, p. 12.

56. Ibid.

57. *Statement on Defence: 1964*, Cmnd. 2270 (HMSO, London, 1964), p. 10.

58. Ian Smart, *The Future of the British Nuclear Deterrent* (RIIA, London, 1977), p. 30.

59. *Amendment to the Agreement for Co-operation on the Uses of Atomic Energy for Mutual Defence Purposes of 3 July 1958*, Cmnd. 4119 (HMSO, London, 1969).

60. *Amendment to the Agreement for Co-operation on the Uses of Atomic Energy for Mutual Defence Purposes of 3 July 1958*, Cmnd. 4383 (HMSO, London, 1970).

61. Message to the Congress of 28 November 1979, *Department of State Bulletin* (February 1980), p. 25.

62. *The Sunday Times* (London), 2 May 1976.

63. *Le Matin* (Paris), 1 April 1980, pp. 10–11, reprinted in *Foreign Broadcast Information Service*, vol. 7 (Western Europe), 10 April 1980, pp. Q4–Q8.

64. *International Defense Review*, no. 2 (1980), p. 165.

65. See Walter Pincus, 'Pentagon's Demand for Plutonium in Mid-'80s Exceeds Present Supply', *Washington Post*, 25 July 1977, p. 1. Pincus reports on Maj.-Gen. Joseph Bratton's (once) secret testimony before the House Armed Services Committee, where the General stated flatly that American plutonium production was insufficient to support planned weapons programmes.

66. Interviews.

67. Gowing II, p. 119.

68. Ibid., p. 299.

69. John Baylis (ed.), *British Defence Policy in a Changing World* (Croom Helm, London, 1978), p. 75.

70. *Statement on Defence: 1955*, Cmnd. 9391 (HMSO, London, 1955), p. 7.

71. A.J.R. Groom, *British Thinking about Nuclear Weapons* (Frances Pinter, London, 1974), p. 190.

72. Michael H. Armacost, *The Politics of Weapons Innovation* (Columbia University Press, New York, 1969), p. 190.

73. *Official Report* (Lords), vol. 233, 5 May 1960, col. 239.

74. C.J. Bartlett, *The Long Retreat* (Macmillan, London, 1972), p. 109.

75. Baylis, *British Defence Policy*, p. 79.

76. Harold Macmillan, *Riding the Storm 1956-9* (Harper and Row, New York, 1971), p. 261.

77. Pierre, *Nuclear Politics*, pp. 219–23. For a general discussion of service politics in Britain at this time, see William P. Snyder, *The Politics of British Defense Policy, 1945-1962* (Ohio State University Press, Columbus, 1964).

78. Groom, *British Thinking about Nuclear Weapons*, p. 281.

79. Pierre, *Nuclear Politics*, pp. 200–1.

80. John Simpson, 'The Polaris Executive: A Case Study of a Unified Hierarchy', *Public Administration*, no. 48 (Winter 1970), p. 383.

81. Interview. After the Nassau Conference, McNamara insisted that Britain pay a portion of Polaris R & D costs analogous to its scheduled share of the production run, that is 12%. Through the medium of an RN Commander at the Special Projects Office, the two navies settled on a token contribution equivalent to 5% of the purchase price of the A-3 missiles. The British Ambassador, David Ormsby-Gore, is said to have then raised the issue in a wide-ranging conversation with the President, gently characterizing McNamara's insistence on 12% as a challenge to Kennedy's authority. The President agreed to resolve the issue directly with the Prime Minister over the telephone. Macmillan suggested, and Kennedy accepted, the 5% surcharge arrangement. With agreement at the services and the heads of government levels, McNamara was isolated and dropped his opposition.

82. Interviews.

83. Interviews.

84. Those prospects were never promising. See Ian Smart, *The Future Conditional: The Prospects for Anglo-French Nuclear Cooperation*, Adelphi Paper no. 78 (IISS, London, 1971).

85. See, e.g., the *Guardian*, 21 March 1982, p. 4.

86. See Defence Minister Nott's remarks in *The Times*, 12 March 1982, p. 4.

87. Gowing II, p. 119.

88. See, e.g., Duncan Campbell, 'How We Spy on Argentina', *New Statesman*, 3 May 1982.

89. Interviews.

90. See, e.g., Richard Neustadt, *Alliance Politics* (Columbia University Press, New York, 1970), p. 134.

91. Interviews.

92. Coral Bell, 'The Special Relationship' in M. Leifer (ed.), *Constraints and Adjustments in British Foreign Policy* (Allen and Unwin, London, 1972), p. 112.

93. Ray Cline, *Secrets, Spies and Scholars* (Acropolis Books, Washington, DC, 1976), p. 124.

94. Gowing II, p. 119.

95. Hewlett and Duncan, *Atomic Shield*, pp. 363-6.

96. Interviews.

97. Leonard Mosely, *Dulles* (Dial Press, New York, 1978), pp. 365-70.

98. See the *New Statesman*, 17 October 1980, p. 7.

99. Robert Hershey, 'British-U.S. Intelligence Links', *New York Times*, 12 March 1979, p. 3.

100. Ibid.

101. Henry A. Kissinger, *Year of Upheaval* (Little, Brown, Boston, 1982), p. 709.

102. Hershey, 'British-U.S. Intelligence Links'.

103. See, e.g., Lord Carrington's testimony in House of Commons, Twelfth Report from the Expenditure Committee, Session 1972-3, *United Kingdom Nuclear Weapons Programme* (HMSO, London, 1973).

104. *New Statesman*, 17 October 1980.

105. Ibid.

106. Interviews.

107. Interview.

108. Gowing II, p. 413.

109. Baylis, *British Defence Policy*, p. 78.

110. The Chiefs of Staff had felt as early as 1952 that targeting co-operation would afford Britain influence over 'the only allied offensive in a world war'. Gowing II, p. 441.

111. Raymond Dawson and Richard Rosecrance, 'Theory and Reality in the Anglo-American Alliance', *World Politics*, vol. 19 (October 1966), p. 24.

112. Bell, 'The Special Relationship', p. 119.

113. Ibid., p. 116.

114. Lord Harlech, 'Suez SNAFU, Skybolt SABU', *Foreign Policy*, vol. 1, no. 1 (Spring 1971), p. 46.

115. *Department of State Bulletin* (February 1980), p. 24.

4 THE DOCTRINAL CONSIDERATIONS

Partly as a consequence of the American connection, all British nuclear forces are committed to the 'international defense of the Western Alliance'[1] and integrated with American forces for planning purposes. All retain national roles as well. There is a view that 'independent deterrence' as a military doctrine was born in the ashes of Suez and expired, with great drama, at the Nassau Conference in 1962. This view does not bear careful scrutiny. Inchoate notions of independent deterrence mark the history of British thinking about nuclear weaponry and, it is argued here, London began gearing procurement decisions to the expectation of independent employment well before 1957. Conversely, the most obvious technical manifestation of British emphasis on national, as opposed to allied, missions occurred with the Polaris Improvement Programme in the late 1970s. The object of this chapter is to examine how these two missions were reconciled as British nuclear weapons doctrine evolved over time and to analyse the doctrinal considerations that influenced third-generation strategic force procurement decisions.

The earliest post-war appraisals of the military impact of nuclear weapons in Britain turned on the country's vulnerability and the insurmountable problems of defence.

> It had become a major tenet of faith among the Chiefs of Staff and Ministers alike that the United Kingdom was peculiarly vulnerable to attack with atomic bombs, rockets, and biological weapons; that a third major war would be utterly disastrous, and that the supreme object of British policy must be to prevent war, in particular by deterring aggression which might lead to war.[2]

When the Chiefs were asked to specify weapons requirements in early 1946, they couched their response in terms of deterrence and made clear their expectation of the putative source of aggression: the Soviet Union. By 1947, the Chiefs argued, in a formal defence policy review, that not only was defence impossible (hence *atomic* attack must be deterred) but that 'the knowledge that we possess weapons of mass destruction and were prepared to use them would be the most effective deterrent *to war itself*'.[3]

Thus, by 1947, the notion of nuclear deterrence had clearly taken hold in British thinking and the putative aggressor had been identified.[4] But *who* was to deter was not yet clear. There is no evidence that American participation in war was expected with confidence in British planning. In 1948, however, American aircraft were deployed to Britain and equipped, eventually, with atomic weapons. The expectation that British forces would be a 'contribution' to an allied force began to colour British planning and shape actual procurement decisions. Lord Portal's review of atomic energy production in that year presupposed an Anglo–American alliance.[5] After thorough review of the Soviet target set, it was estimated that some six hundred weapons would be the minimum necessary to defeat, and hence deter, serious Soviet aggression in Europe — which was not expected until about 1957. The American stockpile was then estimated — without a shred of evidence — at four hundred weapons and Britain's contribution sized at two hundred. This figure was adopted as the atomic energy programme's target.

It is clear, then, that the earliest 'hard' specification of Britain's nuclear weapons requirements presupposed an allied, rather than a national, mission. The ramifications of this decision merit discussion. Quite early, as we have seen, the British conceived of atomic weapons as a deterrent to war itself. They believed that only these weapons could counter Soviet conventional strength. 'The bomb', wrote the Chiefs in 1949, 'is incomparably the most powerful weapon in the world today and its possession in adequate numbers is the only means in the military sphere of offsetting the enormous Russian preponderance in conventional armaments.'[6] But the task of deterring Soviet military power was to be primarily an American responsibility and the British entertained no illusions in 1948 (or later) that they could make more than a 'contribution'. There was an implicit recognition that British forces in and of themselves would be incapable of this mission. No systematic evaluation of national mission requirements was evidently attempted. Either no national use was intended — that is, the force was intended solely as a 'contribution' — or it was simply assumed that the 'contribution' would suffice for national purposes if necessary. The latter assumption, at root, would imply a recognition that what is necessary to deter the Russians from attacking Western Europe and what is necessary to deter them from attacking Britain are quite different things — in short, proportional deterrence.

The experiences of the next three years would seem to belie an argument that no independent mission was envisaged. In 1948-9, with

USAF B-29s in Britain, no doubt about the willingness of the United States to wage war for Europe was evident in British deliberations; indeed, the British at this time were more concerned with American nuclear precipitancy than reticence. The twin shocks of 1949 – the news that American stockpiles were already quite substantial and the success of the Soviets in developing an atom bomb – cast doubt on the priority, if not the very existence, of Britain's project. That American progress should cause such consternation is evidence of the degree to which Britain's forces were seen as a contribution; that the project survived review is evidence of a powerful, if inchoate, sense of the potential for independent uses. At one point, the Chiefs asked: could Britain afford to abandon 'so powerful a weapon when she might one day again find herself fighting alone?'[7] It is only in such sentiments that the germ of independent deterrence is to be found

The Soviet test gave rise to expectations of war in the near term and these were heavily reinforced by the outbreak of war in Korea. The perceived imminence of conflict caused an alteration in priorities and defensive guided-missile research and development were raised to atomic energy's hitherto singular priority. In the rearmament programme mounted by Attlee, massive expenditure was devoted to defensive systems, particularly day and night fighters. What is intriguing here is that, given the emphasis on deterrence which had coloured earlier thought, why was consideration not given to reliance on the *American* deterrent, rich with weapons, based in England and, it was feared, all too ready to go? Scarce pounds might have been better spent on offensive weapons systems. The rationale for emphasis on defence was that war might come before *British* weapons were at hand. If independent deterrence could not be procured in time, then resources should be, and were, shifted to independent defence.[8]

This instinctive unwillingness to trust the fate of a vulnerable island to an ally emerges in the Global Strategy Paper of 1952, a document of great significance for the Atlantic Alliance as a whole.[9] Churchill's government was forced upon taking office first to delay and then to cut back Attlee's massive £4,700 million rearmament programme. Concerned with the economic burden of defence, the Prime Minister ordered a thorough review of British defence policy. The Chiefs of Staff retired to Greenwich and, in the absence of advisers, drew up the 'first systematic elaboration of strategic deterrence in the world', a policy subsequently adopted in Washington as 'the New Look', and at SHAPE as MC-14/2. It became known as the doctrine of 'massive retaliation'.

The Paper commenced with a restatement of objectives: to prevent

Communist success in subversion or war. Prevention of subversion would depend ultimately upon the strength of Western economies. Prevention of war would depend more and more upon Western superiority in atomic air power. Defence against atomic attack would prove impossible for Britain as well as the Soviet Union. Therefore the West should emphasize deterrence forces, making it clear that Soviet aggression in Europe would be met not only or even primarily at the scene of local conflict but punished by massive bombardment of the sources of power in the Soviet heartland. Conventional forces were clearly still necessary: in Europe, they would stay the Soviet advance until the effects of strategic air attack could tell; overseas, they must be available for such limited engagements as Korea, Malaya and Greece. However, the NATO force goals of 90 divisions, imposed by the Americans at Lisbon, were neither militarily necessary nor economically tenable. They were seen in London as an ill-conceived superimposition of conventional upon nuclear strategy.

Britain's part in the new strategy was fourfold: to influence Cold War policy; to meet NATO obligations, with perhaps 50,000 men; to prepare for war should deterrence fail; and to contribute, albeit modestly, to the 'main deterrent': the atomic air offensive.

The Chiefs' discussion of Britain's nuclear role is illuminating. The atomic deterrent was presently entirely American and, for essentially economic reasons, would remain largely an American responsibility. But a British contribution was nevertheless warranted. The Americans could not be counted upon to deal adequately with targets which did not directly affect their interests. Moreover, Britain's influence would depend upon her contribution.

> We feel that to have no share in what is recognized as the main deterrent in the cold war and the only allied offensive in a world war would seriously weaken British influence on United States policy and planning in the cold war and in war would mean that the United Kingdom would have no claim to any share in the policy and planning of the offensive.[10]

The alternative, raised in the 1949 Anglo-American negotiations, of an agreed supply of American weapons was discussed — and rejected. The Chiefs believed that such an agreement was possible after the 1952 elections and contended that even without formal accord, it was 'probable' that the United States would release weapons to the RAF in wartime. Nevertheless, they argued that it would be 'most unwise' for Britain to be 'completely dependent' upon the United States.

The two specific roles advanced for British forces in the Global Strategy Paper presupposed the efficacy of the Alliance, and the American guarantee. They did not, strictly speaking, require British weapons manufacture. Target coverage could have been guaranteed by provision of American weapons to the RAF. Influence could perhaps have been secured either by adoption of the 'common war plans', which were integral to the 1949 negotiation, and/or by the 'contribution' of British aircraft to the Alliance. The bulk of Strategic Air Command's front-line strength was based in Britain, subject to the government's political, and the RAF's physical, control. American stockpiles were vast and growing and, as the Chiefs had themselves argued with commendable prescience, delivery technology was now the 'crux' of deterrence.[11] The V-bombers were expected to be both more effective and less expensive than the USAF's B-47 and a diversion of resources might, at anticipated prices, have substantially increased aircraft production in Britain. Indeed, at this time, Washington was frequently suggesting that Britain should concentrate her energies on her real strength: aircraft design and development. In these circumstances, the Chiefs' recommendation for a doubling of plutonium production must be seen as active pursuit of independent deterrence. No coherent doctrine was yet advanced and no independent employment assumptions apparently made. The Americans were still held to be reliable and British policy would consciously endeavour to ensure their reliability. But the Chiefs were looking ahead, to an era of novel, long-range delivery technology, in the certain knowledge that the United States, the Soviet Union and Britain herself were developing a most revolutionary weapon: the hydrogen bomb.

It is impossible to ascertain with certainty when British nuclear force planning came to emphasize national as opposed to allied missions. Internal documents from the post-1952 period remain classified. It seems clear, none the less, that the development of a doctrine of independent deterrence was linked to the emergence of megaton weapons. On the one hand, Britain's strategic vulnerability was highlighted all the more starkly and classical air defence efforts appeared all the more absurd. On the other hand, however, Soviet vulnerability had increased by orders of magnitude. As Eden put it:

All became equally vulnerable. I had been acutely conscious in the atomic age of our unenviable position in a small and crowded island, but if continents, and not merely small islands were doomed to destruction, all was equal in the grim reckoning.[12]

In the thermonuclear age, any doubt as to Britain's capacity to inflict unacceptable damage upon an opponent vanished.

Eden's observation spoke as eloquently to the American as to the Soviet continent, however. As Churchill argued in 1955:

> In 3 or 4 years' time, it may even be sooner, the scene will be changed. The Soviets will probably stand possessed of hydrogen weapons and the means of delivering them not only on the United Kingdom but also on North American targets.[13]

It is significant that the Prime Minister made this point while announcing that development of hydrogen weapons was under way in Britain. Thermonuclear technology not only provided the capacity, but heralded the need, for independent deterrence. Churchill did not, of course, draw publicly the conclusion that, when American cities become vulnerable, American willingness to wage strategic nuclear war in response to European events must necessarily decline. But that conclusion was drawn privately. In late 1954, the government determined that, in view of the increase in destructive power represented by hydrogen weapons, V-bomber procurement could be cut back from 250 to 180 aircraft. It is likely that the first systematic calculations of the requirements of independently deterring Soviet aggression against Britain and British interests underlay – or at least justified – this decision. Since that time, procurement decisions always reflected national mission requirements. Blue Streak was characterized as being particularly suited to British requirements; Polaris was optimized for countervalue missions – the dispersal pattern of A-3 MRVs was designed to maximize urban-industrial damage for given weights and yields – and the Polaris Improvement Programme was specifically tailored to overcome Moscow's Golosh ABM defences.

In their independent role, British forces were intended to deter serious Soviet conventional or nuclear attack on the British Isles. Conventional attack across the Channel was, of course, unlikely given local British naval superiority. Critics argued that, in view of the peculiar vulnerability of Britain, no government would order a first strike in response to conventional invasion. In light of both the improbability and gravity of the provocation, however, a threatened first strike in these circumstances would not seem inherently incredible. Much more important was the threat of Soviet nuclear attack. Hosting American as well as her own nuclear forces, Britain posed an extremely lucrative target set to the Soviet Union. Attlee's acceptance of USAF B-29s in 1948 had been predicated upon his assumption that Britain would deploy national forces well before a serious Soviet nuclear threat would emerge. When that expectation was shattered by the Soviet test in 1949, the British — and Churchill in particular[14] — evinced grave concern about the extra burden of risk Britain now bore in the 'Airstrip One' relationship. De Gaulle sought to santuarize France from nuclear war by at once raising the risks attending any Soviet attack — by procurement of national forces — and lowering the incentives for such strikes — by removal of American nuclear-capable aircraft. The British could not pursue this strand of Gallic logic; they believed, no doubt correctly, that to do so would fundamentally undermine the Alliance and the American presence in Europe.

As the United States herself became vulnerable, there was no longer any certainty that she would regard strikes on British soil as identical to an attack upon herself. A central national mission for Britain's forces then was to deter Soviet counterforce strikes on the Anglo–American base structure in Britain. A limited reprisal to Soviet counterforce strikes was not possible — with their bases under attack, surviving bombers would have to proceed to their targets — nor was it necessary. Soviet weapons were at this time crude, inaccurate and of heavy yield. To be effective, surface bursts were necessary and the resulting collateral damage might have differed little from a countervalue attack, particularly in view of British demography. Moreover, the British expected political warning and their plans to disperse the V-bombers to anywhere from 40 to 100 bases not only increased the force's survivability but raised the collateral damage attending any Soviet first strike, and hence the credibility of a threat to respond against Soviet cities. This strategy depended, of course, on the survivability of at least some portion of Britain's nuclear forces. Churchill argued the necessity of secure, second-strike forces as early as 1955[15] and thereafter Herculean efforts were devoted to this end, resulting finally in the switch to sea-based deterrence with Polaris.

The British maintained that the independent capacity of their forces to initiate strategic nuclear war was of direct benefit to the security of Western Europe, primarily by ensuring that the Americans would fulfil their commitments. The United States was committed, in NATO doctrine, to undertaking a massive nuclear bombardment of the Soviet Union in response to even conventional aggression. The advent of American vulnerability, exemplified by the flight of Sputnik I, seemed to undermine the credibility of this threat, to 'decouple' Europe from the American guarantee. British forces, by virtue of their capacity to 'trigger' American forces, could 'recouple' American strategic forces to Europe's fate. Essentially two 'trigger' scenarios were advanced. The first posited Soviet inability to distinguish British from American warheads. A British attack would occasion a blind Soviet response against the entire Western target system and, suspecting this result, the Americans would have enormous damage-limitation incentives to pre-empt. The more sophisticated variant incorporated notions of proportional deterrence and conceded Moscow's ability to discern the origins of an attack, either through technical means or direct communication with Washington.[16] However, the Russians would be unwilling to endure the damage threatened by British forces while leaving the United States unscathed. They would mount an attack on the United States — but the United States foreseeing this, would again pre-empt.

The first scenario presupposed not only that nuclear forces were governed by a hair trigger — which was legitimate given the technical state of the art — but also that Washington and Moscow would not communicate — despite palpable incentives to do so. The second scenario had its merits, but unless Britain herself were attacked she had neither the forces not presumably the will to inflict sufficient damage upon the Soviet Union as to cause Moscow concern about the post-war balance. The general utility of a British 'contribution' to the Alliance's deterrent lay in Britain's geographical proximity to the Continent. She was (and is) by orders of magnitude more sensitive politically to European events than the United States and despite her strategic vulnerability, she might be willing independently to escalate conflict for this reason. Macmillan, speaking in Boston in 1960, stressed this 'European dimension' of the independent deterrent.

> We have always been ready in the last resort to fight alone. Our determination to make our own contribution was in a sense instinctive. And perhaps with the Atlantic Ocean between us it has been no bad thing for the people of Europe to see that at least one European member shares the nuclear power with you.[17]

Margaret Thatcher's Minister of Defence, Francis Pym, repeated it, with greater emphasis, in the Commons on 24 January 1980.[18] However sincere the British were in their own estimates of their nuclear 'contribution' to the Alliance, it is also clear that London hoped that emphasis on the strategic significance of the independent deterrent would quell allied criticism of the dwindling size of Britain's conventional contribution.

The British had of course pioneered the doctrine of massive retaliation in the Global Strategy Paper. They did not give it full effect until 1957 largely because of continuing demands on their conventional forces and the slow development of their nuclear forces. In 1954, Britain committed four divisions to the Continent in order to secure French acquiescence in West German rearmament and prevent thereby an 'agonizing reappraisal' of American policy towards Europe. These forces were not warranted militarily in London's view but were politically essential. While Churchill governed, he would brook no talk of scaling down the British Army of the Rhine. He felt that peace depended on American troops in Europe and that American troops would not long remain after a British withdrawal. By 1955, however, it was clear that Britain could no longer afford a large conventional establishment. A peculiarly fierce competition between defence needs and economic health plagued British policy throughout the post-war era.[19] Insupportable on the strength of domestic resources, the British people had to 'export or starve'. Virtually all British exports were manufactures and consequently defence, which drained skilled men and machinery from the export trade, directly conflict with national economic imperatives. By 1956, Eden was determined to reduce the size of the armed forces from 700,000 to 450,000 by 1960-1. Before he could implement his plan, however, the Suez crisis broke, as did, in turn, Eden's health and power. It was left to Macmillan and Duncan Sandys to announce in 1957 the abolition of conscription and concomitant salience of nuclear weapons in Britain's defence posture.[20]

Partly because of its conformity with their national economic circumstances, the British had encouraged the adoption by the Alliance of a first-strike massive retaliation doctrine and subsequently steadfastly resisted revisionism — whether from domestic adherents of 'graduated deterrence' or American proponents of 'flexible response'. The 1957 and, particularly, the 1958 Defence White Papers embodied stark expressions of doctrine:

> The West relies for its defence primarily upon the deterrent effect of its vast stockpile of nuclear weapons and its capacity to deliver them. The democratic Western nations will never start a war against Russia. But it must be well understood that if Russia were to launch a major attack on them, even with conventional weapons only, they would have to hit back with strategic nuclear weapons. In fact, the

strategy of NATO is based on the frank recognition that a full scale Soviet attack could not be repelled without resort to a massive nuclear bombardment of the sources of power in Russia.[21]

British leaders frankly admitted the economic foundation of this policy. An alternative stategy would

> entail a stupendous increase in the demands of defence upon manpower, money and industry. We in Britain might have to maintain between 1 million and 1½ million men in the Armed Forces and spend perhaps £1,000 million more a year on the defence budget.[22]

There were, however, purely doctrinal objections to 'flexible response'. When, in 1955, Churchill had conjured the coming age of mutual deterrence, he did not dwell on its potential dangers but on the likelihood that the peace would be strengthened: 'Then it may be that we shall, by a process of sublime irony, have reached a stage in this story where safety shall be the sturdy child of terror, and survival the twin brother of annihilation.'[23] The British believed that war was unlikely, but that any war — conventional or nuclear — would be utterly disastrous in its consequences for Britain and for Europe. They felt that even an irrational threat would, by inculcating uncertainty, prove a more effective deterrent to war than a defence structure which increased the certainty of Western response only by reducing the risks Moscow need run. Deployment of substantial conventional forces, in an effort to 'raise the nuclear threshold', might as easily legitimate as deter war on the conventional level. By 1960-2, British White Papers spoke of the need for a 'balanced' — nuclear and conventional — deterrent. But London shared with other European capitals a profound distaste for the essentially conventional strategy originally proposed by Secretary McNamara. When the Alliance came, under British leadership, to accept 'flexible response' in 1967, the new doctrine relied on a threat of deliberate nuclear escalation far more than the United States would have wished.

The Nassau Agreement of 1962 committed Britain's nuclear forces to NATO, while reserving the right to national employment where the British government determined that 'supreme national interests are at stake'. It was commonly assumed thereafter that British missiles were targeted by the Supreme Allied Command (SACEUR) against fixed military targets in Eastern Europe and western Russia. National targeting plans for independent missions were assumed to coexist. Britain's

Polaris missiles carried multiple guidance tapes and were readily retargetable. Thus, there was no technical impediment to dedicating the Polaris force to theatre nuclear tasks. There were, however, insurmountable doctrinal obstacles to employment of Polaris for theatre escalation or retaliation strikes. In the benchmark scenario of a conventional/ tactical nuclear conflict in Central Europe, SACEUR would be likely to seek authority to conduct deep theatre strikes for either interdiction or escalatory purposes well before British national employment would be in question. It is simply inconceivable that a British government would divest itself of a 'last resort' deterrent merely in order to participate in theatre strikes. It is precisely in such circumstances that 'supreme national interests' would compel British national command authorities to withhold Polaris from SACEUR.

Thus, Britain's dedication of her Polaris forces to NATO in 1962 either did not entail a commitment to engage in theatre strikes or was militarily meaningless. British governments habitually referred to Polaris as its contribution to NATO's *strategic* deterrent. When, in 1981, the Russians contended that British forces should be included in Soviet–American intermediate-range nuclear forces (INF) negotiations in Geneva, both London and Washington hastened to object that Britain's weapons were strategic in character and not properly part of theatre nuclear balance. It is therefore reasonable to conclude that the commitment of British nuclear forces to the Alliance meant nothing more than continuation of Anglo–American co-ordination of general nuclear response plans. British forces were not analogous to the American Poseidon forces targeted by SACEUR. They were analogous to the remainder of the American submarine fleet, whose mission was to threaten and, if necessary, to inflict assured urban-industrial destruction upon the Soviet Union. In both allied and independent missions, the British were targeted against the Soviet heartland.

Thus, neither 'integration' with American forces in 1958 nor 'dedication' to NATO in 1962 imposed conflicting missions upon Britain's strategic forces. In both their NATO and national missions, these forces were to be employed only at the final hour and only with the deadliest effect. This understanding of the deterrent's Alliance role sheds light on what the British had originally hoped to achieve by an 'independent contribution' and what circumstances were expected to give rise to independent deterrence. If British forces operated as an integral element to American second-strike forces, and the Americans and British responded jointly to strikes on British soil just as they would to strikes on American soil, there would be no occasion for independent action.

The independent contribution would have succeeded in its purpose, linking Britain to the United States in a single strategic unit. If, however, American resolution faltered, and a strategically meaningful distinction between Britain and the United States emerged, independent deterrence would commence. Roughly, the same type of force was suitable for both roles but, in case of doubt, preference was to be given to the demands of the national mission.[24] As allied anxiety about the strategic balance between the United States and the Soviet Union increased in the late 1970s, the British began to voice more forthrightly a view of import of Britain's 'independent contribution' to the Alliance which resolved at a stroke any potential tension between allied and independent missions. The Thatcher government adopted a view of the deterrent which had been quietly bruited by British officials for twenty years: that the utility of British forces for the Alliance lay precisely in their evident capacity for independent action.

> We need to convince Soviet leaders that even if they thought at some critical point as a conflict developed that the U.S. would hold back, the British force could still inflict a blow so destructive that the penalty for aggression would have proved too high.[25]

This rationale had the merit of portraying the pursuit of independent deterrence as fidelity to the Alliance and countering those critics who argued that retention of a modest capability to participate in American strikes would in future suffice.[26]

Theoreticians and commentators exercised themselves greatly over the place and implications of tactical nuclear weapons in French doctrine. British substrategic weapons, on the other hand, never figured prominently in discussions of independent deterrence. After the cancellation of the Blue Water missile in 1962,[27] the Rhine Army's tactical weapons systems were American in origin and operated under 'dual-key' arrangements. The Heath government considered arming the Army's Lance missiles with British weapons but decided against it on economic grounds. RAF Germany's Jaguar aircraft were equipped with British weapons and deployed for battlefield support of the Rhine Army. In addition, Strike Command's Vulcan and Buccaneer squadrons, based in Britain, were armed with British weapons. These aircraft, maintained at high readiness as part of NATO's Quick Reaction Alert (QRA) forces, were targeted in SACEUR's scheduled strike programmes against military installations deep in Warsaw Pact territory. It is also very likely that the RAF also continued to plan for independent employment of, at least, the Vulcan squadrons. British tactical and theatre nuclear forces 'remain[ed] very firmly under British political control'.[28] They could be withheld from SACEUR in the event of compelling circumstances.

Such circumstances were considered unlikely. If, for example, Bundeswehr commanders requested tactical-nuclear air strikes to slow the advance of Soviet armour, a British Prime Minister would probably not refuse authorization. First, land-based Bundeswehr launchers might already have been outfitted with American weapons and tactical nuclear exchanges might already have commenced. Moreover, if SACEUR were to call on the nuclear resources of RAF Germany, then it would be likely that the Soviet breakthrough threatened the Rhine Army as well as the Bundeswehr. Finally, British refusal to authorize nuclear weapons use, while certainly legal, would be an empty gesture, as SACEUR could easily call on American resources. RAF Germany's nuclear-capable aircraft would be denied to. SACEUR only if, in a débâcle analogous to the Battle of France, London wished to retain national resources to cover the Rhine Army's retreat to the sea. That denial would be militarily significant only if American nuclear-capable aircraft were unavailable.

British initiation of tactical nuclear warfare was, on the other hand, a somewhat more likely contingency. The Rhine Army was widely expected to bear the brunt of any Soviet attack on the Central Front and circumstances in which the Army's survival was in peril were easily imaginable. In such circumstances, the Rhine Army's Commander — in his allied guise as Commander, Northern Army Group — would request SACEUR, always an American, for authorization. If SACEUR refused a reasonable request, the British might be compelled to take unilateral action. If he concurred, he would then contact Downing Street. Under a long-standing 'gentlemen's agreement' — a vestige of the Quebec Agreement's consent clause — Presidents and Prime Ministers are obliged to consult about any use of nuclear weapons.[29] The Prime Minister would nevertheless retain full decision-making powers and if he or she ordered nuclear weapons employment, SACEUR would be obliged to obey. His refusal to do so because of American anxieties would be at once ineffective — as the order could be transmitted directly from Downing Street to RAF Germany — and portentous — as the Americans would, with this act, have deserted the Alliance. Thus, negative independence — withholding tactical forces from SACEUR — would be strictly legal but in all probability, militarily meaningless and therefore politically foolish. Positive independence — initiating tactical nuclear exchanges – would be a technical breach of NATO's command structure but would be conceivable only if the Alliance were already crumbling. There was no unavoidable tension between allied and any residual national missions for Britain's tactical nuclear forces.

There was, however, a more substantial possibility of conflict between the NATO and national missions of the RAF's Vulcan and Buccaneer squadrons in Britain. The national deterrence role had, of course, been transferred to the Royal Navy in 1969. The existence of Polaris as an ultimate deterrent released the Vulcans and Buccaneers for penultimate tasks, whether escalatory or retaliatory, allied or independent. There was little distinction, temporal or spatial, between SACEUR and national employment conditions. The British, in a national use scenario, might employ the Vulcans (or, eventually, Tornados) either to signal grave concern with the course of battle in Europe, perhaps raising escalation risks by engaging targets in the Soviet Union; or to conduct interdiction strikes deep in Pact territory; or, assuming survival, to respond to Soviet nuclear counterforce strikes against British soil. SACEUR would be likely to employ RAF aircraft in similar missions against similar targets at about the same stage of conflict. Only if a British government were to attempt to retain 'sanctuary' status would SACEUR's use of British-based aircraft seem to conflict with 'supreme national interests'. The government would, of course, be compelled to restrain American nuclear operations if its denial of the RAF squadrons was to be effective. These circumstances were hardly inconceivable, but they were sufficiently unlikely that the government could plan to optimize any follow-on theatre systems for allied, rather than national, roles.

When the British began, in the late 1970s, to consider alternative means of replacing both their strategic and their theatre nuclear forces, they did so in a threat environment markedly different from the strategic setting of the Polaris procurement decision. Massive American nuclear superiority had given way to the prospect of strategic inferiority in the 1980s. Superiority had afforded some confidence that the United States would, in the event, prove willing to employ nuclear weapons in the defence of Europe. Parity, codified in the SALT process, undermined that confidence substantially. At least, it was incontrovertible that the growth of Soviet offensive capabilities greatly aggravated the risks of damage to the United States accompanying use of American nuclear weapons in Europe. American forces were accordingly less credible as a deterrent to Soviet counterforce strikes on the Anglo–American base structure in Britain.

The Soviet threat to undertake such strikes was, moreover, far more credible than it had been in the 1960s. Soviet SS-4 and SS-5 intermediate-range ballistic missiles were very primitive devices. Laborious — and highly visible — preparations were necessary to ready them for use, during which they were extremely vulnerable to Western counterforce attacks. They were tipped with large-yield warheads and poor guidance packages. It was unclear whether their fusing technology permitted air-bursting; it was certain that in order to have a reasonable chance of success against military targets, they would have to be employed in a surface-bursting mode. The collateral damage attending such an attack would have been astronomical. Thus, a surprise attack by surface-bursting SS-4s or SS-5s limited to installations in Britain housing nuclear weapons systems capable of engaging targets in the Soviet Union — i.e. American and British SSBN, cruise missile and strike aircraft bases — might have resulted in between 5 and 7 million casualties. With warning, these forces would be dispersed and a similar attack would entail many millions more casualties.

The SS-20, a modern, mobile intermediate-range weapon first deployed in the mid-1970s, was a far more discriminating weapon. Its re-entry vehicles could be delivered accurately and air-bursted over their targets. It was virtually invulnerable to pre-emptive attack. It could be employed with far less collateral damage. Hence, a surprise counterforce attack against the target set assumed above — American and British SSBN, cruise missile and strike aircraft bases — might occasion some six hundred thousand casualties. Moreover, surprise was possible with SS-20, while it was not possible with SS-4s and SS-5s. But even if, as would be likely, British and American forces had dispersed upon receipt of political warning, an SS-20 attack on long-range nuclear-strike forces might result in less than 2 million casualties.

The discriminatory attack capability represented by the SS-20 confirmed the wisdom of basing the deterrent at sea. But it also placed a premium on retention of a flexible nuclear posture, capable of responding proportionately to Soviet counterforce attacks. The British had quietly enjoyed such a posture with the combination of the Polaris fleet and the Vulcan squadrons. Strike Command had not taken their formal relinquishment of the independent deterrent in 1969 with undue seriousness. The Vulcan squadrons had been rigorously drilled in low-level strike tactics and maintained at high readiness. The RAF believed that perhaps a third of the bombers might penetrate Soviet defences and reach their targets under independent employment conditions.[30] By the late 1970s, however, the Vulcans were obsolescent and scheduled for withdrawal. They were to be replaced by shorter-range Tornados. It was partly concern with the implications of Vulcan's withdrawal for Britain's national deterrence posture that fed official enthusiasm for a British contribution to NATO's proposed long-range theatre nuclear force modernization programme. It was a measure of British success in resolving the doctrinal tensions of independent deterrence within the Alliance that the Americans welcomed the idea.[31] The British argued that retention of British theatre forces made it inherently more likely that selective attack against Britain would be countered by attacks against the Soviet Union. This argument dovetailed precisely with the fundamental military rationale for modernizing long-range forces at all, for it was felt that Moscow was more likely to be deterred by an allied force structure which credibly threatened retaliation against the Soviet Union proper, than by a similar threat to Eastern Europe.

A discrete replacement for the Vulcan squadrons proved in the event unattainable.[32] Flexibility had, therefore, to be built into Polaris's replacement. It should be pointed out that the sort of flexibility the British sought in third-generation forces did not include a capability to destroy very 'hard' targets. The Soviet Union offered a plethora of large 'soft' military targets and moderately protected political-military command targets. Indeed, it might be argued that Britain should respond to counterforce attack with a limited countervalue strike. For both demographic and weapons-availability reasons, Britain is unlikely ever to be able to sustain a prolonged counterforce 'duel'. It might therefore behove the government to signal immediately its unwilling-ness to tolerate conflict at the counterforce level. But flexibility did require third-generation forces manifestly capable of responding proportionally to Soviet strikes. This meant that, in addition to the fundamental attribute of pre-launch survivability, Polaris's successor had to enjoy a substantial measure of post-launch survivability. Only then could the deterrent pose a 'clear chain of immense risk'[33] to the Russians and deter thereby strikes which, quite possibly, would be critical to the success or failure of Soviet arms in Europe.

Britain's ability to deter any nuclear strike depended upon the proposition that the damage she could ultimately inflict, while perhaps minuscule in relation to the damage threatened by Soviet forces, would be simply unacceptable to the Soviet Union. The difficulties of assess-ing what level or even kind of damage might prove unacceptable to Moscow are legion. In the 1960s, Secretary of Defense McNamara asserted an absolute measure. General Pierre Gallois differed and articulated a notion that had underlain British nuclear policy since 1948: that 'unacceptable damage' is a relative rather than an absolute value, that the risks the aggressor will run vary directly with the stakes and that therefore the two superpowers could endure far more damage from each other than they could accept from third powers.[34] Polaris's replacement had of course to be procured with the expectation of independent employment, that is, with the expectation that it would be used at a juncture when the Americans were not engaged in conflict or, what was more likely, they were not engaged at the escalatory level which the British government felt impelled to approach. British doctrine could not realistically assume that American forces simply did not exist. Moreover, any imaginable situation in which nuclear weapons were used by both London and Moscow would clearly be a crisis of the most serious dimensions. American forces and their prospective employment would loom large on the horizon.

> Indeed, one practical approach to judging how much deterrent power Britain needs is to consider what type and scale of damage Soviet leaders might think likely to leave them critically handicapped afterwards in continuing confrontation with a relatively unscathed United States.[35]

A strategy designed to capitalize on Soviet concern with other and deadlier enemies could take a variety of forms. Thus, Britain might have sought to expose the Soviet Union acutely to American force employment by targeting air defence and ABM radar complexes, C-3 and intelligence installations, interceptor bases, SAM sites, submarine pens, tank marshalling yards, naval air stations, fleet transit points and the like. In circumstances where British strikes would be conceivable, this sort of damage might pose a more chilling threat to the Soviet leadership than straightforward urban-industrial damage. Moreover, it is at least possible that these sorts of strikes would not occasion massive Soviet retaliation against British cities. However, as a primary strategy — and certainly as a guide to procurement decisions — this approach was unsatisfactory. It depended upon two somewhat competing assumptions: firstly, that the United States would be closely involved in conflict as this sort of damage is progressively less significant as American strategic forces are further removed from warfare; and secondly, that American forces would not already be engaged in intercontinental counterforce exchange and attempting to limit conflict at that level. The significance of any British threat, in these circumstances, would lie solely in Britain's capacity to elevate conflict to countervalue exchanges against the wishes of Moscow and very probably Washington as well. Moreover, if the Americans were not engaged in counterforce exchanges, they would be unlikely to welcome British escalation to that level and might therefore deny the British access to intelligence critical to the effectiveness of a counterforce strike. A strategy designed to expose the Soviet Union to its enemies by destroying 'time-urgent' military targets was therefore not tenable.

In the most likely nuclear conflict conditions, Britain had to be prepared to escalate to countervalue strikes if threatened employment of British forces was to have significance. Moreover, it was prudent, given the unavoidable uncertainty in judgements of an opponent's values, to rest deterrence primarily upon a threat to values most universally cherished – people and industry. But these considerations need not confine British doctrine to a pre-programmed, and ultimately purposeless, slaughter, nor need they obviate the genuine strategic advantage afforded Britain by the political-military reality of multiple nuclear threats to the Soviet Union. It was possible to inflict significant urban-industrial damage in a targeting plan designed to threaten the political order of the Soviet Union. A highly centralized command economy, the Soviet Union incorporates an array of ethnically diverse and disaffected groups in an empire bound together, to a considerable extent, by the power of the Red Army. It is therefore doubly vulnerable. A breakdown of central economic direction would paralyse economic life while disruption of government, party and military control might well threaten national unity.

Nuclear strikes against hardened elite shelters, certain critical military C-3 and intelligence facilities, military and paramilitary command centres, national communications nodes, government and party administrative headquarters, rail and road links, as well as Moscow, selected industrial centres and republic capitals could both cripple economic exchange and undermine the ascendancy of the Soviet leadership. With such a diverse and rich target set, the British could not inflict enduring damage but, given the shadow of American power, they need not be concerned with the duration of damage. A critical period – weeks, perhaps months – would ensue when the very foundations of the Soviet state might be in jeopardy. Armies committed in foreign fields might, in the appalling confusion, be temporarily cut off from resupply – a doubly perilous prospect as victories gained could be suddenly at risk and soldiers far from home would be unavailable to reassert Moscow's authority in disaffected regions. Even minor damage to production, coupled with disruption of internal communications, could trip a society afflicted with shortages into genuine privation. At an extraordinarily tense juncture, when Soviet leaders would be uncertain from hour to hour of American intentions, they would hesitate long before risking damage of this kind. It may be that London fashioned its targeting policy to threaten such damage. Certainly, British procurement practices — and the Chevaline programme in particular — suggest a strong commitment to retaining an ability to attack Moscow, the political and economic linchpin of the Soviet system and the Thatcher government let it be known that British deterrence policy rests upon a credible threat to 'key aspects of Soviet state power'.[36]

Speculation about the kind and duration of damage Britain needed to threaten in order to deter the Soviet Union begged the larger question of level — how much damage will suffice? In the worst case — only one submarine at sea and the Vulcan force destroyed — British forces were capable of destroying Moscow and perhaps ten other major urban-industrial complexes. Chevaline would increase the efficiency of attacks on Moscow and therefore permit the British to attack a somewhat larger target set. With any kind of strategic warning, the Navy could generate the Polaris force and guarantee at least two and probably three SSBNs at sea while the RAF would disperse the Vulcan squadrons. In these circumstances, the British could credibly threaten thereafter perhaps forty target-complexes in the defence environment of the early 1980s. One question underlying the Polaris replacement debate concerned the likelihood that Soviet defences would improve and the appropriateness of particular options as hedges against such improvements. A second and analytically distinct question was whether the threat currently posed by the Polaris force was adequate. That threat was awesome, but then so was the historical record of Soviet endurance and resilience.

There was, of course, no way to assess the adequacy of the Polaris threat. All one could ask was, assuming it was once sufficient, would it suffice in future? It could be argued that emerging strategic superiority would increase Soviet endurance of third-country attacks; thus, as the correlation of forces shifted in Soviet favour, the damage requirements for Britain's minimum deterrence rose correspondingly. This argument was, however, flawed. There was no clear reason to assume that the trends of the late 1970s and early 1980s — that is, trends in Moscow's favour — would continue throughout the operational lifetime of strategic forces which would enter service in the 1990s. Moreover, the impact of the growth of Soviet offensive capabilities upon the viability of Britain's deterrence posture would depend upon British doctrine. If London opted for a strategy designed to expose the Soviet Union to imminent American nuclear-force employment, then the significance of the threat posed thereby would vary directly with the margin of Soviet superiority. If Moscow calculated that, even blinded and partially exposed by a British counterforce attack, it could still wage counterforce battle with the United States and prevail, and further reckoned that Washington shared this view, then it would not be deterred by a British counterforce attack. But it was not immediately apparent what the growth of Soviet offensive capabilities had to do with Soviet willingness to endure urban-industrial damage – particularly urban-industrial damage distributed in a manner designed to maximize domestic unrest. Strategic superiority provided the Soviet Union, if anything, with greater confidence that it could fight, limit and win a war at subcountervalue levels, by deterring American escalation. Third-power escalation to countervalue exchanges seemed quite as threatening as heretofore, as it would drive conflict from a level when the Soviet Union might be able to win a great deal relatively cheaply to a level where, for the foreseeable future, 'winning' was liable to be problematical. Indeed, third-power nuclear forces would seem to pose problems to the Soviet Union in the 1980s and 1990s quite analogous to those they posed to the United States in the 1960s.

Soviet strategic superiority could occasion the 'decoupling' of American forces from conflict in Europe and thus it might be thought that in this manner the growth of Soviet offensive forces would inflate the damage requirements of independent deterrence. But here it was appropriate to ask a very basic question – was Britain, as a straightforward economic prize of war worth, say, ten or twenty Soviet cities? Britain's significance both as a threat to the Soviet Union and as a strategic prize would vary directly with the extent of American involvement in war. In the absence of American help, Britain would be unlikely to wage nuclear war in response to Continental events, still less would she reinvade Europe or endeavour long to sustain conventional combat on the Continent. As American involvement in conflict rises, so would Britain's importance as threat and prize, but so also would the relative impact of British escalation. It would therefore appear that the efficacy of Britain's deterrence posture is dependent on neither the growth of Soviet offensive capabilities nor the extent of American involvement in war.

If the level of damage threatened by Polaris did not appear manifestly inadequate, neither did it appear manifestly adequate. It was accepted as a minimum measure of the 'ultimate' deterrent. Rather more firepower, as well as a capacity for selective strikes, would be necessary if Polaris's replacement was also to serve as the Vulcans' successor. The Thatcher government's eventual decision to procure Trident II might be thought to reflect a conscious decision that the level of threat posed by the Polaris fleet and the Vulcan squadrons was now clearly insufficient. It did not. The Trident decision, informed by the several strands of Britain's nuclear story, emerged from a more complex calculus.

Notes

1. 'Statement on Nuclear Defense Systems (21 December 1962)', quoted in Andrew Pierre, *Nuclear Politics* (Oxford University Press, London, 1972), p. 347.

2. Gowing II, p. 187.

3. Ibid., p. 215 (emphasis added).

4. It should be noted that there has long been controversy over this point. In the 1955 parliamentary defence debate, Emmanuel Shinwell, who had served as Attlee's Defence Minister, said: 'We were not thinking in terms of atomic deterrents at that time . . . we did not think that the atom bomb in itself would prove an effective deterrent.' This assertion has been accepted by a number of scholars; see, for example, Richard Gott, 'The Evolution of the Independent British Deterrent', *International Affairs*, vol. 39, no. 2 (April 1964), pp. 238–9. It simply does not square with the historical record.

5. Gowing II, p. 214.

6. Ibid., p. 218.

7. Ibid., p. 228.

8. In this as in any other procurement decision, there were a variety of factors in play: the legacy of the Battle of Britain, the very human instinct to seek even inadequate defence, the near-term threat of conventional air attack. Moreover, Britain was at this time producing excellent jet fighters which had bright export prospects as well as numerous overseas application, provided that unit costs could be held down through long production runs. Nevertheless, the essential point – that the British tended always to emphasize national resources when contemplating nuclear conflict – remains valid.

9. Although the Global Strategy Paper remains classified, researchers have been aware of its general gist for years (apparently from American sources). Gowing has seen the document itself and quotes directly from it. Relevant quotations here are drawn from her excerpts. Ibid., pp. 440–4.

10. Ibid., p. 441.

11. Ibid., p. 442.

12. Anthony Eden, *Full Circle* (Cassells, London, 1960), p. 368.

13. *Official Report* (Commons), vol. 537, 1 March 1955, col. 1897.

14. Gowing II, pp. 412–16.

15. *Official Report* (Commons), vol. 537, 1 March 1955, col. 1898.

16. See, for example, Marshall of the Royal Air Force Sir John Slessor, *What Price Co-existence?* (Praeger, New York, 1961), p. 110.

17. *The Times*, 9 May 1960, p. 1.

18. *Official Report* (Commons), vol. 977, 24 January 1980, cols. 678–82.

19. The economic burden under which the British laboured in the early post-war years bears review. Pre-war defence expenditure averaged about 3% of GNP, and this figure was amply compensated by 'invisible export' receipts from Britain's vast overseas investment portfolio equivalent to 8% of pre-war GNP. The war, however, saw divestment of at least £4,000 million – a figure equivalent to four-fifths of Britain's 1938 GNP – and imposed novel import requirements (to repair damaged plant, etc.). There was, therefore, an overwhelming economic case for reducing defence spending below the pre-war norm (3%) in 1945. In the event, expenditure soared to 11% of GNP by 1952–3 and did not drop below 6% until the mid-1960s. See David Greenwood, 'Defence and National Priorities since 1945', in John Baylis (ed.), *British Defence Policy in a Changing World* (Croom Helm, London, 1978).

20. Largely because of timing, the Sandys White Paper of 1957 is often seen as a reaction to Suez; this is not the case, as the trends in policy date at least back to 1952. However, Macmillan's decision to end conscription altogether was probably dictated by his concern for the Conservative Party's electoral prospects in the aftermath of Suez. In Eden's time, the Chiefs of Staff had agreed to a reduction of Army strength to 200,000. This was tantalizingly close to the 165,000 men the Central Statistics Office believed ˙could be˙ raised voluntarily. The Chiefs were asked to draw up a hypothetical deployment plan for an army of 165,000; they did so and, to their abiding chagrin, Macmillan and Sandys used it as a justification for the end of National Service.

An alternative agreement is often posed – see, for example, Pierre, *Nuclear Politics*, pp. 96–7 – that the British paid too little regard to the 'lessons of Suez'. Given the military irrelevance of nuclear weapons to the Suez campaign and their political irrelevance in the ensuing crisis in Anglo–American relations, the apparently novel emphasis upon strategic forces in post-Suez defence policy seems paradoxical. The real lesson of Suez, however, was economic: American manipulation of sterling had forced the British to quit their efforts. Sterling's weakness seemed to reflect the financial consequences of maintaining, largely out of deference to Washington, a large conventional establishment. This lesson could not have been lost on Macmillan who, as Chancellor, is said to have presented the Cabinet with a stark choice between cease-fire and devaluation. If serious consideration had been given to the lessons of Suez, it would have supported the policy laid down in 1952 and implemented in 1957.

21. *Report on Defence: Britain's Contribution to Peace and Security, 1958*, Cmnd. 363 (HMSO, London, 1958), p. 4.

22. *Official Report* (Commons), vol. 583, 26 February 1958, cols. 382–95.

23. *Official Report* (Commons), vol. 537, 1 March 1955, col. 1899.

24. See, e.g., Defence Minister Lord Carrington's testimony in House of Commons, Twelfth Report from the Expenditure Committee, Session 1972–3, *United Kingdom Nuclear Weapons Programme* (HMSO, London, 1973).

25. Ministry of Defence, *The Future United Kingdom Strategic Nuclear Deterrent Force*, Defence Open Government Document 80/23 (HMSO, London, 1980), p. 5.

26. See Lord Carver's remarks, *Official Report* (Lords), vol. 403, 18 December 1979, col. 1628.

27. Blue Water had been intended for NATO-wide use and was cancelled after the Americans persuaded the allies to buy the Sargeant system.

28. *United Kingdom Nuclear Weapons Programme*, p. 36.

29. Pierre, *Nuclear Politics*, p. 136n.

30. Interviews.

31. Interviews.

32. See Chapter 5, pp. 122–5.

33. *The Future United Kingdom Strategic Nuclear Deterrent Force*, p. 2.

34. See Pierre Gallois, *The Balance of Terror* (The Riverside Press, Cambridge, Mass., 1961).

35. *The Future United Kingdom Strategic Nuclear Deterrent Force*, p. 5.

36. Ibid., p. 6.

5 THE TRIDENT DECISION

The Thatcher government's decision to procure a new generation of ballistic missile submarines equipped with American Trident missiles was hardly startling. It was, on the contrary, a readily predictable progression of an established and successful weapons programme. It represented a historically consistent exercise of the American connection as a means of maximizing the cost-effectiveness of British forces. It confirmed the strategic vision which had underlain the switch to sea-based systems in the 1960s and conformed admirably to the demands of British doctrine in the projected military environment of the 1990s and beyond. It would, in fact, have been a rather obvious and un-controversial choice had it not been so painfully expensive. The logic of that choice is the concern of this chapter.

Strategic Nuclear Force Modernization: the Polaris Replacement Decision

The problem of selecting an appropriate replacement for Polaris began to receive serious and sustained attention from both public and govern-mental quarters in late 1977.[1] In that year, Ian Smart wrote an influen-tial paper for the Royal Institute of International Affairs which argued that only one launch platform – the nuclear-powered submarine – and two delivery vehicles – ballistic and cruise missiles – were realistic options for a third-generation strategic force.[2] After comparing the characteristics of the two forces, Smart concluded that an SSBN fleet of five boats equipped with MIRVed missiles was the better buy for Britain. The study not only dampened rather intemperate enthusiasm for the cruise missile which had recently been evident in Conservative Party circles,[3] but gave the informed public some notion of both the timetable of decisions and the costs likely to be incurred if Polaris was to be replaced at all.

Contemporaneously, the Ministry of Defence discreetly approached the Callaghan government to suggest that the problem merited con-sideration. In response, the Prime Minister convened a small group of Ministers and directed the preparation of studies by the bureaucracy.[4] One study group, chaired by Sir Anthony Duff, Deputy Under-Secretary at the Foreign Office, was charged with considering the international consequences of a decision to renew or discard the deterrent. It ultimately produced a rather bland and unhelpful document. Another, chaired by Professor Ronald Mason, Chief Scientific Adviser to the Ministry of Defence, considered the hardware options. Quite early in its deliberations, Mason's group reached the same conclusion as had Smart: that any successor to Polaris must, like the present force, be based at sea. In so doing, the group despatched the orphaned option of land-based forces and defeated a once-promising campaign by the RAF to reclaim its strategic role after Polaris left service.[5]

The RAF had been encouraged by the advent of modern cruise missiles. The concept of small, armed, pilotless aircraft had originated, of course, with the V-1 weapons developed by the Luftwaffe during the Second World War. In the late 1970s, however, a number of technical advances — highly efficient ramjet engines, new fuels, miniaturized digital computers and terrain-following guidance — combined to create a revolutionary new weapon. Possessed of great accuracy, cruise missiles could now fly several hundred miles at extremely low altitudes while evading known defensive concentrations. Their deployment as standoff weapons seemed to resolve long-held doubts about the penetrability of airborne nuclear forces. In these circumstances, the operational flexibility and distinct command and control advantages of aircraft loomed larger in any force planning calculus. The RAF argued, with some force, that objections to the pre-launch survivability of aircraft had always been overstated in Britain. After all, the Americans continued to believe that aircraft were suitable for strategic missions. Moreover, Bomber Command had for years maintained a very successful strip alert, achieving consistently favourable scramble times. Indeed, Strike Command continued to retain the Vulcan fleet at exceptional readiness pursuant to NATO's Quick Reaction Force requirements. The logistical infrastructure for crisis dispersal remained available. Finally, the emotive argument of the 1960s that, in view of Britain's unique vulnerability, strategic forces had no place in the home islands was hardly persuasive when the government continued to welcome American nuclear deployments.

The RAF's efforts encountered insurmountable obstacles. First, it was regarded as axiomatic that strategic forces must be dedicated entirely to the national deterrent mission. Non-dedicated forces raised intolerable operational conflicts: in any likely wartime contingency, a government would be forced either to hazard the deterrent on conventional missions or to compromise conventional success in order to safeguard the deterrent. Second, it was widely accepted that, for reasons of ecomony, Polaris should be replaced by a single system. The advantages of aircraft could not therefore be presented as part of a diversified force structure. Finally, it was not possible to configure the deterrent with the expectation of strategic warning; indeed, it was only the premium placed upon 'bolt from the blue' survivability of the strategic force which afforded the rest of the forces the luxury of assuming political warning.[6]

Given these premises, aircraft simply could not compare with nuclear-powered submarines in terms of survivability. Reliance upon strip alert had been rejected as too perilous in the 1960s; advances in Soviet weaponry since had only aggravated the problem. The alternative of continuous airborne alert appeared prohibitively expensive. Neither option was tenable in the event of protracted crisis. Most important, neither was an answer to the most likely nuclear threat: selective Soviet counterforce strikes against the Anglo–American base structure in Britain. When, in the early 1960s, Soviet counterforce strikes would have entailed massive collateral damage, the fact that surviving bombers would have been compelled to proceed to their targets did not pose difficulties. A counterforce strike by SS-4s and SS-5s would not have differed much from countervalue attacks; there would have been little left to deter. In the 1990s, a discriminating SS-20 attack would leave a very great deal to be deterred, forcing a government relying upon airborne forces either to bring them down in exceptionally insecure conditions or to commit them in a disproportionate and perhaps suicidal response.[7]

Submarines, by contrast, were thought to be quintessentially 'withholdable' weapon systems. The Royal Navy's *Resolution*-class SSBNs had, by 1980, maintained a secure deterrent threat on-station for over ten years. In all that time, it did not appear that the Soviets had ever detected or trailed a British SSBN,[8] despite the fact that the Royal Navy had apparently been able to trail Soviet SSBNs for extended periods. The Navy was confident that its estimated seven-year technical lead over the Soviets could be maintained; new-generation submarines promised to be even quieter than the Polaris boats; and incremental increases in Soviet capability could be further offset by expansion of submarine patrol areas.[9] Advocates of a return to airborne strategic foces might well conjure with the prospect of a 'breakthrough' in ASW technology,[10] but the fact remained that the Navy — whose principal mission was ASW — could not perceive even the outline of such a 'breakthrough'.[11] The sea is vast and opaque, cluttered by irreducible noise and constantly varying thermal conditions; unlike the atmosphere or deep space, 'it will not become transparent . . . by use of particle beam weapons or lasers'.[12]

The final disadvantage of aircraft was that their viability in the strategic role was inextricably linked to the cruise missile. Since the demise of Skybolt, neither the United States nor Britain had seriously pursued development of air-launched ballistic missiles. Thus as confidence in the penetrability of cruise missiles declined, the projected capital costs of an air-based successor to Polaris escalated, and the financial incentive for a 'second-best' airborne solution shrivelled. New aircraft would in any case have been necessary: the Vulcan fleet could not be long sustained in service and remaining RAF aircraft were highly inefficient cruise missile carriers. (Tornado, for example, could carry only two ALCMs.) New aircraft would impose substantial new manpower demands upon Strike Command at a time when the RAF was already suffering from a severe and chronic shortage of pilots. While it was hoped that service pay increases might restore equilibrium within the current order of battle, there was simply no basis for assuming that the pool of pilots and qualified maintenance personnel could be significantly expanded in the years ahead.

In the light of these considerations that the Mason group advised Prime Minister Callaghan and his colleagues that nuclear-powered submarines should form the basis of any third-generation force. Mason's recommendations went no further, leaving the question of delivery vehicles unresolved. Callaghan's committee, in turn, had gone no further than to accept Mason's advice when the 1979 general election intervened. When, in June 1979, Mrs Thatcher commenced her own, more overt, discussion of possible successor forces, she received the Mason group's papers appropriately adorned with new 'tops and tails', and rapidly endorsed their conclusions.[13]

The consensus in favour of a dedicated submarine fleet effectively foreclosed the formally open question of delivery vehicles. Cruise missiles had attracted a great deal of attention in Britain, principally because of their presumed cost-effectiveness. It was felt that they afforded a mechanism for retaining an independent deterrent without significant disruption of the conventional defence effort.[14] The problem was that virtually all the advantages and disadvantages attributed to a submarine-based, sea-launched cruise missile (SLCM) force turned on widely disputed, highly uncertain estimates of their ability to penetrate Soviet air defences. Ian Smart, in his 1977 study, had suggested an overall reliability-penetrability figure of 0.5;[15] the International Institute of Strategic Studies, in written evidence submitted to the Commons Expenditure Committee in 1979, had advanced a composite figure of 0.2.[16] Estimates in the classified literature ranged literally from 0.0 to 1.0, depending upon assumptions about Soviet air-defence investment, systems performance, defensive tactics, attack parameters and targets. This genuine uncertainty in and of itself hindered SLCM's prospects for the strategic mission. Moreover, it seemed quite likely that, whatever the actual penetrability of American cruise missiles at any given time, it would exceed the performance of British SLCMs, simply because Britain's inventory would be numerically smaller, and launched chronologically earlier, than American forces. Further, it was probable that either British SLCM penetrability would decline over time or total systems costs would rise, as the Soviets could be expected to mount new defences against the American ALCM fleet. Perhaps most troubling was the possibility that strategic intelligence critical to the penetrability of a small SLCM force might be unavailable in independent employment conditions.[17] Finally, the one potential advantage of cruise missiles which was insensitive to penetrability assumptions – hard-target kill capability – was also peripheral to Britain's doctrinal requirements.

In these circumstances, it was very difficult to establish a firm estimate of penetrability for force-planning purposes. A government opting for cruise missiles would therefore be committing itself either to open-ended capital expenditure or to eventual retreat from the principle of a dedicated deterrent force. 'Fine-tuning' the deterrent over time to meet evolving Soviet defences could be accomplished at tolerable expense only if additional SLCMs were to be distributed among platforms with continuing (and vital) conventional missions.

Indeed, even if penetrability could be established with adequate certainty, the operational advantages of an SLCM force were by no means clear. For example, Ian Smart had suggested on the strength of his 0.5 estimate of SLCM penetrability that Britain would require a fleet of seventeen submarines each equipped with twenty-four cruise missiles. At first blush, such a fleet would appear possessed of certain operational advantages. Dispersing the deterrent over some even seven or eight platforms on-station – as opposed to, say, two SSBNs – would seem to complicate the localization problem for Soviet ASW forces. Eight boats are harder to locate simultaneously than are two, assuming equivalent sea-patrol areas. But it rapidly became apparent that any likely SLCM force would not enjoy the sea room available to any available SLBM force. Current-generation land-attack SLCMs had to be launched from fairly close inshore in order to assure proper initiation of its overland terrain-following navigation equipment; in a long flight over water, inertial navigation errors mount and the missile might miss its pre-programmed landfall.[18] Consequently, any pre-launch survivability advantage potentially available from an increase in platforms would be lost through restriction of sea room. It might be possible to restore this advantage by distributing SLCM-armed submarines among forward-deployed SSNs. A deterrent force lurking among a large number of platforms – comprising in total, say, fourteen or fifteen submarines – might well be less vulnerable than two SSBNs deployed further out to sea. But this would, again, entail sacrificing the sensible notion of a dedicated deterrent; SLCM-armed vessels could not 'hide' among SSNs unless they acted like SSNs and pursued conventional missions.

The larger number of platforms associated with the SLCM option would nevertheless be advantageous when account is taken of the requirements of intra-war deterrence. It is certainly true that a British government would be more willing to order a limited retaliatory (or escalatory) strike if by doing so they hazarded only one boat out of eight, instead of one boat out of two. But this genuinely attractive attribute was overwhelmed by the general problem of trans-launch vulnerability in an SLCM force. Launch of an entire boatload of SLCMs could, it was estimated, take hours if the only tested launch mode – via torpedo tubes – were to be employed.[19] In that period, the launching submarine would be exposed to increasingly severe risk from Soviet ASW platforms or 'counterbattery' fire from Soviet land-based nuclear forces. There would be little efficacy to a 'last-resort' minimal deterrent if the Soviets came to believe that they could destroy the fleet in the early stages of its ponderous attack.

It will be apparent that a number of these operational deficiencies could have been remedied by technical modifications, most of which were well within the design capabilities of British industry. British Aerospace Dynamics had undertaken preliminary studies in 1976 pursuant to a Ministry of Defence contract, and had concluded that the resources existed for a successful national cruise missile development programme.[20] BAeD believed that, if it were determined to proceed with SLCMs, second-generation supersonic cruise missiles should be developed.[21] Supersonic capability might have done much to resolve doubts about cruise missile penetrability. Similarly, modifications might have been introduced to increase the absolute range of SLCM and extend the over-water flight capability. Finally, British submarines might have been designed to provide for vertical launch of SLCMs, thereby eliminating trans-launch vulnerability problems. In each case, however, the British would have had to take the lead in novel technologies, incurring quite substantial research and development expenses. The capital costs of an SLCM fleet would inevitably rise steeply, and at the end of the day it was only the fleeting promise of inexpensive deterrence which had made cruise missiles attractive at all.

It thus became clear to the Thatcher government that an SLCM-armed fleet of submarines would not be a financially attractive successor to Polaris. Even if capital costs could be held to a level analogous to those of a new SSBN force, maintenance costs would be considerably greater. Moreover, such a large shipbuilding effort would inevitably exacerbate dislocation in the Navy's SSN construction programme. Finally, and most important, the SLCM option would impose exorbitant demands on service manpower. The Navy already faced a serious shortage of qualified submariners, as was evidenced by escalating re-enlistment bonuses. Even assuming a fleet of, say, seventeen SLCM-armed submarines were to be single-crewed, it would still require nearly a thousand more officers and ratings than would a double-crewed flotilla of five SSBNs.[22] Secretary of Defence Pym alluded to this problem in the Commons in January 1980, pointing out that 'Operating Britain's present strategic nuclear force is exceptionally economic in Service manpower. That is significant because constraints of manpower might be at least as important as constraints of money in shaping the defence effort.'[23] We have seen the peculiar and enduring influence of manpower constraints upon British defence policy throughout the post-war era,[24] and by no means the least important reason behind the Thatcher government's decision to procure SSBNs was the fact that these are labour-reductive as well as capital-intensive weapons systems.

There was, finally, a compelling political consideration driving Britain's choice for ballistic missiles and, indeed, shaping the replacement decision generally. Historically, domestic political support for the independent deterrent has depended critically upon the perceived technical credibility of British forces.[25] It was, after all, the technical failure of the Blue Streak programme which had provided Labour's leadership with a practical reason for opposing independent deterrence and accommodating the demands of the party's left wing. And it was Macmillan's skilful acquisition of the finest nuclear weapons system then available which had quelled controversy and safeguarded independent deterrence for a generation. Glimpsing the political storms ahead and the possibility that major capital expenditures on strategic forces would be required of a Labour government, the Thatcher government may have concluded that there was simply no political margin for experimental weapons technologies.

Six alternative sea-launched ballistic missile systems were potentially available to arm a new generation of British SSBNs. One — the Polaris/ Chevaline system — was an Anglo–American hybrid. Another — a nationally produced SLBM equipped with MIRVs — would have been of wholly British origin. A third — the M-4 — was French. The rest were American: The Poseidon C-3, Trident I C-4 and the developmental Trident II D-5. The option of retaining the Polaris/Chevaline system was rapidly rejected. Not only was there a pennywise, pound-foolish irrationality to emplacing ageing missiles in very new and expensive vessels,[26] and the inevitability of ever-rising missile maintenance expense, but the weapon was unsuitable for the potential military environs of the 1990s and beyond. Chevaline had been developed to counter incremental improvements in deployed exoatmospheric ABM defences. The British had now to hedge against a breakdown of the ABM Treaty regime and possible new deployments by the Soviets. Soviet ABM research and development efforts in the late 1970s had a decidedly endoatmospheric bent.[27] Against such defences, only MIRV would suffice to assure penetrability. Moreover, even against purely urban target sets, MIRV would increase the efficiency of a given stock of re-entry vehicles by permitting more economical warhead distribution. Finally, MIRV, by affording low-cost counter-force targeting options, would enhance the credibility of Britain's implied threat to respond to selective Soviet strikes with strategic forces.

There was no question of Aldermaston's ability to product MIRVs. The British had, after all, been intimately involved in the early stages of MIRV development and Chevaline had provided a mechanism for keeping current with American technology. Moreover, the costs of MIRV appeared likely to be quite manageable. The argument was made within the Ministry of Defence that the costs of *not* MIRVing, of retaining MRV technology, however sophisticated, might ultimately exceed the costs of MIRV. After 1983, all American SLBMs would be MIRVed; Britain would thereafter be in 'a uniquely British business with MRV', and costs would inevitably rise.[28] This was also a subtle political argument. The vitality of the Anglo–American nuclear relationship depends upon reciprocity and common experience of technical and and operational difficulties. To safeguard this relationship, to keep the Americans company in a technical sense, was an important political incentive for MIRV deployment.

The doctrinal and economic arguments for MIRV were none the less central, and in this respect they represented an early evocation of what might be called the 'Chevaline imperative'. The lonely and quite costly development of Chevaline, while stimulating a certain pride in Aldermaston's technical capacities, had also engendered an enduring aversion to what the Ministry of Defence called 'United Kingdom-unique'. strategic weapons innovations. The lesson was drawn from Chevaline that British detours from the thoroughfares paved by the American laboratories were inherently more expensive then concurrent Anglo-American development and deployment efforts. To stay 'in sync' with American development and deployment would, it was felt, lend a certainty to cost-forecasting which was unattainable in the case of unique British systems. Should mid-life modifications to British missiles and warheads prove necessary, then Britain would enjoy the economic benefits of collaborative research, development and procurement. The Chevaline imperative was a decisive influence upon British procurement decisions. It was also, incidentally, a marvellous example of the salience of economic considerations in Britain's approach to the 'special relationship'.

It is therefore not surprising that the Thatcher administration quickly discarded any notion of a nationally manufactured ballistic missile. National manufacture was not inherently beyond British means; British Aerospace Dynamics — which had recommenced procurement of ballistic over cruise missiles[29] — reckoned that a solid-fuelled missile development effort could be got under way immediately.[30] Costs were thought to be prohibitive or, at least as important, unpredictable. Similarly, while the French had intimated that they would welcome a British bid for their new M-4 missile,[31] there was every indication that French SLBMs would cost more, and perform far less effectively, than American missiles.

A number of British politicians and academics were none the less prepared to argue that the time had come for Britain to demonstrate dramatically her European credentials by pursuing co-operation with France or at least by forswearing further dependence upon the Americans. In this view, Anglo–American nuclear co-operation was an enduring political liability in Britain's relations with Europe. As one seasoned analyst put it:

Britain expended a great deal of political capital at Nassau and the political dividends accruing to her by virtue of her possession of nuclear weapons have been 'taxed' ever since. Another Nassau would entail greater capital costs and a higher tax.[32]

This analysis had always been resoundingly rejected by British governments[33] and the Thatcher administration was no exception. To British officials and Ministers (Conservative and Labour alike) any political disadvantages were amply offset by both the cost-effectiveness of American systems and the tangible political benefits of Anglo–American co-operation.[34]

Operational considerations, in concert with the Chevaline imperative, foreclosed purchase of the cheapest of the American missiles: Poseidon. Poseidon was handicapped by a not altogether successful front end — capable of delivering up to fourteen small 40KT warheads — and, particularly, by its restricted range. With a full load of re-entry vehicles, Poseidon had even less operational range than Polaris. Enhanced SLBM range not only increases the pre-launch survivability, but also the post-launch viability, of an SSBN fleet. It is, of course, prudent to assume that any SLBM launch is tantamount to SSBN detection, either through accoustic launch detection, satellite detection of SLBM assent of through 'backtracking' of radar-discerned missiles or re-entry vehicle trajectories. The greater sea-patrol area associated with increased SLBM range has the effect of minimizing the likelihood of active Soviet trailing of the SSBN at the moment of launch. Assuming, however, that there is no active Soviet SSN trail of British SSBNs, three post-launch threats exist. The first involves land-based ICBM nuclear barrages against the detected submarine. In these circumstances, Soviet weapons requirements depend upon the elapsed time between launch detection and the arrival of Soviet 'counter-battery' fire. Greater SLBM range increases both integration time for launch-detection data and time of flight for ICBM attacks, while reducing Soviet missile accuracies. In consequence, increased SLBM range has the alternative effects of either reducing the likelihood of successful nuclear ASW attacks or increasing Soviet weapons requirements, perhaps to a level beyond what the Russians would be willing to allocate if American forces remained on the horizon.

Increased SLBM range similarly increases post-launch SSBN survival in the face of the two remaining threats: aircraft or SSN localization and destruction. Soviet ASW platform requirements increase geometrically as the distance between the SSBN and Soviet bases increases. Moreover, with extended range, an SSBN fleet could operate in areas where the penetration of Soviet aircraft in wartime could prove highly problematical. For example, vulnerable Soviet aircraft pursuing a Trident I or Trident II boat would need either to traverse the United Kingdom Air Defence Region — a risky enterprise — or take a round-about route which, by increasing time of flight, sharply decreases the likelihood of SSBN localization.

Poseidon's prospects dimmed when account was taken of the distinct operational advantages of increased SLBM range. They declined even further when, in late 1979, the government concluded that it would not be possible to replace the Vulcan squadrons with a weapons system capable of engaging targets in the Soviet Union.[35] Polaris's successor would, therefore, be the only element of the British force structure capable of undertaking selective strikes against the Soviet Union properly. It would, in this sense, be successor to both the Polaris and Vulcan forces. This development placed an even greater premium upon post-launch survivability and argued for an excess warhead capacity in third-generation strategic forces.

With these drawbacks, the potential savings involved in Poseidon procurement seemed meagre indeed. Even assuming that the United States would write off all research and development costs, purchase of Poseidon could not have reduced capital expenditure by more than £400 million to £500 million. And these savings — equivalent to 8 to 10 per cent of the projected capital costs of a new SSBN fleet — would be eaten away by higher long-term operations and maintenance expense. As Poseidon would no longer be in US Navy service by the time it went to sea with the Royal Navy, Britain would have to fund the infrastructure for maintenance of quite ancient missiles alone. Finally, the logic of the Chevaline imperative doomed Poseidon: the risks of expensive — and unilateral — mid-life modifications were simply unjustifiable.

The more difficult choice lay between the Trident I C-4 and Trident II D-5 missiles. The Trident I missile was already operational with the US Navy. It could carry a warhead configuration of eight independently targetable 100KT re-entry vehicles over an operational range of up to 4,000 n.mi. It was, in many reaspects, superbly suited to British mission requirements. It was available at a cost the government considered affordable. It had but one disadvantage: there was a distinct possibility that the missile would be withdrawn from American naval service very shortly after its deployment by Britain. A new missile — the Trident II D-5 — was in the long American research and development pipeline and the US Navy, as well as a number of critics of the Carter administration's strategic weapons policies, was lobbying hard for its deployment.

As the Thatcher government deliberated over the replacement question, the fate of Trident II hung in the balance. It was expected to carry up to fourteen 150KT warheads; it was likely that these would be ferried by a post-launch vehicle which, like Chevaline, would be manoeuvrable in deep space. Unlike Chevaline, individual re-entry vehicles would be independently targetable. When operated in conjunction with the Navy's planned NAVSTAR satellite navigation system, the D-5 would be capable of extraordinary accuracies, able to undertake destruction of hardened targets which had hitherto been the preserve of land-based forces. In addition, the D-5 would be able to operate over a range of approximately 6,000 n.mi. Interestingly, the US Navy had pursued such ranges in order to operate their new 18,500-ton *Ohio*-class SSBNs in home waters. The Royal Navy, by contrast, sought increased SLBM range in order to get their SSBNs out of home waters. Geography accounts for the difference. In peace or war, American home waters, far removed from Soviet bases, would offer a sanctuary for the hunted SSBN. British home waters, on the other hand, lie close at hand to Soviet ASW bases and, in wartime, were expected to play host to a third Battle of the Atlantic. Thus, all the advantages of extended SLBM range which had been used to highlight the relative merits of Trident I over Poseidon could be cited in an argument for Trident II. But by far the most persuasive argument for Trident II was the Chevaline imperative: it would be discouraging indeed to lose the advantages of commonality with the Americans after investing so heavily in third-generation strategic forces.

In this case, however, the lesson of Chevaline conflicted with an older and arguably more deeply felt lesson: Skybolt. The memory of Secretary McNamara's seemingly abrupt cancellation of Skybolt in 1962 had left the British understandably reluctant to 'buy in' to an American weapons system whose ultimate deployment was in the least doubtful. It was, moreover, difficult to cost a Trident II purchase at a time when the US Navy had not yet been authorized to procure the missiles themselves. The government did not feel it could afford to await clarification of American intentions before publicly announcing its plans for the future of the deterrent. It had led Parliament to expect a decision sometime in 1980.[36] In addition, the government was more or less committed, in the aftermath of Mrs Thatcher's meetings with President Carter in December 1979, to pursue negotiations with the Carter administration.[37] Finally, there seemed genuine advantage to coming to terms with President Carter. There was striking unanimity among the President's senior advisers on the desirability of assisting

Britain's nuclear efforts[38] and the British could not be certain that such favourable conditions would prevail in the next administration.

The decision was therefore taken to negotiate a purchase of Trident I missiles in 1980. What one American described as a 'very lengthy and very sensitive bilateral discussion' ensued.[39] By all accounts, these negotiations went smoothly.[40] The Americans were quite prepared to transfer C-4 re-entry vehicles in addition to the missiles themselves. Hard bargaining was reserved for matters of money and, perhaps, nuclear materials. It will be recalled that, in the 1963 Polaris Sales Agreement, the British had managed to limit their contribution to Polaris's research and development costs to a token 5 per cent surcharge over the retail costs of the missiles themselves.[41] This had long been recognized as an exceptionally favourable rate and the Americans 'made it clear in the discussions this time that it was a rate they could not give us again – they could not justify it to themselves, nor could they to Congress'.[42] It was initially suggested that Britain pay its *pro rata* share of sunk research and development costs.[43] As these totalled something like $4,000 million,[44] and Britain would purchase nearly 11 per cent of total C-4 production, this would have entailed an 'upfront' cash payment of over $400 million. This was hardly palatable to the British, who were seeking to minimize both absolute and apparent capital expenditure.

It was eventually agreed to retain the framework of the Polaris Sales Agreement, including the provision fixing Britain's contribution to research costs at 5 per cent of the missiles' purchase price.[45] This represented a direct British contribution of about $100 million. In addition, London agreed to man Rapier air-defence systems defending USAF air bases in Britain with RAF personnel. This commitment added another $200 million to Britain's account. The American subsidy in Britain's procurement of Trident I was therefore reduced to a little more than $100 million. This is, of course, a good deal of money. Moreover, the $200 million involved in the Rapier manning arrangement would be spent, in sterling, through the 1990s and into the next century. It was, in short, an advantageous arrangement for the British, particularly in view of their unenviable bargaining position. The Thatcher government sought, however, to make a good deal look better by portraying the American purchase of Rapier missiles as an offset for Trident. This disingenuous gesture angered British Aerospace officials, who had regarded the Rapiers as 'virtually sold' in any event.[46]

The details of the materials exchange arrangement were not disclosed to the public. Final agreement had apparently not been reached at the time the Trident sale was announced.[47] There may have been some difficulty in this area, as the Americans may have anticipated material shortages. It would appear, nevertheless, that the two countries agreed to continue the pattern of co-operation established in the late 1950s and implemented in the Polaris programme. American-enriched uranium of both submarine and weapons quality, as well as other special materials, would remain available to Britain.[48] The British intended, however, to employ domestic materials to the maximum extent possible. Uranium used in the A-3 and Chevaline warheads would be retooled for Trident.[49] Moreover, the decision to withdraw the Vulcan squadrons without replacing them released uranium contained in their thermonuclear weapons for use in Trident. It was probable therefore, that Britain would place few demands upon American materials supplies. Indeed, it was considered likely that the British would be in a position to transfer nuclear materials to the United States in the late 1980s.[50]

On 15 July 1980, the British government announced its intention to build four (or possibly five) new submarines, each equipped with sixteen Trident I missiles, as a replacement for the Polaris fleet. The fact that the government did not commit itself firmly to a force of five SSBNs occasioned some surpise.[51] Operational experience with Polaris had shown that a fleet of four submarines was incapable of maintaining a continuous patrol of two boats. For a period of perhaps six weeks to two months per year, the Navy had only one *Resolution*-class SSBN on-station.[52] Reliance upon a single SSBN for such periods had long been regarded as imprudent because of concerns about the survivability of the boat and the adequacy and flexibility of the threat it represented.

It appeared to the Thatcher administration, however, that technical innovations in new-generation SSBNs, as well as the enhanced capability of Trident missiles, diminished the urgency of a fifth boat. Either of the reactors[53] being considered for the Trident boats would be able to operate longer between refits than could the Polaris vessels; and the refits themselves would take no longer than they had with Polaris.[54] Increased SLBM range entailed longer transit time between home ports and firing stations, but the Navy seemed confident that it could guarantee two boats *at sea* 'nearly, but not quite, all the time'.[55] It is important to recall that, however, persuasive 'worst-case' analyses might be for force-planning purposes, it is, as a practical matter, extraordinarily unlikely that Britain would be caught in a war with only one boat on-station. And even if it were, a single Trident vessel would pose as potent and nearly as flexible as threat as would two Polaris SSBNs. Two Polaris boats could threaten a maximum of 32 separate targets with 96 warheads; a single Trident vessel could threaten up to 128 targets with 128 weapons. In these circumstances, a fifth boat, which would cost some £600 million,[56] seemed rather a luxury and, although the option remained formally open, the government had, in fact, discarded it.[57]

A more telling objection was raised to the government's lukewarm commitment to a fifth boat.[58] Given the distinct possibility of a Labour government coming to power at a time when the Trident programme would still be vulnerable to cancellation, it might have been wise to order the fifth boat as a sacrificial lamb. A future Labour government might then have been able to cancel part of the Trident programme and placate its left-wing constituency while preserving an effective deterrent. The logic of this strategy is compelling. That it was rejected is perhaps an indication of the extent of the government's concern with the expense of third-generation force procurement, and the anxieties it would engender about the future of Britain's conventional contributions to the Alliance.

For all its apparent finality, the government's announcement in July 1980 did not settle the procurement question. Indeed, as problems emerged in the Polaris modernization programme,[59] the logic of Chevaline imperative became ever more persuasive. An irrevocable commitment to the Trident I C-4 seemed most imprudent while American plans remained uncertain. If Washington decided to accelerate development of the Trident II D-5 missile, Britain would be deploying the C-4s only a few years before they left American service. She might then be required to undertake unilaterally mid-life modifications of the missiles and warheads. In these circumstances, it was argued, the through life costs of Trident I would almost certainly exceed those of Trident II.[60] In late 1980, the government advised the Commons Defence Committee that final decisions with respect to missiles and submarine designs had not yet been taken.[61] By mid-1981, the Ministry of Defence was reported to be considering SSBN designs with extra hull capacity in order to hedge against eventual procurement of the D-5.[62] When, in October 1981, Washington announced plans to accelerate development of the D-5, London despatched a team of negotiators to the United States.

The Reagan administration proved even more supportive than had the Carter administration.[63] The Polaris Sales Agreement framework was retained, allowing Britain to purchase missiles at US Navy unit costs. The D-5 was however still in development and it was therefore impossible to allocate a fixed research and development contribution to

Britain's account. The administration none the less agreed to accept a sum of $116 million, fixed in real terms, as Britain's research and development contribution, and to retain the Rapier-manning provisions of the Trident I agreement. As D-5 development costs were certain to exceed C-4 costs, the implicit American subsidy of Britain's nuclear force rose correspondingly. Moreover, the Defense Department waived the facilities charge exacted by the Carter administration and undertook to suspend provisions of the Buy American Act in order to permit British firms to compete for subcontracts on both the American and the British portions of the D-5 production run. The Americans intended to establish a liaison office in London to facilitate placement of British bids. Thus, when John Nott announced the government's decision to buy Trident II missiles on 11 March 1982, no one could question that his negotiators had secured the most favourable terms possible.

The initial capital costs of a Trident II force none the less substantially exceeded those of a Trident I force. A fleet of four C-4-equipped SSBNs had originally been costed at £5,000 million at September 1980 prices and exchange rates; the D-5 force was estimated to cost some £7,500 million at September 1981 prices and exchange rates. Inflation accounted for approximately £800 million of the increase and exchange rate changes — 'real' but potentially reversible charges — accounted for a little more than £700 million. At 1980 exchange rates and prices, the D-5s cost Britain only £390 million more than the C-4s. Real escalation in submarine cost estimates was driven in part by the need for a larger hull section but also by the government's decision to employ the most advanced sonars and Rolls-Royce's developmental PWR-2 propulsion plant. Thus, the government proposed a fleet of four 14,680-tons SSBNs, each driven by PWR-2 reactors and equipped to carry sixteen D-5 missiles.[64]

The government defended the Trident II decision entirely on cost-effectiveness grounds. It eschewed any desire for a substantial increase in its nuclear arsenal. Mr Nott assured the House that

> The number of warheads that the Trident II D5 will carry, and therefore Trident's striking power, remains wholly a matter of choice for the British government; our intention is that the move to D5 will not involve any significant change in the planned total number of warheads than originally envisaged for our Trident II C4 force.[65]

There was some doubt as to whether the government intended to fill only twelve of the sixteen tubes with D-5s, each carrying the maximum warhead package of fourteen 150KT MIRVs, or to deploy the full complement of sixteen missiles armed with a smaller arsenal of MIRVs.[66] The former option would reduce missile acquisition costs (and related exchange risks) but would also reduce future government's' ability to counter ballistic missile defences improvements. Incidentally, it would also mean the government had been disingenuous in its comparison of C-4 and D-5 acquisition costs. The latter option would capitalize on Aldermaston's initial C-4 weapons design research and, perhaps, provide a continuing role for the quite sophisticated penetration aids developed in the Chevaline programme. It would appear that the government chose this course. Mr Nott let it slip in debate that 'Trident II will have the same warhead as Trident I.'[67] Subsequently, the government refused to discuss the warhead/missile mix it intended to deploy: 'Like our predecessors, we do not comment on the number of missiles or warheads carried by our SSBNs at any given time.'[68] However, if the Navy intended to take full advantage of the D-5's range — and patrol with American *Ohio*-class vessels in the western Atlantic — it had to deploy less than the full complement of fourteen re-entry vehicles.[69] Thus, it is probable that the Thatcher administration decided to deploy eight or ten 100–150KT warheads on the Navy's D-5 missiles.

The government's argument for Trident II — well reasoned as it was — did not garner much support. Indeed, Labour's spokesman, John Silkin, announced immediately his party's intention to cancel the programme outright.[70] David Owen was more circumspect but ultimately the SDP declared that it too would cancel.[71] These declarations were of some import. The 1982 decisions — while motivated by a sound desire to hold down total systems costs and attended by a fiscally attractive deferral of missile acquisition expenses — ensured that the programme would be extremely vulnerable to cancellation in 1984 and, indeed, for several years thereafter. Both the right wing of the Labour Party and the SDP premised opposition to Trident upon its costs and consequences for the conventional force budget. Before turning to a discussion of costs, however, it is necessary to trace the course of a second nuclear weapons modernization debate.

Theatre Nuclear Force Modernization: the Vulcan Replacement Decision

Shortly before Prime Minister Callaghan convened his small Cabinet subcommittee in 1977, the Ministry of Defence began to contemplate potential replacements for the RAF's Vulcan bombers, scheduled to leave service in the early 1980s. Strike Command would, of course, commence receipt of its new Tornado IDS strike aircraft in 1980.

However, as part of the price for securing multinational collaboration in production of Tornado, the RAF had been forced to foresake a genuine long-range strike capability. West Germany would not be seen to procure a weapon which was, in the West German–Soviet context, genuinely strategic. Consequently, with the departure of the Vulcans, the British faced the prospect of reliance solely upon the Navy's submarines for strikes against the Soviet Union proper.

This prospect was troubling in two respects. First, by retaining Vulcan in a priority nuclear role, British governments had enjoyed quiet possession of a strategic 'dyad'. Now, just as Soviet development of the SS-20 placed a premium upon an assured British capability to respond in a flexible and restrained manner to Soviet counterforce strikes,[72] the flexibility of the dyad would be lost. Within the parameters of Britain's national deterrent mission, therefore, there was a strong argument for retaining a deep theatre nuclear strike capability in the wake of Vulcan. Second, Soviet development of the SS-20, against the background of strategic parity, had inspired allied concern with a deteriorating 'Euro-strategic' nuclear balance. If the Soviets managed to couple acknowledged conventional superiority with an overwhelming theatre nuclear advantage and, at best, central system parity, they would enjoy an intolerable measure of 'escalation dominance', that is, the capacity to fight, limit and win a war at each level of the escalatory ladder of conflict in Europe. This military hegemony could not fail to cast a long political shadow. This problem, and potential Western responses to it, had been the subject of discussion among the Americans, the British and the West Germans since the last months of the Ford administration. In late 1977, however, West German Chancellor Helmut Schmidt placed the issue squarely and dramatically upon the Alliance's public agenda in a speech before the International Institute of Strategic Studies in London. The issue touched the Vulcan replacement debate directly because the RAF's Vulcan squadrons represented something like a quarter of NATO's existing long-range theatre nuclear weapons arsenal.[73]

Those in the Ministry of Defence – principally but by no means exclusively Chief of the Defence Staff Air Marshall Sir Neil Cameron and Deputy Under-Secretary M.E. Quinlan – who believed that retention of a sub-strategic capability to strike Soviet targets was important for the national deterrent mission were offered a new and quite genuine Alliance rationale for replacing Vulcans.[74] Moreover, as the United States would welcome an opportunity to present theatre nuclear force modernization as an Anglo–American effort within the Alliance,[75] any lingering doubts about the availability of American cruise missiles for

Vulcan replacement purposes vanished. Carter administration officials felt that it would aid the perception by European publics of theatre nuclear force modernization as an evolutionary response to Soviet deployments if it were to include a direct British contribution. Thus, when in 1979 Defence Secretary Pym first hinted at possible replacement of Vulcan, he was already assured of the availability of American technology:

> We have conducted limited studies into the technology associated with cruise missiles, but we see no need to develop an all-British version. We are, however, examining how we can best contribute to the proposed modernization of the Alliance's long-range theater nuclear force and U.S. cruise missiles are among the options being considered for this.[76]

Three cruise missile systems were potentially available to replace the Vulcans: SLCM, ALCM and GLCM. SLCM was affordable only in a non-dedicated mode and even on those terms inspired little interest in the Royal Navy. When the NATO High Level Group (HLG), which was formulating the theatre nuclear force modernization proposal, established an overriding preference for dedicated theatre forces, SLCM was discarded as an option.

ALCM, for some time, appeared to be Britain's favoured option. It was, of course, the most 'evolutionary' replacement for the Vulcans, and, in its early deliberations, the HLG tended to emphasize this criterion for modernization. It was not an option available to the Americans because, under the proposed SALT II agreement, any ALCM carriers dedicated to NATO would have to be offset by reductions in American central systems. But this was not a fundamental obstacle; Britain could have varied from the American norm. The modernization package would then have comprised RAF ALCMs in Britain and USAF Pershing II ballistic missiles and GLCMs deployed both in Britain and on the Continent. The problem was that ALCM was not nearly as cost-effective as GLCM. If Tornado or Buccaneer, both inefficient carriers, were employed, an intolerable reduction in conventionally dedicated air strength was unavoidable. If Tornado or Buccaneer were not employed, new aircraft procurement was inevitable. In either case, an ALCM force would be more expensive in manpower and maintenance costs than GLCM. Strike Command did not, however, find GLCM at all attractive and resisted the quite compelling arguments in its favour advanced by Ministry of Defence civilians and seconded by the Americans.[77]

Two debates therefore raged during 1979. In one, Cameron, Quinlan and others endeavoured to persuade the Treasury, the Navy and the Army of the strategic merits of replacing Vulcan at all. In the other, the same protagonists tried to convince the RAF to accept GLCM. Both debates were settled when account was taken of Aldermaston's limitations and the burdens to be imposed on it by the Trident programme. Developmental work on the Trident warhead was to be conducted at Aldermaston while production was to be shared out among Aldermaston and the specialized Royal Ordnance factories at Burghfield and Cardiff.[78] Aldermaston's facilities were obsolescent and production was to take place upon a single-stream basis rather than the assembly-line processes employed in the United States. Construction of a new plutonium-machining plant at Aldermaston and a new assembly plant at Burghfield was necessary just to accommodate the Trident programme.[79] A quite significant new investment would have been necessary to accommodate theatre nuclear weapons development as well. Moreover, as there was already some doubt about attracting an adequate staff to support Trident,[80] there was no basis for assuming excess capacity in the skilled work-force. Finally, an accident involving radioactive dust at Aldermaston in early 1978[81] had not only aggravated recruiting problems and delayed the Chevaline programme, but made it very unlikely that the NATO deployment deadline of 1983 could be met.

These difficulties rendered the question of Vulcan replacement moot and, to the genuine disappointment of American officials,[82] the December 1979 ministerial meetings, where the Alliance undertook to modernize its long-range forces, came and went without a British commitment to replace Vulcan. The logic of retaining a long-range nuclear strike capability is persuasive and efforts to fill the void left by Vulcan may well be made in future; but the strain imposed upon Britain's defence budget by the Trident programme is unlikely to permit new nuclear weapons programmes in the years ahead. The expense of GLCM's acquisition could have been accommodated most easily in the very early 1980s and that moment has now passed.

Notes

1. Various aspects of the problem had, of course, been discussed in the scholarly press well before 1977. See, for example, Geoffrey Kemp, *Nuclear Forces for Medium Powers*, Adelphi Papers nos. 106 and 107 (IISS, London, 1974), for a formidable *tour d'horizon* of the technical requirements of independent deterrence. See, similarly, Ian Smart, *The Future Conditional: The Prospects for Anglo-French Nuclear Cooperation*, Adelphi Paper no. 78 (IISS, London, 1971).

2. Ian Smart, *The Future of the British Nuclear Deterrent* (RIIA, London, 1977).

3. See, e.g., J. Bellini and G. Pattie, *A New World Role for the Medium Power: The British Opportunity* (Royal United Services Institute, London, 1976).

4. See Chapter 2 above; P. Hennessey, 'Planning for a Future Nuclear Deterrent', *The Times*, 4 December 1979, p. 3.

5. Interviews.

6. Ministry of Defence, *The Future United Kingdom Strategic Nuclear Deterrent Force*, Defence Open Government Document 80/23 (HMSO, London, 1980), p. 7.

7. See Chapter 4 for a fuller discussion of the implications of improving Soviet accuracies for British doctrine.

8. See the testimony of Deputy Under-Secretary of Defence M.E. Quinlan and Rear Admiral J.S. Groves, in House of Commons, Fourth Report from the Defence Committee, Session 1980-1, *Strategic Nuclear Weapons Policy* (HMSO, London, 1981), p. 80.

9. Ibid.

10. See, e.g., Air Vice Marshall S.W.B. Menaul, 'The Future of Britain's Strategic Nuclear Force', *Strategic Review* (Summer 1979). This is an interesting public exposition of the RAF's case.

11. *Strategic Nuclear Weapons Policy*, p. 88.

12. Ibid., p. 83.

13. Hennessey, 'Planning for a Future Nuclear Deterrent'.

14. See, e.g., 'Don't Forget the Cheap One', *The Economist*, 29 March 1980.

15. Smart, *The Future of the British Nuclear Deterrent*.

16. House of Commons Sixth Report from the Expenditure Committee, Session 1978-9, *The Future of the United Kingdom's Nuclear Weapons Policy* (HMSO, London, 1979), p. 89.

17. See the discussion of Anglo–American intelligence collaboration in Chapter 3 above.

18. *The Future United Kingdom Strategic Nuclear Deterrent Force*, p. 16.

19. Ibid.

20. Memorandum by British Aerospace Dynamics Group, *The Future of the United Kingdom's Nuclear Weapons Policy*, p. 241.

21. *The Future United Kingdom Strategic Nuclear Deterrent Force*, p. 16.

22. Derived from Ministry of Defence evidence, *Strategic Nuclear Weapons Policy*, p. 76.

23. *The Times*, 25 January 1980, p. 8.

24. See Chapter 4 above.

25. See Chapter 2 above.

26. The Ministry of Defence felt it 'would have been too small a step to be cost-effective'. *Strategic Nuclear Weapons Policy*, p. 81.

27. See, e.g., Clarence Robinson, 'Soviets Grasping Strategic Lead', *Aviation Week and Space Technology*, 30 August 1976.

28. Interviews.

29. *The Future of the United Kingdom's Nuclear Weapons Policy*, p. 242.

30. 'UK Trident Purchase Under Investigation', *International Defense Review*, no. 3 (1981), p. 244.

31. French Defence Minister Yvons Bourges conveyed this impression to his British counterpart, Fred Mulley, in April 1979. See the *Daily Telegraph*, 2 May 1979, p. 1.

32. Interview.

33. Even Edward Heath, who went to quite extraordinary lengths to dispel the atmospherics of the special relationship and cultivate a European image (see, e.g.,

Henry A. Kissinger, *White House Years* (Little, Brown, Boston, 1979, pp. 932–8) had been prepared to 'buy American' had the need arisen.

34. Indeed a Cabinet Office paper prepared in early 1979 concluded that the American connection afforded Britain one of her four principal bargaining chips in her relations with West Germany as Bonn was thought to value highly Britain's role as a 'softening influence between Germany and the United States on nuclear matters'. *The Economist*, 9 November 1979, p. 55.

35. The Vulcan replacement decision is discussed below.

36. See Defence Secretary Pym's remarks, *Official Report* (Commons), vol. 977, 24 January 1980, col. 110.

37. See the White House's communiqué of 17 December 1980, *Department of State Bulletin* (February 1980).

38. Interviews.

39. *The Baltimore Sun*, 16 July 1980, p. 1.

40. Interviews.

41. See Chapter 3 above.

42. Testimony of M.E. Quinlan, *Strategic Nuclear Weapons Policy*, p. 94.

43. Ibid.

44. *The New York Times*, 16 July 1980, p. 1.

45. See exchange of letters between the President and Prime Minister Thatcher, 14 July 1980, *Weekly Compilation of Presidential Documents*, 21 July 1980, pp. 1343–5.

46. The Chairman of British Aerospace Dynamics sputtered: 'To say that *Rapier* is an offset is the greatest load of codswallop I have heard in all time.' *International Defense Review*, no. 3 (1981), p. 244.

47. *The Baltimore Sun*, 15 July 1980, p. 1.

48. Interviews.

49. *International Defense Review*, no. 3 (1981), p. 244.

50. Interview.

51. See, e.g., the *Financial Times*, 16 July 1980, p. 20.

52. Estimate derived from Smart, *The Future of the British Nuclear Deterrent*, pp. 27–30, and Farooq Hussain, 'Implications of Successors to Polaris', *The Future of the United Kingdom's Nuclear Weapons Policy*, p. 187.

53. Two reactors were being studied at this juncture: Rolls-Royce's experimental new PWR-2 and the *Trafalgar*-class power plant. See *International Defense Review*, no. 8 (1981), p. 977.

54. *Strategic Nuclear Weapons Policy*, p. 76.

55. Interview.

56. *Strategic Nuclear Weapons Policy*, p. 76.

57. Interviews.

58. See *The Times*, 17 July 1980, p. 5.

59. See Chapter 1 above.

60. See Defence Secretary John Nott's speech to the Commons, *The Times*, 12 March 1982, p. 4.

61. Ministry of Defence Memorandum, *Strategic Nuclear Weapons Policy*, pp. 76–9.

62. *International Defense Review*, no. 8 (1981), pp. 977–8.

63. *The Times*, 12 March 1982, p. 4.

64. Ministry of Defence, *The United Kingdom Trident Programme*, Defence Open Government Document 82/1 (HMSO, London, 1982).

65. *The Times*, 12 March 1982, p. 4.

66. See *International Defense Review*, no. 3 (1982), p. 256.

67. *The Times*, 12 March 1982, p. 4.

68. *Statement on the Defence Estimates 1982*, Cmnd. 8529-I (HSMO, London,

1982), p. 5.

69. With a full load of warheads, the D-5's range was limited to approximately 4,000 nmi – the C-4's maximum range. Ibid., p. 4.

70. *The Times*, 12 March 1982, p. 4.

71. *The Times*, 2 February 1983, p. 4.

72. See Chapter 4 above.

73. In 1978, 56 Vulcans and 170 USAF F-111s were based in Britain and dedicated to long-range missions.

74. Interviews.

75. Interviews.

76. 'UK/NATO Nuclear Options for the 1980s', *International Defense Review*, no. 9 (1979), p. 1488.

77. Interviews.

78. *Strategic Nuclear Weapons Policy*, p. 79.

79. Ibid.; *International Defense Review*, no. 3 (1981), p. 244.

80. *Strategic Nuclear Weapons Policy*, p. 79.

81. *International Defense Review*, no. 9 (1979), p. 1463.

82. Interviews.

6 COSTS AND CONSEQUENCES

Even among those well disposed to the notion of independent deterrence, the Thatcher government's decision to build a new generation of nuclear submarines equipped with Trident missiles generated controversy. Few doubted that Trident was, militarily, the best system that Britain could buy.[1] The question was whether she could afford it. That concern moved the Carter administration to exact, and the Reagan administration to retain, a formal commitment that 'the economies realized through cooperation between our two governments will be used to reinforce the United Kingdom's efforts to upgrade its conventional forces'.[2] Journals editorially committed to retention of the deterrent vented their anxieties about the 'opportunity costs' of the Trident decision.[3] The Social Democratic Party explicitly,[4] and and Parliamentary Labour Party implicitly,[5] based their opposition to the government's nuclear programme upon its potential implications for Britain's conventional-force posture. Even the British public, while staunchly supporting retention of independent strategic forces, seemed to balk at the expense of Trident.[6] This chapter examines the costs and consequences of the Trident decision.

The government estimated the capital costs of Polaris's successor at £5,000 million in September 1980 sterling. With the decision to procure Trident II, costs escalated to an estimated £7,500 million at September 1981 prices and exchange rates. Table 6.1 identifies the major components of this total. These estimates met with some scepticism.[7] Substantial cost escalations had plagued the Chevaline programme and these were cited as evidence of the habitual optimism of procurement-cost forecast.[8]

The Thatcher administration, however, argued forcefully that Polaris rather than Chevaline was the appropriate analogy to the Trident programme. Chevaline's costs had mushroomed because 'it was essentially a U.K.-unique programme of very high technological ambition . . . [Trident would not be] anything like so big and so bold a step.'[9] The Trident force, like Polaris, would be developed in the closest collaboration with the United States and Polaris had come in at just above its originally estimated cost. Moreover, nearly every aspect of Britain's Trident programme would utilize proven technologies and draw upon vast reserves of British and/or American expertise. The submarines

129

Table 6.1: Estimated Cost of Trident II

	Cost (£ millions)	Percentage of Total
Missiles	1,275	17
Submarines	2,575	35
Weapons system equipment (including tactical weapons)	1,275	17
Shore construction	600	8
Warhead design and production, unallocated contingency	1,725	23
Total	7,450	100

Source: Derived from *Statement on the Defence Estimates 1982*, Cmnd. 8529-I (HMSO, London, 1982), p. 6.

would employ to a very large extent components already developed in the SSN construction programme.[10] Vickers Barrow — which would suspend SSN construction entirely in the late 1980s to concentrate on the SSBN effort — had an excellent record, having built by 1982 some twenty-two nuclear submarines without any real cost increases at all.[11] Rolls-Royce had virtually completed development of the PWR-2 propulsion plant and any risk of cost escalation there was amply provided for in the 'enormous contingency allowance' built into the total figure of £7,500 million.[12] The United States had a fairly good record of bringing in strategic missiles at cost and the Trident II sales agreement insulated the British from any risk of development cost escalation.[13] Finally, as the British intended to deploy essentially the C-4 warhead on their D-5s, the government foresaw no reason for warhead design and production expenditure to rise.[14] Indeed, the greatest uncertainty was thought to lie in the estimate for shore construction. In any case, while acknowledging that risk was unavoidable, the government felt confident that any overruns in the Trident programme would be modest and manageable.

In so far as it is possible to weigh the grounds for the government's confidence, it would seem to have been well placed. The Ministry of Defence had costed the Trident programme carefully and conservatively and its representatives defended the estimates ably.[15] It is unclear whether the Ministry's 1982 estimates included the out-year costs of RAF personnel committed to man Rapier air defence units[16] or any net expenditure incurred in Anglo–American nuclear materials exchange arrangements.[17] If not, the cost of Trident would increase by perhaps £150 million to £200 million. That caveat aside, the Thatcher

Figure 6.1: Tornado and Trident: Illustrative Impact on the Defence Budget

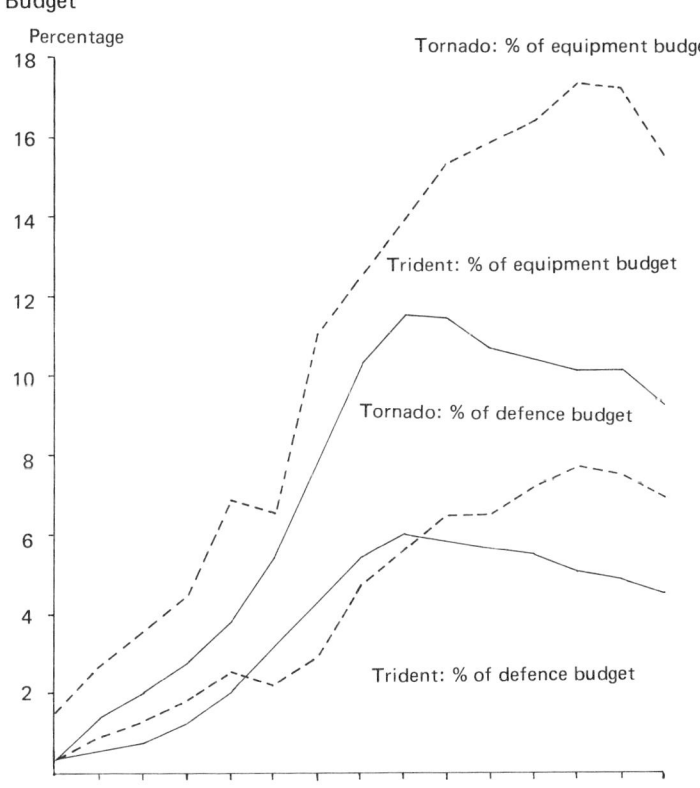

Tornado: 1970–85
Trident: 1980–95

Source: *Statement on the Defence Estimates 1982.*

administration would appear to have represented the capital costs of Trident quite fairly.

What concerned most observers, however, was not the absolute costs of Trident but their incidence in the defence budget and their impact upon Britain's conventional capabilities. The Thatcher government took the view that Trident was simply an ordinary charge on the budget: 'The accommodation of large re-equipment programmes is a normal part of defence planning and budgeting.'[18] The capital costs of Trident were, relatively speaking, quite modest. They compared quite favourably, for example, with the costs of building the V-bomber force in the 1950s or indeed the ongoing costs of the Tornado strike and air defence aircraft procurement programme (see Figure 6.1). It was estimated that the Trident programme would absorb, on average, no more than 3 per cent of the defence budget over the years 1980-95. In peak capital expenditure years, Trident was likely to consumer perhaps 6 per cent of the total budget or, a more important indicator, 12 per cent of the equipment budget.[19] By comparison, France was currently devoting 20 per cent of its entire defence budget to nuclear-weapons procurement.[20]

There were, inevitably, opportunity costs to Trident procurement: 'money spent on this is money not spent on other things'.[21] The government stressed, however, that because it intended to increase real defence spending by 3 per cent a year through 1985/6, expenditure on the conventional forces would rise by 'several billions of pounds' in real terms despite the decision to proceed with Trident.[22] It could, in any case, see 'no other use of our resources which could possibly contribute as much to our security and the deterrent strength of NATO as a whole'.[23]

> [T]hose who argue that expenditure on Trident would be better devoted to strengthening our conventional forces must consider whether future Soviet leaders are more likely to be deterred by an invulnerable second strike SLBM force or, for example, two additional armoured divisions with 300 extra tanks (even if this were a sensible alternative), given that the Warsaw Pact already outnumbers NATO in tanks by some 30,000.[24]

On these terms, Trident seemed an eminently prudent use of national resources.

It was, however, by no means generally accepted that these were the terms on which the opportunity costs of Trident had to be weighed. The opposition parties and their allies in the press contended that retention rather than expansion of Britain's conventional contributions to the Alliance was the genuine issue at stake in the Trident debate.

> The war that obliterates Britain — whether unilaterally disarmed or not — will either start between the two superpowers, or by accident and miscalculation in the European theatre. The long-term cost of Trident is a substantial withdrawal from that theatre. The long-term nightmare is that Trident will then prove a fatal irrelevance to our survival.[25]

Even supporters of the Trident decision evinced uneasiness about its implications for the conventional forces and urged the government to air the issues fully. Only then would there be 'at least a chance of an emerging consensus on an issue fundamental to the generation to come'.[26] Divergent assessments of Trident's real costs floated around London and generalized distrust of the government's position prevailed. It was felt that the government was being 'disingenuous'.[27] To some extent this criticism was warranted, but it also reflected partisan efforts to capitalize on anti-nuclear sentiment. The peculiar sensitivity of the 'opportunity cost' issue arose principally from the fear that, sometime in the 1980s, another in the long series of budgetary crises which had driven British defence policy throughout the post-war era would emerge. This time, it was feared, budgetary crisis would require radical structural change in Britain's defence posture and that, surprisingly enough, was a novel prospect.

The basic dilemma of post-war British defence policy was simple: domestic economic growth could not keep pace with the inexorable rise of the real costs of defence. Each generation of defence equipment — with such notable exceptions as nuclear submarines — cost far more in real terms than had its predecessor. Type-22 frigates, for example, cost three times as much as the *Leander*-class vessels they replaced; Harrier aircraft proved four times more expensive than Hunters; even artillery shells doubled in price from one generation to the next.[28] Governments had the choice either to allow defence expenditure to rise — and thereby further inhibit domestic growth and increase pressure on the balance of payments — or to restrain spending and cut back on military commitments. Broadly speaking, governments tried both approaches. Real defence spending increased by 37 per cent between 1950 and 1980 and, as the abolition of conscription reduced the salience of personnel costs, the equipment budget doubled in real terms. That growth was none the less insufficient and reductions in planned defence expenditures were regular occurrences. Thus, Churchill cut back on Attlee's massive Korean rearmament programme. Eden, immediately upon succeeding Churchill, began to review his spending plans; his efforts were completed in the wake of Suez by Macmillan and his Defence Secretary, Duncan Sandys. The fundamental realignment of defence policy announced in the Sandys White Paper in 1957 was, in due course subjected to prolonged review by the Labour governments of the 1960s. Labour withdrew British forces East of Suez and announced, in 1969, that 'reorientation of our defence policy is now complete and the armed forces can look forward to a period of stability and progress'.[29] Within five years, however, a new Labour government ordered another round of defence cuts which completed the withdrawal of British forces from all but the last vestiges of empire and focused their energies entirely upon the European theatre. The 'long recessional'[30] had, it was hoped, come finally to an end.

The process of adjustment which culminated in the 1975 defence review was geographical and scalar, rather than structural. Budgetary savings were achieved in the main by abandoning extra-European commitments and reducing the size of British forces accordingly. The individual armed services retained their broad, multidimensional force structures. Balance, both within and among the services, was maintained despite constant fiscal pressure and periodic doctrinal challenges. Indeed, it could be argued that regionalization of British defence policy was a necessary condition for the maintenance of such balance. This was most obviously the case with the Army. The Army had maintained substantial forces on the Continent for avowedly political purposes and, properly speaking, no military purposes at all. It was deployed beyond the Rhine to assuage European concerns about the Germans and to keep the Americans company. In the event of war, it had only to die or, more precisely, to die alongside the US Seventh Army. It therefore did not require expensive equipment. The Army's peacekeeping duties beyond Europe not only did not require high-quality weapons but could not justify retention of large formations in the order of battle. The end of conscription in 1962 left the Army short of men as well as *matériel*. Regionalization and the doctrinal revolution underlying NATO's embrace of 'flexible response' were then something of a godsend. Withdrawal from overseas stations reduced (though it did not eliminate) manpower constraints just as the Army's hostage role in Europe was evolving into a complex of genuine conventional warfighting missions. The Continental commitment demanded a range of capabilities – e.g. large and well equipped armoured, artillery and mechanized infantry formations, sophisticated anti-tank weaponry, organic airlift and air defence capabilities, smaller specialized assault units – which conformed admirably to the Army's own force structure preferences. In Europe, the General Staff found both doctrinal justification and external political support for the kind of army – qualitatively on a par with any in the world – it had struggled to preserve throughout the post-war era.

The RAF had also suffered through periods of fiscal neglect and doctrinal doubt before finding succour in its European vocation. Bomber Command's strategic nuclear mission had, of course, given the

RAF pride of place among the services in the 1950s. Even then, how-ever, the Air Staff had had to abide the decline of Fighter Command in order to validate the stark doctrine of deterrence voiced in the Sandys White Paper and physically embodied in the V-bomber force. The strategic role was lost in 1962 and thereafter the RAF's prospects looked very grim indeed. As one procurement programme after another was cancelled, the Air Staff was reduced to competition with the Fleet Air Arm for missions East of Suez. It achieved brief success in 1966 when the Wilson government endorsed its dog-eared 'island plan' and ordered F-111 strike aircraft in lieu of the Navy's coveted carriers. In 1968, however, the mandate for operations East of Suez was with-drawn and so was the order for F-111s. In the same year, the Navy formally assumed control of the deterrent. Flexible response and the growth of Soviet conventional air power, however, began to generate a range of missions in the European theatre which required a variety of sophisticated aircraft and skilled pilots. In its European vocation, the RAF required capabilities along virtually the whole spectrum of air missions. Strike Command had now to plan on continuing theatre and tactical nuclear roles as well as conventional battlefield support, ground attack, deep interdiction, maritime strike and reconnaissance and air defence missions.[31] Only the strategic nuclear role proved elusive. In consequence, the Air Staff had under way in the late 1970s and early 1980s 'the most comprehensive re-equipment programme for the Royal Air Force ever undertaken for 30 years'.[32]

The Royal Navy faced perhaps the most severe and persistent doctrinal challenges in the post-war era and managed, through sheer bureaucratic skill as well as the inherent flexibility of the fleet, to over-come them all. The implications of nuclear weaponry for a capital ship navy committed to offensive operations were resisted well into the 1950s by the Admiralty's evocation of prolonged post-nuclear 'broken-backed' warfare.[33] The Navy recognized, however, that it had to 'slim itself down and reorient for the new strategic era if it was to stave off an inevitable call for more drastic cuts'.[34] The Admiralty cut its reserve fleet, trimmed its shore structure, disposed of overseas stations, and reduced the number of major surface combatants in the active fleet. Most important, it forsook total war in the Atlantic in favour of limited war in the Indian Ocean. It therefore survived the 1957 White Paper's renewed emphasis on massive retaliation admirably. In 1962, it grudgingly accepted a strategic mission while lobbying for a new generation of carriers. With the Wilson government's decisions to cancel carrier procurement and to withdraw British forces East of

Suez, however, the role and future of the Navy came into serious question for the second time in a decade.

The promise of prolonged conventional warfare in Europe implicit in flexible response and the spectacular growth of Soviet naval forces gave the Navy new purpose. Like Fisher on the eve of the Great War, the Admiralty in the early 1970s recalled the fleet from its distant imperial stations to confront a gathering naval threat in home waters.[35] General warfare capabilities built into ships laid down in the East of Suez era facilitated the fleet's rapid retooling for ASW and sea-control missions in the Atlantic. The Admiralty set to work designing a new class of 'ASW cruisers' — the *Invincible* class — which strikingly resembled light carriers; indeed, they eventually embarked Sea Harrier aircraft and entered service with carrier pennant numbers. After thirty years of doctrinal flux, the Royal Navy approached the 1980s with unquestionably the most powerful fleet after the superpowers', and arguably the most modern and sophisticated, ship for ship afloat. It remained, moreover, a 'balanced' fleet, deploying capital ships with organic air defence and power projection capabilities alongside a large complement of surface escorts, a quite impressive flotilla of nuclear and diesel-driven submarines and, of course, strategic nuclear forces.

Expenditure reductions through regionalization therefore permitted and perhaps encouraged maintenance of force structures congruent with the services' own preferences. This happy circumstance un-doubtedly mitigated service opposition to the retreat from empire. It may also have helped to sustain broader political support for the direction of British policy. The logic and lessons of decades of military experience[36] as well as the exigencies of Britain's relations with her neighbours lent primacy to the Continental commitment. But the decisions of successive governments to forsake a wider world role for Europe never lacked for critics. The 'open sea' beckoned from time to time to Englishmen of widely varying political persuasions. Avoidance of structural change probably facilitated political acceptance of those decisions because the prerequisites of military independence — independent strategic forces supported by a military establishment replicating, albeit in miniature, the force postures of the great powers — were preserved. In this sense, there was nothing genuinely irrevocable about the progressive Europeanization of British defence policy. To be sure, independent roles and missions in various parts of the world were abandoned and the political conditions which had sustained them were unlikely to recur. Particular force components — large aircraft carriers, long-range transport aircraft — were discarded. In the main, however, capabilities once identified with global missions were retained and simply recast in European roles. If events ever took an ugly turn, the organizational framework and residual capacity for military autonomy were still at hand.

The expedient of reduction through regionalization also entailed acceptance of certain risks and constraints. First, the painstaking avoidance of major structural changes in the individual services over so many years could only increase the political salience of such changes should they eventually prove necessary. Second, regionalization gave the services substantial political leverage in their procurement efforts and generated requirements for technically demanding and very expensive weapons systems. As such systems tended to be prone to unforeseeable cost escalation, regionalization also compounded governments' difficulties in managing the equipment budget. Third, commitment of virtually all British forces to the Alliance undermined the flexibility of future governments. Henceforth, reductions, reconfigurations and redeployments would carry political costs within the Alliance. Moreover, as the distribution of political risk in the Alliance did not necessarily track domestic political priorities, governments caught between domestic and allied pressures would tend to postpone decisions likely to raise questions about the compatibility of NATO priorities with British security interests. The 1975 defence review, which completed the regionalization process, was therefore something of a watershed. There had never been easy choices but henceforth decisions would be exceptionally difficult. Indeed, when Prime Minister Callaghan intimated during sterling's spectacular collapse in 1976-7 that, in the absence of international assistance, further defence cuts might be necessary, he encountered substantial resistance. Serious dissension surfaced in military circles and NATO's Secretary-General, Dr Joseph Luns, took the extraordinary step of advising the government publicly that 'any further cuts by the United Kingdom would not be understood by its allies or find any measure of support on their part'.[37]

The advent of North Sea oil revenues eased pressure on both the defence budget and the balance of payments. The Callaghan government avoided substantial defence cuts and restored the funding levels envisaged in the 1975 defence review by joining with the allies in a pledge to increase defence spending by 3 per cent in real terms annually. However, Labour did preside over 'hidden' defence cuts by allowing service pay and benefits to decline significantly relative to civilian remuneration. Consequently, by 1979, the RAF was short of pilots and specialists, while the Navy was 5 per cent under strength, with recruitment some 18 per cent short of target and voluntary wastage running at 7 per cent. In that year, nine ships of the active fleet were placed on standby largely because of manning problems. The Regular Army was almost 10 per cent, and the reserve Territorial Army a full 19 per cent below establishment. Only 78 per cent of the tanks deployed with the Rhine Army were manned.[38] Moneys released in this manner from the personnel budget could be used to fund a swelling equipment budget. The Ministry of Defence's ten-year spending forecasts, the 'long term costing projections', promised maintenance of the programme laid down in 1975: a broadly balanced fleet, a multimission air force and fully equipped land army in Europe supported by adequate reinforcements and specialist units in Britain. Provision was made for the modernization of major force components. The Navy was to receive new classes of light carriers, destroyers, frigates and SSNs, equipped with state-of-the-art sensors, communications, fire control and weapon systems. The Army was to be equipped with new main battle tanks, mechanized combat vehicles, field howitzers, rocket launchers, anti-tank and anti-air weapons. The RAF would take receipt of the Tornado GR-1 strike and F-2 fighter aircraft, Nimrod AEW aircraft and VC-10 tankers. Provision had also been made for replacements of both the Jaguar and Harrier aircraft. In view of Labour's explicit, albeit ultimately equivocal,[39] commitments not to replace Polaris, however, the long-term costings which the Thatcher government inherited in 1979 made no provision whatsoever for strategic force modernization.[40]

The Thatcher government came to power pledged to make defence 'the first charge on [the] nation's resources'.[41] It endorsed the main features of its predecessor's defence plans, extended Labour's commitment to increase real defence expenditure by 3 per cent per annum and added an explicit commitment to replace Polaris as and when necessary. The Conservatives also honoured an election promise to restore service pay to levels comparable with civilian pay and indicated that the forces' capabilities for extra-European intervention missions would be reinforced.[42] By mid-1980, however, problems were already emerging. The government had originally intended to exempt defence from the expenditure reductions envisaged in its economic programme. However, when the expected contraction in the money supply failed to materialize by 1980, the Treasury demanded sacrifice from defence as well as the civilian departments. Defence Minister Pym resisted rather too fiercely and earned the Prime Minister's displeasure. He was replaced before the year was out. Moreover, management of the defence budget itself was proving difficult. Recession-plagued contractors began to submit invoices to the Ministry of Defence ahead of schedule. This, along with the 'catch-up' pay rise given to the services, caused the Ministry to overspend its budget in cash terms. Pym accepted a modest reduction in defence expenditure and imposed a moratorium on equipment and supply contracts which severely constrained military training, exercise and deployment.[43] Table 6.2 compares the expenditure authorized in the April 1981 White Paper with the government's original programme and Labour's projections.

Table 6.2: British Defence Budget Projections (£m at 1981-2 estimates prices)

Origin	1980-1	1981-2	1982-3	1983-4
Labour's programme 1979	12,385	12,487	12,497	12,522
Conservative programme 1980	12,107	12,517	12,890	13,270
Conservative programme 1981	12,265[a]	12,274	12,650	13,050

Note: a. Reflects cash overspend.
Source: Derived from David Greenwood, *Reshaping Britain's Defences*, Aberdeen Studies in Defence Economics (ASIDES), no. 19 (Aberdeen University, Aberdeen, 1981), p. 6.

The minor spending revisions announced in April 1981 were stopgap measures. A new Minister of Defence, John Nott, had taken office in January and had undertaken a thorough review of defence expenditure. It became clear that actual defence expenditure would substantially exceed the defence funding authorized in the April 1981 White Paper by 1985 (see Figure 6.2). Contrary to the impression prevailing at the time, the Trident programme was not the source of this imbalance. Rather, the difficulty lay in the conventional equipment budget. Equipment costs were increasing at an average rate 6 to 10 per cent higher than inflation.[44] Rates of increase varied among equipment types, but overall some 60 per cent of the equipment budget was liable to real cost increases well in excess of 3 per cent per annum. As defence spending could not keep pace, Nott had no choice but to reduce conventional equipment expenditure. To his credit, he resisted political temptation and eschewed the option of simply underfunding existing programmes. Nott confronted the problem of structural change directly. He reviewed the Trident programme and satisfied himself as to its indispensability. As he was committed to achieving a relatively permanent solution of

Figure 6.2: British Defence Budget Expenditures (£m at 1981-2 estimates prices)

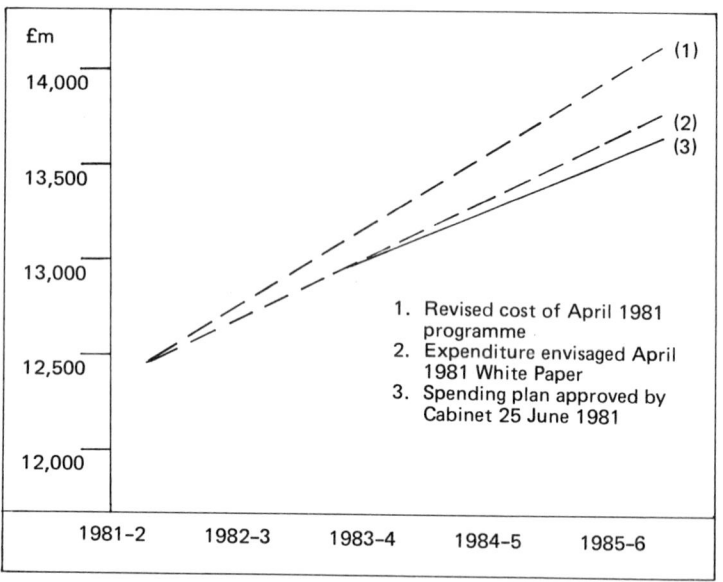

Source: *The Times*, 7 July 1981, p. 2.

the defence budget problem, he was bound to accommodate strategic spending in his revised budget projections. The Minister instructed each of the service procurement executives to prepare, given differing assumptions about funding, detailed zero-based models of their equipment requirements for the 1990s.[45] It was made clear that there were to be no 'sacred cows' in this process. This was to be structural change with a vengeance.

Nott and his advisers were principally concerned with the rising costs of weapons platforms, which increasingly absorbed funds needed for the weapons they were meant to carry. The objective of the review was to restore equilibrium between armaments and platforms expenditure. Particular force components were scrutinized to see if they represented the most cost-effective method of weapons delivery. The Minister's objective reflected a series of doctrinal assumptions about the nature and likely locus of East–West conflict. Nott and his advisers took the view that any war between the Soviet Union and the West was certain to be extraordinarily intense, consuming weapons at unprecedented rates.[46] Protracted conflict was possible only if the Western powers invested in sufficient weaponry to weather the first crucial hours and days of conflict. Time was an ally of the West just as geography was an ally of the East. Therefore, the Soviet Union would be loath to embark upon European war unless rapid victory appeared probable. Deterrence was thus best served by maximizing the front-line forces of the Alliance. War, if it came, would in all likelihood come in central Europe. Conflict would, of course, be global in scope but the stakes would be West Germany and the Low Countries. They alone would warrant the risks.

By these lights, the Navy fared poorly indeed. The Minister, formerly an investment banker, was clearly dubious about the cost-efficiency of surface combatants. Tens of millions were being spent on warships 'whose principal lethal armament [was] one missile launcher'.[47] Quite substantial sums were regularly absorbed by mid-life modifications of older hulls in Navy yards when for the same money private firms were prepared to build equally effective and less labour-intensive warships. Surface ships absorbed money better spent on weapons and perversely influenced defence priorities. The Minister was said to have been particularly dismayed to learn that expenditure on fleet air defence exceeded spending upon the air defence of Britain proper.[48] Moreover, the Navy was vulnerable under the doctrinal standards Nott employed to establish mission priorities. Virtually all the ready forces of the Army and the RAF were committed to missions directly relevant to the course of conflict in early days. This was obviously the case with RAF Germany, the Rhine Army and British-based units earmarked for rapid reinforcement of the Central Front. Similarly, Strike Command's squadrons were critical to any hope of blunting the advance of Soviet armour in Europe. But British air defence, which emerged as one of the Minister's principal concerns, was also essential as British and American offensive air operations out of British bases could not be sustained unless the RAF retained mastery of the air. The Navy's very substantial investment in escorts could be justified in the NATO context only by reference to convoy protection duties, a mission which presupposed prolonged conflict. Nott apparently reasoned that maintenance of a large fleet of escorts could not be justified if it came at the expense of land, air and maritime missions directly relevant to the initial stages of conflict. If the Continent was lost, there would be no reinforcements. Operation Overlord could not be replayed in the nuclear age.

Naturally, political considerations entered the Minister's calculations. Reductions in the surface fleet, partially offset by increases in submarine and maritime air forces, would be acceptable to the Americans and would not concern the rest of the Alliance at all. The distribution of naval roles and missions in the Atlantic was a matter for London and Washington resolve. On the other hand, reductions in the Rhine Army, 'so essential to the Alliance's military posture and political cohesion',[49] would involve political costs of an entirely different order, costs the government was not yet prepared to accept.

As the direction of Nott's thinking became clearer, anxieties at the Admiralty mounted. 'Worst case' naval expenditure models were circulated around Whitehall and found their way to the press. Spirited debate, generally favourable to the Navy's cause, ensued.[50] Confrontations between Nott and the Minister for the Royal Navy, Keith Speed, grew more heated and frequent. Rumours of savage cuts in fleet strength were seemingly confirmed when Mr Speed, ill-advisedly, went public with his concerns. Mrs Thatcher promptly sacked him and, with typical thoroughness, went on to abolish the traditional sub-Cabinet positions for individual service Ministers. In the event, rampant speculation rebounded admirably to the government's benefit. The cuts Mr Nott announced in June 1981 were not nearly as catastrophic as the public had been led, perhaps deliberately, to expect. They were substantial none the less.

The principal features of the defence programme laid down in *The Way Forward*[51] may be summarized as follows.

Royal Navy: Destroyer and frigate strength was reduced from 59 to 42 hulls, with eight remaining in the standby squadron on 30 days' minimum notice. Four fleet auxiliaries were scheduled to be withdrawn by 1985. While all three ships were to be built, only two of the *Invincible*-class carriers were to remain in service. The carrier *Hermes* and specialist assault ships *Intrepid* and *Fearless* were to be phased out by 1984. Expansion of the SSN fleet to 17 ships by the early 1990s was confirmed. A seventh Type-22 frigate, already under construction, was to be the last of its class. No more orders would be placed for Type-42 air-defence destroyers. Instead, the programme to design and produce a new, simple export-suitable Type-23 frigate was to be accelerated. The Portsmouth dockyard was to be run down, and the Chatham dockyard closed altogether, with a resultant loss of 13,000 civilian jobs. Henceforth, expensive mid-life modifications of surface combatants were to be avoided. Navy strength was to be reduced by 8,000–10,000 by 1986.

Army: The Rhine Army was to be maintained at its Treaty strength of 55,000 men, but a divisional headquarters was to be withdrawn to Britain and the 1(BR) Corps was to be consolidated into three divisions. All of the Army's planned re-equipment programmes were to continue with the addition of three batteries of tracked Rapier SAMs, increased warstocks and a larger purchase of Milan anti-tank missiles. Regular Army strength was to be run down by 7,000 men by 1986, while Territorial Army strength was to increase from 70,000 to 86,000 men, with added funding for reserve training.

Royal Air Force: Purchase of 60 AV-8B V/STOL aircraft as replacements for the Harrier force was confirmed, but a discrete Jaguar replacement was cancelled. Hence, after the mid-1980s RAF Germany was to rely entirely on Tornado IDS and first- and second-generation Harriers for offensive air operations. British air defence was to be augmented substantially by increasing the purchase of Tornado F-2 fighters from 165 to 185 and retaining two Phantom squadrons in service. An additional 36 Hawk trainers were to be equipped with Sidewinder missiles for air defence. The Tornado IDS buy was to be reduced from 220 to 200, but IDS previously earmarked for maritime strike roles were to be released for land-attack duties by Buccaneers retained in service and equipped with Sea Eagle anti-shipping missiles. The Nimrod MK II fleet was to be increased to 34 aircraft, in further support of the Navy's ASW missions. Additional civil VC-10s, held in storage for parts, were to be converted for transport and/or tanker duties. RAF strength was to decline by some 2,500 men by 1986.

There was no brooking the fact that the Navy suffered far more than the other services; it bore 57 per cent of the expenditure cuts. The government contended, however, that, in *mission* terms, Britain's capabilities in the Atlantic would suffer no marked degradation. Different force elements would henceforth be devoted to maritime missions. There was considerable merit to the government's argument. The Admiralty had long planned to mount a three-tiered defence against the Soviet Navy. It developed and justified a force structure able to:

(1) conduct offensive ASW and anti-surface ship operations against the Soviet Northern Fleet in its putative sanctuary in the far northeast;
(2) mount, in co-operation with the RAF's long-range maritime

patrol (LRMP) aircraft, barrier defences across the Greenland-Iceland–UK (GIUK) gap;
(3) provide local protections for convoys.[52]

The government attached lower priority and accordingly provided fewer resources for the third of these missions. But the first two – probably far more important to Soviet calculations on the brink of war – retained their priority. The government intended to structure a less costly but arguably more effective force posture to deny sanctuary and close the GIUK gap. Nott simply believed that RAF's Nimrod MK II LRMP aircraft equipped with Searchwater radar and armed with Stingray torpedoes and similarly armed SSNs could do the job at least as well as surface combatants. The government confirmed its commitment to increase spending by (nearly) 3 per cent per annum[53] and assumed in its cost projections that approximately 40 per cent of the equipment budget over the years 1980–5 would be devoted to maritime missions.

Nott's defence review proved acceptable to the Alliance. American officials welcomed the emphasis on British air defence and listened, albeit warily, to the arguments for reducing the surface ship fleet. They were mollified by an unexpected bonus: restructuring of the ASW commitment in the Atlantic would free the *Invincible*-class carriers for out-of-area deployments.[54] A Royal Navy carrier task force was scheduled to deploy East of Suez in 1982. Domestic political reaction was unenthusiastic but not immediately threatening. Debate was joined on the balance to be struck between the Continental commitment and the 'open sea'. In effect, the 1981 defence review had preserved Britain's contributions to the Alliance and its ability to fund modernization of the independent deterrent at the expense of broadly balanced, multidimensional naval forces. Structural change along these lines naturally angered admirals; it had, however, more serious implications. Mr Nott's innovations made sense only with reference to allied missions in the Atlantic and northern seas. Rapid reconfigurations of the kind undertaken by the Admiralty in the 1950s and 1960s would no longer be as simple or even possible. The Navy Mr Nott envisaged would lack a substantial residual capacity for independent action. That was not a comfortable prospect for an island race, depending upon the sea for life itself and schooled over a long history not to trust greatly in alliances.

Pressure for reconsideration of the direction taken in the 1981 defence review was contained throughout the year. It was the common impression of defence analysts that the review's 'broad strategic thrust' would be maintained by the Conservatives or any likely successor.[55] The government was sufficiently concerned with pressure from the 'naval lobby' to use some of the funds released by the decision to procure Trident II – Trident II missile expenditure would be incurred later than would Trident I spending – to sustain surface ships. Thus, early in 1982, the Ministry of Defence ordered an eighth Type-22 frigate and decided to retain the amphibious assault ships *Fearless* and *Intrepid*. But it also confirmed plans to sell the carrier *Invincible* to Australia and to pay off the carrier *Hermes* after *Invincible*'s sister ships *Illustrious* and *Ark Royal* entered service. The Royal Navy, veteran and victor of so many budgetary campaigns in the post-war era had, it seemed, finally lost. As one naval officer commented forlornly after the Chiefs' unsuccessful appeal to the Prime Minister in June 1981, 'What we need now and quickly is a small colonial war requiring a lot of ships.'[56]

On 2 April 1982, Argentine forces invaded the Falkland Islands, a British dependency in the South Atlantic, and overwhelmed a garrison of seventy Royal Marines.[57] The next day, Members of Parliament gathered for the first weekend session of the House of Commons since the Suez crisis in 1956, and supported the government's decision to despatch a naval task force to the South Atlantic. There followed 'one of the most remarkable logistical feats of modern times'.[58] A task force, composed of the carriers *Hermes* and *Invincible*, the assault ships *Intrepid* and *Fearless*, some two dozen destroyers and frigates, and practically all of the fleet auxiliaries, were fitted out and put to sea in little more than 72 hours. Still more extraordinary was the rapid requisitioning and conversion of civilian ships – some 54 in all, including the luxury liners *Canberra* and *Queen Elizabeth 2* – to carry troops and supplies. The task force sailed 8,000 miles and successfully effected amphibious landings against defended positions under sustained and valorous air attack in Antarctic conditions. Deficiencies in warship design and weapons performance there clearly were: the fleet suffered terribly from the absence of an organic airborne early warning capability and inadequate air defences. When all was said and done, however, the fact remained that British forces had performed superbly in exceptionally difficult conditions. The Admiralty could point out without fear of contradiction that the operation could have been sustained had war come after all of Mr Nott's originally planned reductions had taken place.

The government could not hope to resist demands for changes in its defence programme in the wake of the Falklands campaign. The sight of the fleet setting sail undeniably stirred national feeling.

> Somewhere deep in the collective subconscious lay an understanding
> that we are an island people who, when threatened, have to look to
> the sea not just to locate the threat but to discover the instrument of
> our own security. We have the sea around us, and we have to have
> a navy for all seasons and all seas.[59]

Restoration of at least some of the cuts in fleet strength was politically imperative. In July, Minister Nott let it be known that HMS *Invincible* would be retained in the active fleet. It had been sheer luck that the Argentine invasion had come when both *Invincible* and *Hermes* were operational. Normally, only one would have been available. With three decks, two would always be operational.

In December 1982, the government announced a series of changes, substantially upgrading the forces' capabilities for intervention missions.[60] These were:

Royal Navy: Retention of HMS *Invincible*, along with HMS *Illustrious* and *Ark Royal* was confirmed. All of the Sea Harriers lost in the Falklands campaign were to be replaced and an additional seven were to be ordered. Each of the carriers was to be fitted out with an organic airborne early warning system: the Searchwater/Sea King system cobbled together during the war. The five destroyers and frigates lost in the campaign would be replaced by new heavyweight Type-22 frigates. One of the replacements was to be a 'batch 2' Type-22 (to round out a set of six in the fleet); the remaining four were to be 'batch 3s' with Sea Wolf anti-missile and anti-aircraft missiles, a new 4.5-inch gun, eight anti-ship missiles and a close-in point defence system. Point defence weapons, probably Seaguard, were to be added to all thirteen *Sheffield*-class (Type-42) destroyers, as well as to all three carriers, the light cruiser *Bristol* and the assault ships *Fearless* and *Intrepid*. Total escort strength was to stay at 55 ships until 1985. Thereafter, Nott's plans called for reducing escort strength to 50 but apparently the idea of keeping only 42 of those ships operational was discarded. Finally, although the Chatham dockyard was still to be closed, cuts from the 7,000-man workforce at Portsmouth were to be less severe: nearly 3,000 were to stay on instead of the 1,500 originally envisaged.

Table 6.3: The Surface Fleet 1981–6: Comparison of Force-size Projections *c*. 1981 and *c*. 1982

Type	In Service Mid-1981 (standby)	Under Construction Mid-1981	1981 Review In-service Mid-1980s	Falklands Review In-service Mid-1980s
Larger Fleet Units				
Invincible-class carriers	1	2	2	3
ASW/commando carriers	1	—	—	--
Assault ships	2	—	—	2
Subtotal	4	2	2	5
Escorts				
County-class destroyers	5	—	—	1
Type-82 destroyer	1	—	1	1
Sheffield-class (Type-42)	7	7	14	13
Leander-class	26	—	12 (8)	20
Rothesay-class	7 (3)	—	—	—
Amazon-class (Type-21)	8	—	8	8
Broadsword-class (Type-22)	2	5	7	12
Type-23 (design stage)	—	—	?	?
Subtotal	56 (3)	12	42 (8)	55
Total	60 (3)	14	44 (8)	60

Note: Figures in parentheses indicate ships in standby.
Source: Derived from Greenwood, *Reshaping Britain's Defences*, p. 44, and *The Economist*, 18 December 1982, pp. 29–31.

Army: The RAF's helicopter and airlift upgrades (q.v.) were designed to increase the Army's rapid intervention capability. The Army's main intervention unit, 5th Infantry Brigade, currently composed of the two-battalion Parachute Regiment and a regular infantry battalion, was to be upgraded into a full-strength airborne brigade. It was to receive a substantial complement of engineers, an armoured reconnaissance regiment (400 men with light tanks and armoured cars), an artillery regiment with 18 light 105 mm guns and a squadron of a dozen helicopters. The resulting force would be formidable in European contingencies but particularly useful for out-of-area interventions, perhaps in co-operation with the American rapid deployment force. Twenty-four additional Rapier anti-aircraft missile launchers were ordered, some for the RAF but most for the Army. An extra £10 million was also earmarked to increase weapons stockpiles above pre-Falklands levels.

Royal Air Force: The RAF was to receive six new heavy, dual-capable airlifters, able to serve both as tankers and cargo aircraft. Tristar aircraft from British Airways were to be converted for this purpose. The Tristar purchase represented a major increase in both the RAF's airlift capability and its aerial re-fuelling capacity. The RAF was also to receive a total of eight heavy-life Chinook helicopters in place of the three lost in the Falklands and a dozen second-hand American Phantoms for air defence of the Falklands Islands.

The government let it be known that funding for the Falklands campaign and replacement of equipment was to be met not by the defence budget but by the Treasury directly. There was, however, considerable doubt as to the extent of this commitment. Preliminary estimates suggested that the costs of the war itself — that is, the costs of fuel, warstocks, ammunition and the requisitioning and chartering of civilian ships — amounted to £700 million; and that the equipment purchased outlined above would cost approximately £900 million. In 1983-4, the cost of the Falklands Islands garrison was estimated at £424 million — a figure which included such capital costs as barrack, airfield and radar installations construction.[61] There was concern that while 'the Treasury may have unwillingly agreed the principle, they [had] yet to agree the detail';[62] thus, it was likely that some portion of the Falklands bill would be borne eventually by the defence budget. Moreover, manpower, operations and maintenance costs would increase markedly over Mr Nott's 1981 projections because HMS *Invincible, Fearless* and *Intrepid*, and several escorts, were to be retained in the active fleet. The impact of these costs would not be severe in the early 1980s — many of these ships had been originally scheduled to operate until the mid-1980s and five escorts had been lost in the South Atlantic — but after 1985-6 manning and operations costs would undoubtedly exceed the government's estimates. These costs were certain to be borne by the defence budget. There was, moreover, widespread anxiety that, quite apart from any Falklands costs, the equipment budget was once more getting out of hand. It was estimated that because insufficient account had been taken of defence equipment inflation in the 1981 defence review, the programme authorized therein would be underfunded by perhaps 10 per cent by 1984-5.[63] The gap might be larger if the defence budget was forced to bear a portion of the Falklands costs.

Minister Nott maintained fiercely that, even after the Falklands costs were taken fully into account, his budget was not underfunded.

> The truth is — in spite of the fact that some critics see it otherwise — the defence budget is not now under strain. I know it suits the argument of the anti-Trident lobby to assert that it is. But the pressures on me are, in fact, to add to the programme within the already agreed defence totals — there are no financial pressures to cut the forward plans which are in balance. With the three per cent real growth until 1986 to which we committed, we can maintain all our present defence roles, if we resist the temptation to add to our equipment programmes further at this stage. Beyond 1986, whilst equipment costs escalation could always cause problems, we have been very careful not to over-programme in the longer term. It was why we cut around £10 billion out of our forward plans. And in budgetary terms it has been successful.[64]

This position was not very persuasive. Along the government's back benches '[t]he need for a major new defence review within a year or so of the next general election [was] already accepted'.[65] Indeed, Nott himself admitted that his calculations did not take account of possible development of British Aerospace's P-110 experimental fighter-bomber. The Defence Ministry has an obligation, as the Minister once put it, to pursue an 'industrial strategy'[66] and for those reasons alone, a British government might feel compelled to authorize development of the P-110. That would add approximately £1,500 million to the equipment budget[67] — just as peak Trident expenditure was getting under way.

The prospect of a major review — and radical choice among Britain's four main defence roles — stimulated opposition to Trident and quickened debate on the direction of British defence policy. It may be that '[i]t will never be the case that money released by abandoning Trident will support for long substantial conventional forces'.[68] But if the funds earmarked for Trident could sustain 'two additional armoured divisions'[69] on the Central Front, they would suffice to retain two existing armoured divisions for some period of time. Serious consideration was being given to withdrawal or reduction of the Rhine Army. A revisionist school had emerged in the wake of the 1981 defence review which argued that if a choice had to be made, Britain must give preference to maritime forces.[70] As *The Times* put it, in a much remarked editorial, 'The single most important strategic consideration in British defence policy is that we are an island off the continent of Europe.'[71] It was senseless to cut British naval forces in order to maintain a Continental army, while encouraging Continental powers to build up naval forces. The Continental commitment had been undertaken at a time when Britain maintained a much larger defence establishment and for political reasons which no longer seemed relevant.

> Times have changed now, both in Britain and in West Germany. The latter is an economic giant in the alliance which should no longer be treated as a military dwarf, through a device which allows the smaller members of NATO to think, in their hearts, that the Rhine Army is as much to protect them against West Germany as it is to protect West Germany against the Russians.[72]

For these reasons, the editors called for reductions in the Rhine Army. The revisionists cast their position in an Alliance aspect, stressing the global nature of the threat and NATO's need to respond.

> Maritime and rapid intervention land and air transport forces are, therefore, the two elements of military power which the Western countries require to counter Soviet expansion beyond the NATO area . . . Given the likely constraints on defence spending for the rest of this decade, they would represent the most cost-effective British contribution of conventional forces to any new strategic plan for the Western Alliance.[73]

But while there was some merit to their view — the Reagan administration would certainly have welcomed a more pronounced British presence beyond the NATO area — their rhetoric betrayed a hankering for independence and a legitimate sense that something had gone terribly wrong when the Continental commitment was allowed to turn traditional British defence priorities round full circle. It was nationalism which rallied men to the Navy's cause and it was the peculiar xenophobia of the British left which explains the emergence of Labour as a 'Navy party'.[74]

Adherents of the Continental commitment cautioned that, whatever the budgetary decisions of the next few years, the fleet's capacity for independent action would be limited.[75] Moreover, at least one lesson of the Falklands campaign was that surface ships were highly vulnerable to missile attack. This, Minister Nott argued, confirmed the 'broad strategic thrust' of the 1981 defence review.

The Argentines had two modern submarines and five, just five air-launched missiles. At the present time the Soviets have some 2,000 submarine- and air-launched missiles including the most up-to-date standoff systems; the weight of missile strike against surface platforms would be immense.[76]

The Minister, in his last major speech before retirement, argued that it was not Britain's global power projection capabilities which required emphasis, but the defence of the home islands.

These islands are in a crucial position as the unsinkable aircraft carrier of the Alliance, the route through which American reinforcements would come in the event of conflict, and as the key rear base of European NATO.[77]

Citing the rise of neutralist sentiment in Europe, and isolationism in America, Nott contended:

Certainly now more than at any other time it would be pure folly for us to destabilize the current situation on the Central Front. With 55,000 British troops committed to the forward defence of Germany we provide our share of a political contribution, mirrored by the American contribution of over 200,000 committed to the same task.[78]

British withdrawal could trigger American reductions, encouraging a shift among the Continental powers to greater political and economic integration with the East, undermining 'the current balance of power against the interests of the United Kingdom; and through the centuries it has been our constant preoccupation to maintain that balance'.[79]

Hovering over the Trident debate, then, was the prospect of major structural choice among Britain's principal defence roles. Sustained economic growth could obviate the need to choose, but if choice proved necessary, it could only be agonizing. An 'island people' had looked for centuries to the fleet as the flexible guardian of its far-flung interests and the final mainstay of its independence. With a powerful fleet, streamlined interventionary forces, an effective air force and credible strategic forces, Britain might well be able to meet a range of threats to Western interests beyond Europe's shores and yet survive if the worst befell the Continent. Revisionists argued that a shift of resources from Continental to maritime forces could be accomplished at tolerable political cost through an agreed framework of 'global burdensharing'.[80] If that were possible – if, for example, British withdrawals from Europe could be offset by increases in American as well as West German forces – the revisionist case was very appealing. There was a great deal the British could do in the Persian Gulf, for instance, which the Americans by virtue of their close relationship with Israel, could not do or could not do as well. But, in point of fact, pressures – from advocates of a 'maritime strategy'[81] and indeed from unabashed isolationists[82] – were growing in the early 1980s for withdrawal of American forces from Europe and Britain's revisionists wanted to join them. And, in that regard, the revisionists betrayed a fundamental misconception of the role of the Rhine Army and British power generally in Europe.

The Rhine Army represented much more than a substantial contribution to the forward defence of Western Europe. It embodied the military lessons of the twentieth century:

> After the Second World War neither the political nor the military leaders of the United Kingdom shrank any longer from a Continental commitment. They had learned their lesson . . . We are unlikely ever again to have statesmen – or come to that, strategists – who maintain that the security of the United Kingdom can be considered in isolation from that of our Continental neighbours east as well as west of the Rhine.[83]

British forces had been deployed in Europe in a quite conscious effort to establish the political-military conditions for post-war West European and Atlantic military co-operation, to finalize what was, in effect, the post-war settlement in Western Europe. Over the years since 1954, able statesmen had elaborated a complex institutional superstructure both to redress West German anxieties and to contain West German energies. But they were building on a crude and ultimately uncertain foundation: the United States Seventh Army. It was only the visible and substantial engagement of American power in the European balance which permitted co-operation within the West and collective defence against the East and thus allowed revisionists to contemplate redirecting British efforts towards the open sea. Historically, British forces had both anchored and supplemented the American presence. Thus, the logic of the post-war settlement ran directly counter to the revisionists' instincts: Britain could not encourage or even accompany American withdrawals; she must resist and, if necessary, offset them.

The Trident programme, though hardly a principal cause, was expected to be the principal casualty of the gathering crisis in British defence policy.[84] However, Trident represented the best and very probably the only means of preserving credible, operationally independent strategic nuclear forces; its cancellation would be very likely to result in the abandonment of the independent deterrent. And that was a course as laden with risk for Britain — and indeed the Alliance — as any she faced.

Notes

1. Some did question Trident's military suitability, quite apart from its costs. See, e.g., Lord Chalfont, 'Is Trident the Right Answer?' *The Times*, 4 August 1980, p. 14.

2. Letter from President Reagan to Prime Minister Thatcher, *The British Strategic Nuclear Force*, Cmnd. 8517 (HMSO, London, March 1982), p. 8.

3. See, e.g., *The Economist*, 29 March 1980, pp. 18–19; *The Times*, 16 July 1980, p. 17.

4. *The Times*, 2 February 1983, p. 4.

5. See John Silkin's argument for cancellation, *The Times*, 12 March 1982, p. 4.

6. See, e.g., the *Guardian*, 4 February 1982, pp. 1, 26; 24 January 1983, p. 4.

7. See, e.g., the *Guardian*, 21 March 1982, p. 1.

8. See, e.g., D. Greenwood, *Reshaping Britain's Defences*, Aberdeen Studies in Defence Economics (ASIDES) no. 19 (Aberdeen University, Aberdeen, Summer 1981), p. 26.

9. Testimony of M.E. Quinlan in House of Commons, Fourth Report from the Defence Committee, Session 1980-1, *Strategic Nuclear Weapons Policy* (HMSO, London, 1981), p. 93.

10. Ibid.

11. *The Times*, 12 March 1982, p. 4.

12. Ibid.

13. See *The British Strategic Nuclear Force*.

14. *The Times*, 12 March 1982, p. 4.

15. See, e.g., *Strategic Nuclear Weapons Policy*, pp. 80–98.

16. See Chapter 5, p. 000.

17. See Chapter 3, p. 000.

18. Ministry of Defence, *The Future United Kingdom Strategic Nuclear Deterrent Force*, Defence Open Government Document 80/23 (HMSO, London, 1980), p. 26.

19. *The Times*, 12 March 1982, p. 4.

20. Ibid.

21. *The Future United Kingdom Strategic Nuclear Deterrent Force*, p. 25.

22. *The Times*, 12 March 1982, p. 4.

23. Ibid.

24. *Statement on the Defence Estimates 1982*, Cmnd. d. 8529-I (HMSO, London, 1982), p. 3.

25. 'Trident — The Wrong Choice, the Wrong Time', *Guardian*, 21 March 1982, p. 1.

26. 'Trident's Fourth Dimension', *The Times*, 8 March 1982, p. 10.

27. See, e.g., D. Greenwood, 'A Taxpayer's Guide to Trident's True Cost', *The Times*, 8 March 1982, p. 8.

28. *Statement on the Defence Estimates 1982*, p. 27.

29. *Statement on the Defence Estimates 1969*, Cmnd. 3227 (HMSO, London, 1969), p. 1.

30. The phrase is Professor Laurence Martin's; see his *British Defence Policy: The Long Recessional*, Adelphi Paper no. 61 (IISS, London, 1969).

31. See Derek Wood, 'Reshaping the Royal Air Force', *International Defense Review*, no. 3 (1982), pp. 311–16, for a brief résumé of the RAF's missions and programmes in the 1980s.

32. *Statement on the Defence Estimates 1982*, p. 16.

33. See J.G. Garnett, 'British Strategic Thought' in John Baylis (ed.), *British Defence Policy in a Changing World* (Croom Helm, London, 1978), pp. 158–66.

34. John E. Woods, 'The Royal Navy since World War II', *Proceedings* (March 1982), p. 85.

35. Ibid., p. 87. First Sea Lord John Fisher along with Winston Churchill, then First Lord of the Admiralty, oversaw the Navy's preparations for the First World War.

36. See Professor Michael Howard's classic essay, *The Continental Commitment* (Temple Smith, London, 1972).

37. *Proposed Reduction of United Kingdom Defense Expenditure for 1978/79* (NATO, Brussels, 16 September 1977).

38. *Statement on the Defence Estimates 1982*, p. 9.

39. The Callaghan government's attitude toward the Polaris replacement issue is discussed in Chapter 2.

40. Testimony of David Greenwood in *Strategic Nuclear Weapons Policy*, p. 62.

41. Quoted in Lawrence Freedman, *Britain and Nuclear Weapons* (Macmillan, London, 1981), p. 84.

42. See *Statement on the Defence Estimates: Defence in the 1980s*, Cmnd. 7826 (HMSO, London, 1980).

43. *Statement on the Defence Estimates 1981*, Cmnd. 9212-I (HMSO, London, 1981), pp. 1, 64.

44. *Statement on the Defence Estimates 1982*, pp. 27–31.

45. P. Hennessey and D. Greenwood, 'Uncovering the Real Defence Cuts', *The Times*, 7 July 1982, p. 2.

46. See Greenwood, *Reshaping Britain's Defences*, for an informed and detailed analysis of the 1981 defence review.

47. Ibid., p. 42.

48. Ibid., p. 29.

49. *The United Kingdom Defence Programme: The Way Forward*, Cmnd. 8288 (HMSO, London, 1981), p. 1.

50. See, e.g., 'The Navy Comes First', *The Times*, 19 May 1981, p. 10.

51. Cmnd. 8288 (June 1981).

52. Greenwood, *Reshaping Britain's Defences*, p. 40.

53. See Hennessey and Greenwood, 'Uncovering the Real Defence Cuts'; Nott announced that by 1985–6 defence spending would be '21 per cent higher, in real terms' than actual expenditure in 1978–9. That works out to be slightly less than 3 per cent per year.

54. Interviews.

55. Interviews. See also Woods, 'The Royal Navy since World War II', p. 83, and Greenwood, *Reshaping Britain's Defences*, pp. 53–4.

56. Quoted in P. Hennessey, 'New Strategy Could End Disputes', *The Times*,

18 June 1981, p. 6.

57. See, e.g., M. Hastings and S. Jenkins, *The Battle for the Falklands* (Michael Joseph, London, 1983).

58. L. Freedman, 'The War of the Falkland Islands', *Foreign Affairs*, vol. 61, no. 1 (Fall 1982), p. 201.

59. 'Strategy in a Silver Sea', *The Times*, 1 July 1982.

60. *The Economist*, 18 December 1982, pp. 29–31.

61. *The Financial Times*, 20 December 1982, p. 4.

62. L. Freedman, 'British Defence Policy after the Falklands', *The World Today* (September 1982), p. 334.

63. *The Financial Times*, 20 December 1982, p. 4.

64. British Information Service, *Policy Statements*, 53/82, 22 December 1982, p. 3.

65. *Financial Times*, 20 December 1982, p. 4.

66. *International Defense Review*, no. 12 (1981), p. 1695.

67. Wood, 'Reshaping the Royal Air Force', pp. 311–12.

68. Freedman, 'British Defence Policy', p. 336.

69. *Statement on the Defence Estimates 1982*, p. 3.

70. See, e.g., M. Chichester and J. Wilkinson, *The Uncertain Ally: British Defence Policy, 1960–1990* (Gower, London, 1982).

71. *The Times*, 1 July 1982, p. 10.

72. Ibid.

73. M. Chichester, 'Britain and NATO: The Case for Revision', *The World Today* (December 1982), p. 417.

74. Freedman, 'British Defence Policy', pp. 333–4.

75. Ibid., p. 339.

76. British Information Services, *Policy Statements*, 53/82, p. 5.

77. Ibid.

78. Ibid.

79. Ibid.

80. See, e.g., Chichester, 'Britain and Nato'.

81. See, e.g., Stansfield Turner and George Thibault, 'Preparing for the Unexpected', *Foreign Affairs*, vol. 61, no. 1 (Fall 1982), pp. 122–35.

82. See, e.g., Earle C. Ravenal, 'The Case for a Withdrawal', *New York Times Magazine*, 6 March 1983, p. 58.

83. Howard, *The Continental Commitment*, p. 146.

84. See, e.g., *The Economist*, 18 December 1982, p. 31; *Financial Times*, 21 December 1982, p. 12.

THE INDEPENDENT DETERRENT AND THE
     ATLANTIC ALLIANCE

National nuclear forces in Europe were once considered perhaps the most divisive and intractable problem facing the Atlantic Alliance, the subject of bitter political struggle and sustained academic attention. They were condemned in 1962 by Secretary of Defense McNamara as 'dangerous, expensive, prone to obsolescence and lacking in credibility as a deterrent'.[1] American hostility was so intense and vocal that even seasoned observers reckoned it would prove a permanent feature of transatlantic relations.[2] Yet, in 1982, McNamara's successor formally advised his British counterpart that 'the United States attaches great importance to the maintenance by the United Kingdom Government of an independent nuclear deterrent'[3] and NATO's Nuclear Planning Group declared the modernization of Britain's deterrent a matter 'of fundamental importance' to the Alliance as a whole.[4] Indeed, Mrs Thatcher's was the first British government to commit itself to a major strategic nuclear weapons procurement programme with the explicit support of its allies on both sides of the Atlantic. It is intended here to seek an explanation for this rather striking change of heart and to weigh its import for Britain and the Alliance.

Anton de Porte, towards the end of a comprehensive analysis of European–American relations, excused his cursory treatment of the great nuclear debate of the 1960s with the following remark: '[I] n the end, this great debate on fundamental issues, which at the time severely strained NATO, had so little lasting impact on it, or the Western sub-system.'[5] This observation is particularly relevant to a study of Britain's nuclear story. After all, it was principally American officials and scholars who objected to independent European forces – or at least it was American objections which absorbed the attentions of governments and set the tone of allied debate. Yet, their articulate arguments never significantly affected American policy towards Britain. At the height of the transatlantic nuclear controversy, the United States agreed to transfer its most sophisticated strategic missile system on terms fully consonant with Britain's operational independence. Even Gaullist France, long denied American assistance, was eventually offered Polaris and actually supplied with tanker aircraft critical to the credibility of the nascent *force de frappe*. Indeed, it is a measure of both the endemic confusion and extraordinary influence of Washington that a constellation of bureaucratic interests could so thoroughly dominate the Alliance's agenda without ever managing to give sustained direction to American policy.

It is useful none the less to recall the thrust and context of American objections to national nuclear forces in the 1960s. For one thing, allied opinion has traditionally figured prominently in Britain's domestic nuclear debate and the Thatcher government quite naturally relied upon American and European support in justifying its nuclear weapons programme.[6] Thus, an appreciation of the sources, nature and likely endurance of allied support is directly relevant to any assessment of the Trident programme's prospects. Moreover, with the exception of the unilateralist left, critics of Trident basically questioned the government's judgement that 'no other use of our resources could possibly contribute as much to our security and the deterrent strength of NATO as a whole'.[7] In this respect, it is important to recognize that de Porte's brief discussion of the nuclear controversy of the 1960s is justified precisely because he was writing a book about the structure of post-war Atlantic relations and that American objections to national nuclear forces were largely − though not exclusively − byproducts of a spirited but ultimately unsuccessful effort to reform the structure of Europe and hence the Alliance. In the political-military setting of the 1980s, the premier task facing the Alliance is to sustain the structure which survived the challenges of the 1960s and in this endeavour, both British and French nuclear forces play constructive, even critical, roles.

The central elements of the post-war settlement in Western Europe were cobbled together into a recognizable system (or subsystem) in the closing months of 1954. In August of that year, after prolonged and impassioned national debate, France rejected the European Defense Community (EDC) treaty. The EDC had originated as a French proposal, put forward in 1950 largely in order to thwart American efforts to rearm West Germany and gather her into the Atlantic Alliance. The plan had accordingly met with American suspicion. The British, averse to any form of supranational integration, had politely declined participation. Over time, however, the United States developed a profound attachment to the idea of an integrated European army, not simply as a device to make West German rearmament relatively palatable, but as a decisive step towards European unification. Americans began to lobby fiercely for its acceptance. Chanceller Adenauer had led the West Germans, after long deliberation, to accept rearmament and alignment with the West; partly because of American enthusiasm and partly because of his own genuine dedication to European union, he welcomed the EDC. The French, on the other hand, had come to dread the loss of national independence inherent in a fully integrated European defence establishment quite as much as they feared West German military autonomy.[8] The French government recognized that some form of West German rearmament was inevitable; it had emerged as a condition precedent to long-term American involvement in European defence and it was generally understood that an American military commitment was presently the only alternative to Soviet domination. Thus, French rejection of the EDC was less a final, futile protest against West German rearmament than a refusal to subscribe to a particular structural solution to the related problems posed by Soviet power in central Europe and West German power in Western Europe.

The diplomatic search for an alternative to integration as a framework for West German rearmament, while driven and informed by American pressure, was directed by Europeans, principally Anthony Eden and French Premier Pierre Mendès-France. The solution they came up with relied, like its grander forebears, upon a balance of power. West Germany was invited to join the Alliance as a sovereign equal, save in one important respect: she was forbidden to develop and deploy national nuclear forces without the consent of her European allies. Without a national nuclear capability, West Germany could never escape the exceptionally insecure conditions of her birth. Her existing dependence upon her allies and the United States in particular would now be permanent and under those circumstances she could be accommodated in a *Europe des Patries*.[9] As it was most unlikely that Bonn would willingly accept any substitute for American protection, the American military guarantee, purchased by West German rearmament, emerged in 1954 as the principal external restraint upon the political-military flexibility of West Germany rearmed.

Under pressure from France and the Low Countries, Britain undertook, for the first time, to maintain substantial armed forces on the Continent in peacetime. France, unwilling to consider integration in the absence of the British, was equally unwilling to trust in a balance of power which did not include Britain. The Rhine Army served a variety of purposes. It represented a residual hedge against renewed German adventurism while contributing directly and substantially to the defence of West Germany. It therefore supplemented the American guarantee and, in political terms, helped to anchor it. Perhaps most important, it afforded the British standing to monitor and, if necessary, to moderate the developing and already very special West German-American relationship. After all, the demise of the EDC had raised two alternative nightmares in Europe: either the Americans would go home or they would forge ahead and rearm West Germany on their own terms. If the West Europeans were to trust in the West German-American security relationship as their primary guarantee against German ascendency, it would bear watching. For all her insularity, Britain was far more sensitive to the demands of intra-European balance than the United States and, as a nuclear power and the United States' closest ally, she was ideally placed to ensure that legitimate West German security needs were addressed without undermining that delicate state of dependence upon which Europe now relied. Britain was therefore engaged in the 'inner balance of Europe' even though the British had refused to participate in the European Coal and Steel Community (ECSC) and would shortly decline membership in the European Economic Community (EEC). That division of roles was tenable, if arguably ill-advised, because the Atlantic Alliance was chosen in 1954 as the fundamental framework for West European relations. European economic integration and political collaboration would henceforth be an important but essentially supplementary mechanism for accommodating West German power; for precisely that reason, de Gaulle could exclude Britain from the EEC in the 1960s with impunity.

France, of course, retained her military autonomy and preserved it thereafter jealously. It is probable that West German rearmament galvanized French efforts to develop nuclear weapons. In any case, Mendès-France took decisions in late 1954 which, for the first time, gave the quickening French atomic energy programme a discernible military bent.[10] It is not really important what considerations moved Mendès-France or even his successors. What mattered was that, after 1954, Western Europe was in the military sphere a *Europe des Patries* and, if Franco-West German co-operation was to rest on a balance of power rather than full-scale integration, nuclear weapons would afford Paris a meaningful and permanent advantage over Bonn. National nuclear forces were not yet considered inconsistent with membership in NATO — Britain as well as the United States had them — and they were accepted in 1954 as the centrepiece of allied strategy. Rejection of the EDC had been more than anything else an affirmation of French political-military independence and it would be difficult to argue with the proposition that a strategic nuclear capability was a necessary, if not manifestly a sufficient, condition for independence in the nuclear age.

The settlement achieved in 1954 accommodated short-term American objectives — West Germany joined NATO the following year — but was not, from Washington's perspective, an altogether satisfactory arrangement. The United States had undertaken in 1949 to defend Western Europe against Soviet aggression; it had not consciously undertaken to assume a structural role in Western European politics. The duration of the United States' military commitment was admittedly open-ended, but it was not generally supposed to be permanent. Yet in 1954 the Western Europeans implicitly assumed the permanence of both West German military vulnerability and American military involvement and incorporated them as integral elements of the political structure of Western Europe, as permissive conditions for West Germany's attainment of genuine sovereignty and acceptance into the Western state system. This rather dramatically changed the terms of the United States' engagement in Western Europe. The relatively straightforward business of deterring Russians would henceforth be informed and complicated by the exquisite subtleties of Continental diplomacy. Military questions would now be analysed not only or even primarily on their own terms — will this measure improve military efficiency without unduly destabilizing mutual deterrence along the Central Front? — but also for their second-order political implications within Western Europe — how will this affect West German confidence or West German prominence and how will that go down in Paris or Brussels or Copenhagen? The problems of defence and deterrence in the nuclear age were complex enough. If military decisions had to emerge from two analytically distinct calculuses, they might not emerge at all. In any case, they could only be imperfect and ambiguous. And, in a loose confederation of states regulating their affairs fundamentally by a balance of power mechanism, the competitive tension underlying defence co-operation would afford both motive and opportunity for the exploitation of ambiguity — as, indeed, General de Gaulle demonstrated in the 1960s.

The United States' long, conflicted romance with European unification need not be chronicled here. It should be clear, however, that unification as an alternative structure for accommodating West German power and potential in Western Europe held significant advantages for the United States. Something like the EDC could be expected to reduce the steadily increasing financial costs and military risks attending the United States' presence in Western Europe and restore that presence to its original pristine vocation as a bulwark against the East. It would minimize or eliminate the second-order political difficulties afflicting military decision-making in the Alliance and perhaps, someday, free the United States from European involvement altogether. Many Americans, as well as Europeans, concluded from the EDC's demise not that integration was an inherently unworkable solution for post-war Europe, but that integration without Britain was untenable. There was then a revisionist disposition among Americans in the early 1960s, a sense that the arrangements of 1954 promised only permanent and exasperating entanglement. American objections to national nuclear forces first surfaced in the course of the thorough review of American military doctrine which culminated in the Kennedy administration's adoption of 'flexible response' in 1962. But the political difficulties attending presentation of flexible response fed revisionist sentiments within the administration and political objections to British and French forces reflecting those sentiments needlessly complicated practical resolution of military disagreements.

'It was primarily the introduction of the missile, rather than the political overtones of European projects, that made American nuclear experts insistent on centralized command and control of nuclear weapons.'[11] The United States had, of course, enjoyed an extraordinarily favourable strategic position during the 1950s. With more than 1,500 interceptors and nearly a hundred surface-to-air missile (SAM) batteries countering the small and primitive Soviet long-range bomber force,[12] the continental United States was, a practical matter, impervious to attack. On the other hand, Soviet nuclear forces, including the thousand medium bombers and steadily increasing arsenal of intermediate-range ballistic missiles (IRBMs) threatening Western Europe, were exceedingly vulnerable to pre-emptive attack by the Strategic Air Command (SAC) and RAF Bomber Command. Even as the number of IRBMs began to undermine the survivability of forward-based SAC forces and the RAF's V-bombers,[13] the invulnerability of the American homeland rendered Soviet nuclear weapons use futile — as retaliation would be devastating to the Soviet Union and risk-free to the United States — and the West's commitment to respond to conventional attack with nuclear strikes entirely credible.

The advent of Soviet intercontinental ballistic missile (ICBM) capabilities transformed the United States' strategic position.[14] Nuclear weapons use anywhere in the world now posed risks to the American populace. Deterrence of Soviet nuclear strikes was best served by development of a force posture manifestly able to ride out any conceivable counterforce strike and still suffice to inflict unacceptable damage upon the Soviet Union. With Polaris and Minuteman, the United

States had suitable second-strike forces in train. Even SAC's home-based bomber squadrons could, with improved readiness and warning procedures, be expected to survive ICBM attack. Forward-based air-craft, however, would enjoy substantially less tactical warning of missile attack and were therefore less likely to survive. Consequently, they injected an element of instability into the system by placing a meaning-ful premium upon a Soviet first strike. SAC's B-47s and B-58s, Bomber Command's Victors and Vulcans and, above all, France's Mirage IV bombers were considered incompatible with a stable deterrent posture.

In the event that deterrence failed and the Soviets initiated a major counterforce attack against the United States, the United States reserved its options but it was generally intimated that surviving American forces would execute an assured destruction retaliatory response, designed to destroy the Soviet Union's military capabilities as well as perhaps 'one-fifth to one-fourth of her population and one-half of her industrial capacity'.[15] The Soviet conventional threat to Europe posed a more demanding set of problems. American officials reckoned that, given an emerging threat to the continental United States, the credi-bility of the American pledge to respond 'massively' to conventional incursions must decline. Moreover, quite apart from Soviet perceptions, the United States government had no desire to be driven rapidly into potentially suicidal countervalue exchanges. Assistant Secretary of Defense John McNaughton put the point succinctly: 'The first interest of the United States Government is the protection of people.'[16] The United States therefore called upon the Alliance to increase conven-tional 'shield' forces on the Central Front from 23 to 30 divisions. It also scaled downwards its official estimates of Soviet conventional strength.

If nuclear weapons use proved unavoidable none the less, damage limitation would loom large as an allied objective. At Ann Arbor, in 1962, Secretary McNamara declared his conviction that 'principal military objectives, in the event of a nuclear war stemming from a major attack on the Alliance, should be the destruction of the enemy's military forces, not of his civilian population'.[17] A discriminating counterforce campaign would attrit Soviet retaliatory capabilities and, if coupled with substantial, invulnerable reserve forces, city-avoidance would give the Soviet leadership the 'strongest possible incentive' to avoid countervalue strikes against the West. By holding Soviet cities hostage, the United States would retain, in the context of inter-continental exchanges, the capacity to influence Soviet behaviour. The fundamental concern of the Secretary and his advisers was to prevent the escalation of thermonuclear warfare to countervalue exchanges, to create and, through painstaking control of nuclear-weapons employment, to sustain a clear and universally respected 'firebreak' between counterforce battle and the deliberate slaughter of civilian populations. European forces were simply too small and too vulnerable to be employed in a controlled manner; the United States feared, with some reason, that European nuclear weapons employment would fatally undermine American efforts to restrain nuclear violence and that the American people would suffer in consequence.

The British and French shared American concerns about the vulnerability of their forces; British governments had recognized the utility of second-strike forces as early as 1955. Bomber Command could reasonably expect a substantial portion of its forces to survive a Soviet IRBM attack until the late 1960s, by which time Polaris would be in service. The French could argue the survivability of their Mirage IV bombers only by exaggerating probable warning time and grossly underestimating Soviet missile accuracy. Nevertheless, both countries were quite right to contend that the Russians could never be certain of destroying their forces and might well be deterred from trying by the prospect of even a small countervalue retaliatory strike. The United States reserved the right to respond against Soviet cities in the event of a major counterforce attack; it was not at all clear why Britain and France should not reserve the same right, particularly when, given the yield and accuracy of Soviet weapons and the demography of France and Britain, counterforce attacks were liable to result in massive civilian casualities. Moreover, as both Britain and, for a while, France hosted American nuclear forces, abandonment of their independent forces would not necessarily reduce the likelihood of Soviet attack. To the contrary, it was argued that the risk of a small countervalue retaliation tended to sanctuarize forward-deployed American systems because once such a response had been launched and the 'firebreak' breached, the United States would have the 'greatest possible incentive' to follow up with a massive counterforce strike against Soviet forces so as to limit potential damage to American population centres.

In the early 1960s, French doctrine and, more ominously, French manoeuvres suggested that countervalue strikes would commence as the enemy approached France's north-eastern frontiers. This was, perhaps, the principal nightmare of American strategists.[18] They argued that an American threat to initiate unrestricted nuclear war in response to conventional aggression in West Germany was inherently incredible, and yet they worried about French pronouncements. To discredit British and French forces in the eyes of the non-nuclear allies, American spokesmen emphasized their strictly national character. 'Britain has retained its national command structure and the right to withdraw [its nuclear forces] at its option,' argued Robert Bowie in a speech to the Western Europe Union Assembly; 'this means they certainly could not be counted on by any of the others to be available in case of need'.[19] If the United States feared 'premature' escalation to urban-industrial strikes, and yet British forces were 'certainly' not to be used until Britain herself was threatened, precisely when were countervalue strikes warranted? The answer, Europeans suspected, was never, which is to say that unless American counterforce strikes could force the Red Army to a halt and then force it to withdraw, Europe was left with a conventional defence against Soviet attack, or none at all. The French took the view that imminent Soviet conquest and occupation of metropolitan France was an event serious enough to warrant the most damaging attack France could mount. And if the Americans, who rather snidely belittled the significance of French forces, responded with apoplexy to France's threat to initiate countervalue war in response to conventional attack, why then were they so certain that the Russians would never credit an American threat to do the same?

The United States could escape the contradictions of its policy only by demonstrating that a counterforce campaign would be decisive or by openly advocating a purely conventional (or conventional/tactical-nuclear) defence of Europe. They could do neither. For a few years in the 1960s, American forces were probably capable of destroying all Soviet forces in an initial attack and American officials sometimes intimated that such superiority would be retained. But, if that were the case, what was the need for increased conventional strength? Once it was clear that a major assault was under way, the United States could launch a disarming first strike and then, with Soviet cities at risk, coerce Soviet withdrawal. On the other hand, if, as almost everyone conceded, the number, sophistication and survivability of Soviet strategic and theatre forces would increase over time, then counterforce exchanges would eventually prove inconclusive and largely irrelevant to the course of conventional conflict. For while the United States could do great damage to Soviet power projection capabilities, American power projection capabilities were liable to prove at least as vulnerable, if only because of geographic conditions.

Even inconclusive counterforce exchanges were likely to lead to war termination — neither the Russians nor the Americans were liable to escalate — but not on terms favourable to the West. Unless the United

States managed to develop leverage in the exchange, war termination would merely ratify the results of conventional battle. As no one argued that NATO would throw back a determined Soviet assault with thirty divisions,[20] the conventional 'pause' advocated by the United States was worse than pointless; it simply afforded the Russians an opportunity to advance deeper into Western territory before allied conventional resistance broke altogether. American officials countered this argument by contending that 'an enemy is likely to find our threat of nuclear retaliation more credible when he must crash through a thick shield of conventional forces in an unmistakably major attack'.[21] But it was at least as likely that the credibility of the United States' threat to escalate conflict would decline after sustained conventional combat. 'If nuclear war was too risky at the start of the conflict, why should it not be even more risky when the local issue has in effect already been decided against us and when the devastation caused by a nuclear exchange may make the local situation seem irrelevant?'[22] It was, in any event, difficult to convince the British and French that an extra handful of divisions would contribute more to their own security than independent nuclear forces demonstrably sufficient to cause at least one superpower great anxiety.

Many Europeans concluded from this analysis that the United States envisaged a completely conventional defence of Europe.[23] For Europe, such a strategy was both financially and politically unacceptable. Europeans believed that war was unlikely but that any war — conventional, tactical-nuclear or strategic — would prove fatal. They came to dispute the intellectual premiss of flexible response. Perhaps because of the unique experience of the 1950s, when the American guarantee was risk-free and therefore entirely credible, Americans tended to assume that a threat was effective only if its execution were certain. Perhaps because after the 1950s they simply had no choice, Europeans contended that even irrational threats could deter by inducing uncertainty and that such threats were preferable to a declaratory strategy and force posture which increased the likelihood of Western response only by reducing the values that the Soviet Union must place at risk. American efforts to 'raise the nuclear threshold' might as easily legitimate conventional warfare in Europe as deter it. Given these premisses, West German support for independent British and French forces, which injected a certain incalculability into European conflict, was perhaps inevitable and indeed, as acute American antipathy eased and Soviet military power grew, West German governments came to favour both the British and French forces as useful contributions to deterrence.

'[T]he speeches of Secretary McNamara at successive NATO meetings have been generally hailed as extraordinarily brilliant,' observed Henry Kissinger, 'yet they have almost invariably been followed by periods of intense restiveness in Europe.'[24] The Kennedy administration's effort to redefine the terms of the United States' military engagement in Europe was profoundly unsettling, precisely because that engagement was critical to both the external defence and internal equilibrium of Europe. Inevitably, questions were raised about the depth of American commitment and, in particular, the credibility of the nuclear guarantee. The presentation of 'flexible response' accordingly proved heavy going and contributed to Americans' dissatisfaction with the existing structure of American–European relations, evoking among officials a discernible 'weariness with the complexities and intrigues of the "entangling alliance" '.[25] Fear compounded fatigue as General de Gaulle shrewdly exposed and exploited the vagaries of American policy in his effort to woo Adenauer's West Germany and hence achieve the leadership of Europe, furthering the general sense that 'discord among the Atlantic nations [arose] from a basic issue: how to organize the West'.[26] An opportunity for structural change seemed at hand after Harold Macmillan startled the world in 1961 by applying for British membership in the European Community.

Political opposition to national nuclear forces in Europe emerged in the context of a bold, though misconceived, 'grand design' for Atlantic relations. The Kennedy administration hoped that British membership might transform the EEC from a mildly integrated customs union into a powerful, politically unified entity intimately linked to the United States in a partnership of equals. The President, in his Independence Day address in 1962, observed that a strong and united Europe had been

the basic objective of our foreign policy for seventeen years ... We see in such a Europe a partner with whom we could deal on a basis of full equality on all the great and burdensome tasks of building and defending a community of free nations.[27]

It was thought, not without reason, that Europe's restiveness, her concern with control of nuclear weapons and her resistance to American policy initiatives, reflected a chaffing sense of dependence. 'Emerging Europe deeply wants a more self-respecting role in the world.'[28] The testiness and quarrelling which marred the defence debate in NATO could only be avoided in a true partnership of equals, and that required a genuinely federal structure for Europe.

> Only such a [fully cohesive] Europe will permit full reciprocity of
> treatment across the ocean, in facing the Atlantic agenda. With only
> such a Europe can we have a full give-and-take between equals, an
> equal sharing of responsibility and an equal level of sacrifice.[29]

Thus, the administration committed itself by 1963 to a rigid 'concept
of European integration which [was] rejected by *both* France and
Great Britain'.[30]

Enthusiasts of integration within the State Department regarded
national nuclear forces as formidable political obstacles to European
union. European governments had to recognize that, with limited
national resources, genuine independence and sovereignty were unattainable in the modern world of superstates. National nuclear forces
sustained illusions of power and influence. Thus, the decisions of the
Eisenhower and Kennedy administrations to resume nuclear co-operation with Britain in 1958, and to sell her Polaris missiles in 1962, had
only bolstered 'an outdated image of her influence and options' and
had 'cut across the more basic objective of fostering a united Europe, so
necessary for an effective partnership'.[31]

The success of these enthusiasts in setting the administration's policy
agenda — despite the established positions of Britain and France —
owed much to mounting anxieties about the role and significance of
national nuclear forces in Europe. The *force de frappe* had provided de
Gaulle with standing to wage a systematic campaign to impugn American reliability. American vicissitudes over Berlin and the abrupt and
unsuccessful presentation of flexible response naturally aroused
Adenauer's suspicions. De Gaulle steadfastly supported the Chancellor's
'intransigence' over East–West relations, highlighting Anglo-Saxon
wavering, and proferred his nuclear force as a potential supplement or
successor to the waning American guarantee. French nuclear weaponry
supported Paris's claim to the leadership of a *Europe des Patries*; British
nuclear weaponry seemed to make Britain's accession to the EEC
impossible. De Gaulle would not tolerate British competition for the
leadership of Europe. Without Britain, France would lead Europe with
West German support; with Britain, as the Italian Ambassador in Paris
observed, Europe 'would be dominated by Britain and Germany'.[32]

The centrality of nuclear weapons to the organization of Europe was
apparently confirmed by a succession of events in December 1962 and
January 1963. At Nassau in December, the United States and Britain

renewed their nuclear relationship and agreed upon the transfer of Polaris. Moreover, the two countries seemed to agree between themselves upon a new nuclear policy for the Alliance as a whole. France was invited to accept Polaris on the same terms as Britain. On 14 January 1963, General de Gaulle held a press conference in which he rejected the Nassau offer and vetoed British membership in the EEC. On 23 January 1963, Adenauer and de Gaulle, in a solemn ceremony at Paris, signed a treaty designed to establish a close Franco–West German alliance. The terrifying prospect of a Franco–West German *entente nucléaire* as the centrepiece of a European 'third force' gripped Washington in early 1963.

De Gaulle's German policy did not long survive the collapse of the 'grand design'. Adenauer's supporters joined with the Social Democratic opposition to affix a preamble to the Franco–West German treaty declaring West Germany's unshakeable adherence to the Atlantic Alliance and her firm support for British membership in the European Community. The preamble was adopted by unanimous vote of the Bundestag on 8 May 1963 and, at least as far as de Gaulle was concerned, robbed the treaty of meaning.[33] But the nightmare of Franco–West German nuclear collaboration gave way to an even more frightening prospect: independent West German nuclear forces. An accepted historiography lent this prospect some plausibility. The French had, it was believed, undertaken development of national forces in emulation of the British in order to gain equivalent status in the Alliance. Sooner or later, West Germany would follow suit. 'Many Germans say frankly that they cannot accept second-class status within the Alliance indefinitely.'[34] Independent West German forces would cripple political-military co-operation in the Alliance; 'No prospect arouses greater passions throughout Europe than this.'[35] They would hopelessly compromise American efforts to control nuclear weapons employment.[36] Moreover, the resolution of the Cuban missile crisis had seemed to pave the way for a meaningful East–West arms control dialogue – as evidenced by the quickening pace of nuclear test-ban negotiations among the United States, Britain and the Soviet Union. Nothing could squelch that developing dialogue faster than the emergence of an independent West German nuclear capability.

The fear of an independent West German weapons programme reinforced American hostility towards national nuclear forces and led to the revival of an ill-starred American proposal for a Multilateral Force (MLF). Any indication of American approval would encourage the West Germans and ratify the Anglo-French position that national forces were sources of military security and political influence. If American opposition could not force the British and French to forsake their independent efforts, some means had to be found to accord the West Germans 'equal status' in the Alliance. This could be accomplished through the MLF, proposed as a mixed-manned, jointly financed and jointly controlled fleet of twenty-five surface ships equipped with Polaris missiles.[37]

American fears of West German nuclear ambitions were, of course, largely groundless. No Western government shared them at the time and scholars since have found no evidence to sustain them.[38] Indeed, it is difficult to avoid the conclusion that Europeanists in the State Department deliberately exaggerated such evidence as there was in order to promulgate and prolong an initiative conducive to their own vision of Europe's future. It was hoped that the MLF might emerge as a repository for national nuclear forces, the nucleus of an eventually independent European deterrent.[39] Not surprisingly, the issue of political control of this force was never resolved, not only because the military and political strands of American policy conflict – the Defense Department opposed *independent* nuclear forces, whether nationally or multilaterally controlled, while the State Department opposed *national* nuclear forces, whether independent or integrated with SAC – but fundamentally because the Europe envisaged by American integrationists was the stuff of dreams. The real Europe was taking a different course or, more precisely, was advancing along the one charted in 1954, where close co-operation and even a genuine European identity could emerge, but only on the basis of collaboration among sovereign states sustained by a balance of power in which the United States played an essential role. And in the real Europe, West Germans recognized that the incentives for a national nuclear programme were 'clearly outweighed by the restraints imposed by [their] special circumstances'[40] and everybody else regarded the MLF as a misguided initiative likely to cultivate West German interest in nuclear weapons and hence as a threat to European stability.[41] The plan was effectively abandoned when Lyndon Johnson, preparing to meet Harold Wilson in December 1964, learned that it had little support in Europe and even less in the Senate. An alternative arrangement for enhancing allied participation in nuclear weapons employment plans was developed in the NATO Nuclear Planning Group and the spectre of a national West German force was laid to rest when West Germany signed the Nonproliferation Treaty (NPT) in 1969.

It was in 1969 that the United States and indeed the rest of the

Alliance began to recognize the constructive role played by British and French nuclear forces in the Western system. It was not just that fears of West German nuclear ambitions subsided after Bonn accepted the NPT — though it was widely recognized both within and without West Germany that the commitment given in the NPT to the Soviet Union was a more permanent and final undertaking than the original pledge to the WEU powers. Rather, it was because in 1969 West Germany seemed to come of age as an independent agent in international affairs. West German economic strength and political confidence were now so substantial that, for the first time, Bonn resisted concerted American, British and French demands and refused to revalue the Deutschmark during the currency crisis of 1968-9. Then, in September 1969, the Social Democrat Willy Brandt was elected Chancellor with the support of the Free Democrats (FDP). The tentative openings to the East made in the days of the SPD's grand coalition with the Christian Democrats began to blossom into a distinctive and genuinely independent foreign policy: *Ostpolitik*. These two events convinced the French that the time had come to bring Britain more directly into the intra-European balance. General de Gaulle began the process when he summoned British Ambassador Christopher Soames on 4 February 1969 and voiced a vision of Europe regulated by agreement among the larger powers and sustained by Anglo-French cooperation. He invited a British initiative for comprehensive — and confidential — bilateral talks. That conversation 'occasioned a veritable cascade of diplomatic incidents',[42] because the British, who had learned through painful experience to be wary of the General, felt obliged to apprise their allies of the substance of his *démarche*. But the ensuing controversy did not reverse the trend of French policy. De Gaulle's successor, Georges Pompidou, redoubled French efforts to forge a new entente with Britain and, moreover, moved to reconcile Franco-American differences. In a meeting with the new American President, Richard Nixon, and his National Security Advisor, Henry Kissinger, in 1970, Pompidou expressed his fears.

Pompidou went straight to the heart of his concern, which turned out to be *Ostpolitik*. Like all his colleagues he claimed that he trusted Brandt but feared that Brandt's policies might unleash nationalistic tendencies that it would prove impossible to contain . . . German nationalism might break forth again and, if through calamity it had learned patience, it might prove even more dangerous. It was fear of a resurgent Germany, Pompidou averred, that caused him to reverse de Gaulle's opposition to Britain's entry into Europe.[43]

Brandt also favoured British membership in the EEC, if only to reassure his critics that he remained a man of the West. Thus, the growth of West German economic power and the emergence of *Ostpolitik* facilitated British entry into the EEC. The practical demands of the balance of power mechanism adopted in 1954 accomplished in the early 1970s what all the passion and pressure adherents of the Grand Design brought to bear in the 1960s could not manage.

Pompidou found a sympathetic audience in Washington. Neither Nixon nor Kissinger shared the doctrinaire positions on European and allied integration voiced in the 1960s and still prevalent in the American bureaucracy. At the time of Soames affair, Nixon was preparing for a European tour and was 'deluged with proposals from inside and outside the government to seize the opportunity to reaffirm our commitment to a federal Europe'.[44] On Kissinger's advice, Nixon did nothing of the sort, making it clear that the United States would henceforth refrain from interfering in internal European affairs. He also 'tackled head-on the so-called special relationship between Britain and the United States that was so contentious within our government – by referring to it explicitly twice and in the most positive terms'.[45] In short, the administration signalled early in its tenure that it intended to deal with Europe as it stood, not as it might or ought to be. This attitude was conducive to a Franco-American *rapprochement*, as Washington was now prepared to approach problems of military co-operation in a pragmatic spirit, sparing the French the 'liturgy of NATO integration'. In 1970, Pompidou and Nixon agreed to begin bilateral military discussions at the staff level.[46] It is very likely that these discussions eventually embraced problems of operational co-ordination in strategic nuclear weapons employment conditions, an area where substantial co-operation and technical information exchange might have been possible without Congressional approval. Thus, political realism probably resolved one of the major problems posed to American military planners by the advent of the *force de frappe*: how and when did the French really intend to employ nuclear weapons?

The Nixon administration shared French concerns about the direction of Brandt's West Germany.[47] What was more important, however, was that it sympathized with French policy prescriptions. Advocates of the Grand Design had argued that unless Washington opposed implacably British and French nuclear forces and the notions of national sovereignty which sustained them, Europe might 'revert to its historic pattern of nation-states competing for primacy', with 'bitter consequences' for the West.[48] Where his predecessors had feared chaos, Kissinger recognized stability. Without obvious dismay, he noted that by 1970

> traditional patterns of European politics were beginning to reassert themselves . . . The British had told Nixon that they might resume their historical role of balancing the continental powers. The French were speaking of the need to keep open the line to Moscow so as to watch German–Soviet relations. Both the Germans and the French, in the wake of their talks in Washington, were clearly moving toward Britain, each for their own essentially national reasons.[49]

In Kissinger's time, Washington accepted the arrangements of 1954, not least because the system operated fairly smoothly to accommodate West Germany's growing economic power and her increasingly significant role in East–West relations. Henceforth, Europeans would complain not of the United States' excessive zeal for European unification, but of her indifference to European political collaboration.[50]

By accepting the settlement of 1954, the United States necessarily came to terms politically with the British and French national nuclear forces. For the political-military stature of both Britain and France was now a matter of systemic import. European stability could be maintained only so long as Britain and, above all, France remained powers of rank and influence comparable to West Germany and only so long as West German governments and parties retained confidence in the efficacy of the Western guarantee of West German security. Whatever one thought of the political significance of nuclear weapons state status, no one could seriously maintain that by abandoning independent nuclear forces France and Britain could actually *enhance* their standing among the nations. In any event, Americans had always considered possession of nuclear weapons politically important. Nothing makes this clearer than the nuclear diplomacy of the early 1960s. Enthusiasts of the MLF tended, for example, to regard Anglo–American nuclear collaboration as the cause, rather than a symptom, of the special relationship and hence saw the nuclear character of the Nassau Agreement, rather than its broader political implications, as the cause of de Gaulle's veto of British membership in the EEC.[51] Similarly, American officials believed or at least argued that nuclear weapons afforded Britain and France so pronounced a political advantage that West Germany would have no recourse but to violate her commitments to the WEU, alienate her allies and enrage her enemies by seeking national nuclear forces. The MLF proposal was, itself, an eloquent affirmation of the political import of nuclear arms, for its fundamental rationale was that only access to nuclear weapons could give West Germany 'equal status' in the Alliance. It might be objected that the MLF was merely intended to address the political views of Europeans and did not necessarily reflect American opinion. But, in point of fact, Americans generally considered nuclear weapons very important elements of national power;[52] and, in any case, for the purposes of maintaining political equilibrium in Europe, European sensibilities were (and are) decisive. It was primarily recognition of their political significance within the Alliance[53] which led the United States to approve national nuclear forces for the first time in the Ottawa Declaration of 1974.[54]

Concern about the stability and even the ultimate viability of the post-war settlement in Western Europe mounted as the 1970s drew to a close. The structure worked out in 1954 was coming under increasing strain. West Germany's steadily growing economic preponderance and corresponding political influence within the EEC and the Western Alliance generally threatened to undermine that 'inner balance of Europe'[55] upon which political co-operation depended. Indeed, it was expressly in order to preserve the 'equilibrium' of Europe's confederal structure that President Giscard d'Estaing embraced the austere Barre Plan and dedicated France to the elusive objective of economic equality with Germany by 1985.[56] Wealth and the increasing strength and quality of her military forces gave West Germany a more pronounced role in defence matters — as evidenced by the quiet creation of a West German Deputy SACEUR position alongside the traditional British post and, dramatically, by Chancellor Helmut Schmidt's presence at the Guadeloupe summit conference with President Carter, Prime Minister Callaghan and President Giscard d'Estaing. The centrality of Bonn's role as Moscow's *interlocuteur valable* in the West emerged in relief as Soviet–American *détente* withered, reinforcing concern about both West Germany's power and her potential course in Europe. These factors, together with the decline of American military and economic strength and the perceived incompetence of American leadership, contributed to 'the sudden realization that the Federal Republic [had] come to play a much more important role, not just within the Alliance, but on the world stage generally'.[57]

West Germany's new prominence complicated and constrained allied military policy. West German governments were becoming increasingly hesitant to undertake defence initiatives which would highlight Bonn's pronounced political-military role. As one senior American official put it, West German sensitivity to intra-European balance considerations resulted in 'a self-imposed ceiling on the size and even the shape of German armed forces'.[58] This 'ceiling' limited the flexibility of NATO's order of battle along the Central Front. Chancellor Schmidt stressed the point in 1979:

> Let me add in this context that the Federal Republic is interested in preventing a shift in the balance within NATO as well. This is also of great significance in Western relations, and I cannot imagine that any Federal government in the foreseeable future could be prepared to enlarge essentially the German contingent in the ground forces in central Europe.[59]

Similarly, NATO's long-range theatre nuclear force (LRTNF) modernization efforts were complicated by Bonn's requirement that West Germany not be placed in a 'singular' role in Europe; deployment could not go forward unless West Germany was joined by at least one other non-nuclear host country. Defence Minister Hans Apel considered this a fundamental prerequisite to modernization.

> [An individual, singular German role] would be deadly in my opinion for the alliance . . . for relations between the United States and Western Europe, and also for relations between the Federal Republic and Western Europe.[60]

West German officials lamented American insensitivity on this point. 'We try to make the United States understand that this is not an excuse,' observed a West German officer. 'It is a fundamental fact of European politics. An imbalance within Europe would be far worse for the Alliance, and for US interests, than SS-20.'[61]

In these circumstances, it is hardly surprising that Britain's independent nuclear force came to be regarded as a very important contribution to political stability. As Walter Schulze advised the House of Commons Expenditure Committee in 1979:

> The most valid contribution of the British nuclear deterrent is doubtlessly that it provides a balance within the Atlantic Alliance, especially in offsetting the greater financial and economic potential and the bigger conventional forces of the FRG. It is absolutely essential

that this assymetrical intra-alliance balance of power is maintained.[62]

West German officials and politicians believed that 'the fact that two European powers are nuclear weapons states helps maintain equilibrium',[63] and West German governments – whether dominated by the Social Democrats or the Christian Democrats – strongly supported retention of independent nuclear forces by Britain and, *a fortiori*, by France. The United States had independent reasons for desiring a strong British voice in Europe and the Alliance; British and American governments tended to take complementary views of world events and some American officials felt that nuclear weapons were 'all that keep the Brits alive'. Increasingly, though, American officials saw the political case for the independent deterrent in terms of the intra-European balance and its implications for West German defence efforts. British and French weapons were regarded as 'permissive conditions for the stable expansion of the Bundeswehr'.

The French, too, supported modernization of Polaris; they had no desire to be the only nuclear weapons state in Europe. It was 'overwhelmingly in France's interest that Britain remain strong'.[64] Indeed, Defence Minister Bourges is said to have formally advised the Callaghan government of French views on this matter in 1979, seconding a similar communication at the 'highest political level'.[65] The French were, in fact, concerned that Britain remain a nuclear power not only to balance Bonn's political-military prominence but to help arrest what the French government and bureaucracy regarded as an alarming decline of West German confidence in the efficacy of the collective security guarantee. The late 1970s and early 1980s saw the re-emergence of the German Question,[66] and in those circumstances declining West German confidence in the American guarantee aggravated West Germany's unwelcome prominence, just as prominence helped to undermine confidence by complicating the politics of defence in Europe.

West German concerns about the steadfastness of the American guarantee in the late 1970s and early 1980s arose from a variety of factors. The 1970s had introduced new tensions into the West German-American relationship and much of the problem was simply the cumulative effect of a decade of disputes about economic, energy, trade and monetary matters as well as foreign and defence policy issues. West Germans, and Europeans generally, wondered whether there might be some structural flaw that prevented development and pursuit of consistent American policy responses to the challenges of the era.[67]

Declining confidence also reflected apprehension about the implications of an acknowledged, serious and perhaps permanent divergence of views with respect to *détente*. Despite its initial reservations, the Nixon administration had supported Brandt's *Ostpolitik* but its original hopes of cultivating a rich Soviet–American relationship never materialized, partly because of Congress's decision to link trade concessions to Soviet emigration practices. Thus, Soviet–American *détente* never amounted to anything more or less than SALT and, *faute de mieux*, SALT was perceived as the only medium by which Washington could express displeasure with frequently outrageous Soviet behaviour. The treaty was withdrawn from Senate consideration in the wake of the Soviet Union's invasion of Afghanistan. For West Germany, however, there was no turning back from *Ostpolitik*, a policy which had yielded very substantial economic and, more important, humanitarian gains and represented, albeit in the faintest hues, national hopes for eventual reunification. The United States' response to Afghanistan differed rather fundamentally from West Germany's and each side feared the conclusions the other might draw.

At the root of West German concern lay the deteriorating military balance between the United States and the Soviet Union. A decade of Western neglect and unprecedented Soviet expansion had established very substantial Soviet superiority in conventional and theatre nuclear forces and formal superpower parity in central strategic forces. West Germans suspected that SALT had 'neutralized' American and Soviet central strategic systems and were anxious about the military reality and political shadow of the Soviet Union's overwhelming advantage in the European theatre.[68] The vulnerability of American Minuteman ICBM forces tended to undermine the credibility of the American guarantee because their use in deliberate escalation strikes – the ultimate deterrent in Europe – was becoming ever more doubtful. Since 1962, it had been American policy to limit deliberate escalation attacks to military targets – missions for which land-based forces were most suitable both because of their accuracy and because of their superior command and control responsiveness. Secretary of Defense Schlesinger's innovations in the mid-1970s refined, rather than revised, this policy.[69] But in the 1980s, American ICBM counterforce attacks would not only be inconclusive; they would expose the remaining ICBM force to potentially devastating retaliation. Europeans justifiably questioned Minuteman's use in such circumstances. SAC's ageing B-52 bomber fleet could deliver very substantial payloads with commendable accuracy, but its response time was slow and its penetrability doubtful.

Sons were now piloting aircraft their fathers had once flown. The Navy's SSBN fleet performed superbly its allotted task — that is, it preserved a secure, second-strike threat of 'assured destruction' — but was hardly optimal for use against hardened or mobile targets. As against this background, the discriminating theatre nuclear counterforce capability represented by the SS-20 looked especially ominous, for it completed a spectrum of violence along which the Soviet Union had achieved something like 'escalation dominance'. At each escalatory threshold — conventional, tactical-nuclear, theatre-nuclear, intercontinental counterforce — the Soviet Union now seemed to hold the advantage and the Americans might be loath to escalate to levels where they knew they could not prevail. At the countervalue level, no meaningful advantage seemed possible but the United States had for twenty years done everything in its power to minimize the likelihood of either side resorting to countervalue exchanges. It was to mitigate this imbalance that Chancellor Schmidt's government began to press for modernization of the Alliance's theatre forces. It was hoped that deployment of survivable theatre forces of a range sufficient to engage Soviet targets would make NATO's threat of deliberate escalation more credible and its threat of theatre retaliation both more credible and more menacing to the Soviet Union.[70] Substantial Western theatre forces contributed to deterrence by making the prospects of cheap victory less certain or simply uncertain.

British and French national nuclear forces were thought to contribute to deterrence in much the same manner. Multiple decision-making centres seemed to strengthen deterrence by making the course of European conflict unpredictable or less predictable to the Soviet Union and national forces were accordingly considered by the West Germans and the rest of the Alliance to be useful supplements to the American nuclear guarantee.[71] This was the principal justification given by the Thatcher government for modernizing the Polaris force.[72] The polite formulation held that the Soviet leadership might miscalculate American resolve but be deterred none the less by fear that the British or French would escalate conflict and trigger American nuclear intervention. The cruder variants assumed American irresolution and saw in British and French forces a mechanism to trigger American strikes, either because Washington would fear Soviet retaliation against the Western system as a whole or because the Russians, mortally wounded, would in fact so retaliate. In any event, national nuclear forces diminished confidence in the Soviet Union's ability to fight, limit and win a war in Europe. Most observers agreed that French forces were more

important in this context because for a complex of geographical, doctrinal, political and cultural reasons – for all the reasons, as one American official put it, that 'there isn't any Franco-American special
relationship' – it was easier to imagine French nuclear weapons use in
the absence of American action. As one German official observed,
'geography and the special relationship make it very unlikely' that
Britain would act independently of the Americans and 'the Soviets
know that'.[73]

If the French had the advantage of independence, however, the
British retained the advantages of integration. These were several.
First, in peacetime, the British were positioned to mediate West
German-American relations in the nuclear arena, a role London did in
fact undertake successfully with respect to theatre nuclear force
modernization in 1978-9.[74] In war as in peace, the British were more
likely to influence the United States than the French and given the
security afforded by an independent deterrent and the extent to which
British interests would be imperilled by Soviet success in Europe,
British advice could be expected to be steadfast. Moreover, precisely
because of the factors which make French independent action more
probable, the United States could more easily disassociate herself from
France. British independence, while less likely, would be more risky
for both Moscow and Washington. Moscow, in the extraordinary
circumstances of nuclear conflict, might simply confuse British action
with an American strike or, more likely, perceive it as a harbinger of
eventual American nuclear intervention. For Washington, British action
would be fearful not only because it would set in train the Soviet calculations just described but also because it would force the United
States to consider the implications of standing aside and leaving Britain
to her fate. After all, this discussion assumes that the United States
is prepared to countenance the loss of Germany and, in those circumstances, it might well be prepared to suffer the loss of France as well.
For a variety of reasons, Washington might regard Britain differently.
Britain hosts installations rather critical to the course of a global
Soviet-American war which, at this juncture, would loom very large
among American fears. More importantly, loss of Britain might well
entail loss of sea control in the Eastern Atlantic and would then effectively ratify American withdrawal to the Western hemisphere. Thus, if
the British did resolve to run the risks of an independent escalatory
strike, their resolution would have greater weight in American councils
than would a French decision and, at the end of the day, it is American
decisions which matter to both the West Germans and the Russians.

It is ironical that American officials now saw military advantages in the capability of allied nuclear forces to disrupt limited war in Europe and, potentially, to trigger engagement of American forces at escalatory levels which the United States had hoped to avoid. In part, this change of heart reflected the emergence of relatively invulnerable British and French forces. Withholdable, second-strike forces not only reduced the incentives for a Soviet first strike, they also reduced the likelihood of precipitate French or British action. Withholdable forces, in short, were more likely to be withheld. British and French forces also significantly restricted Soviet theatre nuclear war-fighting flexibility, as Soviet strikes against British or French targets were much more likely to trigger responses against the Soviet Union proper. National forces had then the capacity to sanctuarize British and French territory. With respect to Britain, this was a very significant contribution to the deterrence and war-fighting posture of the Alliance. American power protection in the European theatre depended critically upon the integrity of the 'unsinkable' aircraft carrier, with its extraordinary concentration of American (and British) strategic and tactical reconnaissance assets, signals and electronic intelligence collection facilities, ocean surveillance systems, satellite monitoring stations and C-3 installations, as well as front-line offensive air and ASW forces. Conventional/tactical-nuclear war in Europe could not be fought without Britain and the independent deterrent both strengthened British resolve and raised significantly the risks attending Soviet nuclear strikes against the Anglo–American base structure in Britain. With France, which in peacetime hosted no American forces, the advantage of sanctuarization was less clear. The French had hoped to isolate French territory from regional nuclear conflict by reducing the incentives for Soviet strikes as well as increasing the risks attending such strikes. None the less, French territory could provide a sanctuarized rear area contiguous to the battlefields in West Germany. Thus, there were genuine war-fighting benefits to British and French forces contributed to the Americans' favourable attitudes.

It could be argued that American acceptance of the military case for allied, but independent, forces was ultimately a consequence of the loss of strategic superiority. If a deliberately escalatory counterforce campaign could not be decisive – if it could neither blunt Soviet power projection in Europe nor attrit Soviet nuclear forces to the point where the United States would enjoy a coercive advantage – the threat to escalate conflict lost any proper military purpose and became, instead, a terroristic device, an American threat to die and take the Soviets along with them. By the standards of the McNamara era, such threats were inherently incredible. But Europeans never accepted those standards and Americans had sooner or later to forsake them. In the 1980s, American officials cared less passionately about controlling nuclear conflict in Europe, partly because it was not at all clear how they would prevail in a conflict subject to rational American control. Consequently, the prospect of uncontrolled conflict seemed a more effective deterrent to the Soviet Union. In these sense, American perceptions of the strategic utility of independent forces were simply mirror-images of their fears of the 1960s: national nuclear forces complicated the Soviet Union's capacity to wage a controlled nuclear war in Europe.

The French had monitored West German anxieties closely and, as the decade drew to a close, began to debate how France might help to maintain confidence in the Alliance. French military doctrine had, of course, evolved substantially since de Gaulle's time. General Ailleret's provocative strategy *à tous azimuts* had given way in 1969 to the sober recognition that France must prepare to counter a threat 'coming from the East'.[75] The introduction of the Pluton tactical nuclear missile in the early 1970s had facilitated development of a strategy of 'graduated response' in place of the pure Gaullist doctrine of massive retaliation. Under Giscard, the trend towards doctrinal conformity with NATO and an overt guarantee of West German security accelerated. Conventional force expenditures increased markedly relative to the nuclear budget and, in 1976, Chief of Staff General Méry bruited the notion of *'sanctuarisation élargée'*. The preamble to the 1976 military *loi de programme*, said to have been written by Giscard himself, acknowledged that:

> It would indeed be illusory to hope that France would maintain more than a reduced sovereignty, if her neighbors had been occupied by a hostile power or were simply under its control. The security of Western Europe as a whole is therefore essential for France.[76]

After 1976, however, doctrinal movement ground to a halt amid sharply conflicting visions of French defence policy.[77] In part, controversy reflected genuine intellectual fidelity to the purity and rigour of Gaullist doctrine; in part, doctrinal disputes were simply handy clubs for the gathering neo-Gaullist political opposition. Much of the difficulty, however, centred on Franco–West German relations. Certainly, Communist support for the *force de frappe* was directly linked to fears of German dominance; Socialist support sprang from similar, though less rabid, concerns.[78] Centrist and conservative elements also perceived tension between the two political-military roles ascribed to French forces: the more closely France involved West Germany with the *force de frappe* (to buttress West German confidence), the less potent it seemed as a political advantage over West Germany. In this sense, the paralysis of French doctrine merely mirrored the incipient bankruptcy of French foreign policy. France could no longer broker Soviet–West German relations or compete with West Germany for Soviet attention; she still served as Moscow's *interlocuteur valable* in the West from time to time but only by West German default. Nor could she long maintain even the illusion of pre-eminence within the EEC. And, as West German anxieties grew, the old Gaullist gambit of juxtaposing Bonn's Atlantic and European allegiances by calculated bursts of anti-Americanism began to seem risky. Indeed, Socialist France emerged as the most vocal European supporter of allied rearmament and theatre nuclear force modernization, in particular.

The government of François Mitterand was no more able than its predecessor at reconciling the contradictory currents in French defence policy. The government planned reductions in conventional forces and renewed emphasis on nuclear weaponry.[79] A sixth SSBN was ordered but it appeared that the M-4 SLBM would be equipped with MRV, rather than MIRV, warheads. This decision, taken on financial grounds, boded ill for a resumption of the trend towards extended deterrence. Weapons developments tend to spawn doctrinal innovation – consider the Pluton – and the operational flexibility associated with MIRVs might have led to a French nuclear commitment to West Germany. Doctrine, however, was ultimately a second-order issue. Geography probably did more to link French nuclear forces with West Germany's fate in Soviet minds than any posture statement could have done. The most important contribution France would make to West German security was maintenance of effective strategic forces, regardless of their declared missions. For the present, they would complicate Soviet calculations. For the future, they represented insurance. The French, like most Europeans, feared that at some point West German confidence would slip below a critical threshold, compelling Bonn to chart a new course, perhaps with the East, perhaps alone. No one thought this imminent, but even so, French fears were no doubt exaggerated. The post-war settlement remained fundamentally sound, 'Doubts about the credibility of the American shield are not going to tempt the Germans to abandon it,' reasoned Professor Stern. 'They are unlikely to commit suicide out of fear of death.'[80] But what if it is the Americans who abandon the West Germans? And might there not come a day when, fearing abandonment, any West German government would feel duty-bound to seek alternatives to the very choice Stern poses? As a hedge against that distant and desperate moment, both British and French forces helped to buttress confidence in the existing security arrangements in Europe. Only in that prospective sense were they substitutes as well as supplements to the American guarantee.

The Russians sought to hurry things along when they proposed, in late 1982, to limit their SS-20 forces in the European theatre to the total number of launchers deployed by Britain and France. This was a proposal with great potential for mischief. Its apparent symmetry and substance were appealing, especially in light of the serious political problems attending deployment of new American forces.[81] The British and French had long made it clear that their forces were not subject to negotiation in Geneva, where Russians and Americans were discussing Russian and American missiles. But the basic Soviet contention that some account had to be taken of expanding European arsenals was hardly outrageous. Moreover, as has just been argued, these forces did serve much the same strategic purposes as would new American weapons. None the less, Moscow's proposal was rejected within hours by the British, French and Americans and condemned as a ploy by Chancellor Kohl's new government in Bonn.[82]

The speed of the West's response is instructive, for it rather nicely illustrates the peculiar and limited functions of national nuclear forces in Europe. It was suggested earlier that both European national forces and American theatre forces strengthened deterrence by introducing uncertainties into the military balance; both types of forces also possessed ranges sufficient to engage Soviet targets, threatening a kind of damage considered qualitatively more serious to Soviet decision-makers than the damage promised by shorter-range systems. Finally, both were reckoned more likely to be used than American strategic forces, because either the weapons themselves or their national command centres would be closer to, and more immediately threatened by, conflict in central Europe. But, from the perspective of the non-nuclear allies, neither was especially helpful in their own right. Their value lay in the likelihood that their deployment would restrict Soviet war-fighting flexibility while their employment might trigger engagement of American central systems. They were, in short, 'coupling' devices, linking American strategic forces with European conflict.

Acceptance of the Soviet proposal would have quite the opposite effect. It would have entailed formal recognition of a 'balance' between

Soviet theatre and European national forces, creating the impression that American and Soviet central systems, regulated under SALT and its successors, were reserved for direct superpower conflict. It would, in short, have been 'decoupling'. All this is not mere sophistry; it had genuine political impact. In his 1977 speech to the Institute for Strategic Studies sounding the call for theatre nuclear force modernization, Chancellor Schmidt had spoken of the need for balance. Subsequently, Bonn retreated from the notion of an autonomous European balance lest anyone conclude that United States' theatre nuclear commitment represented the limit of her liability in European conflict. Accordingly, the modernization programme approved by the Alliance in 1979 was sized quite independently of Soviet force levels. The West was not seeking a discrete theatre balance, but merely an analogous 'countervailing' theatre capability.

If an autonomous Soviet–American theatre balance was troubling, still more so was the prospect of a formal Soviet–European balance. In those circumstances, the impression might grow that the United States' nuclear commitment was restricted to its short-range theatre forces, rendering the likelihood of central system employment even more remote. Moreover, it would imply an overt form of dependence upon Britain and France quite unacceptable to Bonn. Time and again, West German officials and parliamentarians stressed in interviews that British and French nuclear forces were welcome additions to the West's deterrence posture only as long as they were not considered substitutes for American forces. West Germans did indeed draw comfort from the notion that Anglo-French forces were held, in Edward Heath's phrase, 'in trust for Europe'. But it was all in the future tense. Particularly the Christian Democrats, who had authored the original commitment to the WEU only to agonize over the implications of the NPT, felt that an iron-clad bargain had been struck: West Germany had yielded its right to national forces in return for American protection. She would not now willingly rely solely upon her European neighbours.

The broader question of when and how British and French forces were to be accounted in East–West arms control had hovered on the sidelines of the SALT process since its inception. In the wake of SALT I, Moscow issued a statement asserting unilaterally its right to increase SSBN strength in line with any increases in British and French forces. Washington never accepted that position.[83] The issue was postponed in SALT II. Most American officials assumed that it would resurface in SALT III, where, at least if the Russians had been willing to agree to deep reductions in central systems, some accommodation might have been made. An unhappy sequence of events brought the question of British and French forces to the fore. Before NATO confronted the issue of theatre nuclear force (TNF) modernization, there was speculation that SALT III might be wholly or partly multilateral. Early in the Alliance's TNF deliberations, however, this idea was dropped, if only because West Germany could neither attend such talks (this would aggravate the problem of 'prominence') nor divorce herself from them (because she was intimately concerned). The ultimate decision for bilateral TNF negotiations presumed, however, that parallel SALT III negotiations would be under way. With SALT's demise, the Russians could hardly avoid demanding that British and French forces be addressed in Geneva, the more so as both London and Paris announced very significant modernization programmes. The national forces therefore emerged as obstacles to an agreement, in the absence of which politically disruptive deployments were unavoidable. The Russians were unlikely to yield on this question without a commitment that British and French forces would be addressed elsewhere. Thus, the only solution was renewed momentum in central strategic force negotiations and, at this writing, there was little sign of such movement.

Mrs Thatcher enjoyed an advantage over her predecessors as she committed her government to procurement of a new generation of strategic nuclear weapons. Mr Attlee had been forced to proceed in the face of determined, though inarticulate, American opposition. Mr Macmillan, on the other hand, had obtained direct and substantial American assistance, but in the teeth of policy pronouncements which indicated that Washington fundamentally objected to independent deterrence in the Alliance. Only Mrs Thatcher managed to secure both American hardware and American approval. American approval reflected a more widespread conviction that Britain's deterrent played useful military, and increasingly critical political, roles within the Alliance and was therefore very likely to endure. Indeed, the strength of American support was tested during the 1981 defence review and survived; the Reagan administration agreed to the transfer of Trident II missiles despite the contraction of Royal Navy forces in the Atlantic. In the wake of the Falklands campaign, and the defence policy adjustments it spawned, another defence review was considered likely.[84] If, this time, the decision is taken to favour nuclear and maritime forces over the Continental commitment, the independent deterrent will become more controversial in Europe. If confronted with a trade-off between nuclear forces and the Rhine Army, West Germans have little choice but to favour Britain's conventional contribution.[85] The Rhine Army has its own political significance, as it prevents the Central Front from becoming an exclusively West German–American responsibility and has been traditionally viewed as an anchor for American forces. Moreover, as a front-line state, West Germany must ultimately accord conventional forces priority because, while the threat of nuclear weapons employment is the best guarantee of West German security, the reality can only mean the devastation of West German society. For the rest of the Alliance the choice would be much less clear; perhaps few would dispute that the revisions undertaken by Mr Nott represented the best solution of a difficult problem.

In any event, the perceived trade-off among maritime, Continental and nuclear forces was ultimately artificial. 'It will never be the case that the money released by abandoning Trident will support for long substantial conventional forces.'[86] Nuclear forces entailed substantial capital costs and minimal operations and maintenance costs; conventional forces required heavy and relatively constant equipment expenditure and enormous personnel, operations and maintenance funding. If one assumed Britain's economic decline was irreversible, then sacrificing Trident would only postpone eventual contraction of conventional contributions to the Alliance, and nothing could unsettle political cohesion and military effectiveness more than the ultimate abandonment of both the independent deterrent and the Rhine Army. If, on the other hand, one assumed that economic decline could be arrested or even reversed, then maintenance of independent nuclear forces would be a temporary budgetary difficulty best addressed by a short-term increase in defence spending. In no circumstance should transient fiscal pressures warrant abandonment of a capability which contributes substantially to both the political-military stability of the Alliance and the security of Britain.

At the end of the day, the fate of the independent deterrent will be determined by the complex of fears and concerns which gave it rise. For nearly forty years, it has proven a sturdy child of terror, a physical manifestation of the convictions of British governments of both parties that nothing in life is permanent. No nation has done more than the British to cultivate and sustain the intermingling of European and American destinies which has maintained the peace since 1945. Through it all, British governments have husbanded a resource which, while not without immediate utility, was fundamentally a hedge against the collapse of their own designs. It would be a supreme irony if that resource were now to be abandoned just as the dynamics of power in

Europe have supplanted controversy with consensus and reconciled pursuit of independent deterrence with fidelity to the Atlantic Alliance.

Notes

1. McNamara's remarks were made in a commencement address at the University of Michigan at Ann Arbor. *Department of State Bulletin*, 6 July 1982, p. 8. The Ann Arbor speech closely paralleled the Secretary's formal presentation of the new American strategy of 'flexible response' to NATO Ministers in Athens in May 1962.

2. See, e.g., Alastair Buchan, 'Partners and Allies', *Foreign Affairs*, vol. 41, no. 4 (July 1963), p. 623.

3. Letter of Secretary of Defense Caspar Weinberger to Minister of Defence John Nott, *The British Strategic Nuclear Force*, Cmnd. 8517 (March) (HMSO, London, 1982), p. 5.

4. Quoted in K.G. de Vries, 'Security Policy and Arms Control' in M.M. Olive and J.D. Porto (eds.), *Nuclear Weapons in Europe* (Lexington Books, Lexington, Mass., 1983), p. 61.

5. Anton W. de Porte, *Europe between the Superpowers* (Yale University Press, New Haven, 1979), p. 191.

6. See, e.g., Defence Minister Pym's remarks, *Official Report* (Commons), vol. 977, 24 January 1980, col. 978.

7. *The Times*, 12 March 1982, p. 4.

8. de Porte, *Europe between the Superpowers*, p. 159. See, generally, Daniel Lerner and Raymond Aron, *France Defeats EDC* (Praeger, New York, 1957).

9. See, e.g., Charles de Gaulle, *Memoirs of Hope* (Simon and Schuster, New York, 1971), pp. 171–2, for the General's assessment of the importance of West Germany's pledge not to pursue nuclear weapons development.

10. Lothar Reuhl, *La Politique Militaire de la Vème République* (Presses de la Fondation Nationale des Sciences Politiques, Paris, 1976).

11. Buchan, 'Partners and Allies', p. 622. See also, for representative presentations of the American military case against British and French forces, M.W. Hoag, 'Nuclear Policy and French Intransigence', *Foreign Affairs*, vol. 41, no. 2 (January 1963), pp. 286–98; A. Wohlstetter, 'Nuclear Sharing', *Foreign Affairs*, vol. 39, no. 3 (April 1961), pp. 355–87.

12. *The Military Balance 1961–62* (IISS, London, 1962), pp. 4, 10.

13. See A. Wohlstetter, 'The Delicate Balance of Terror', *Foreign Affairs*, vol. 37, no. 2 (January 1959), pp. 211–34.

14. See William W. Kaufman, *The McNamara Strategy* (Harper and Row, New York, 1964) for an excellent and informed account of the evolution of American doctrine in the Kennedy years.

15. Robert S. McNamara, *The Essence of Security* (Harper and Row, New York, 1968), p. 76.

16. Kaufman, *The McNamara Strategy*, p. 144.

17. Cited in Hoag, 'Nuclear Policy', p. 290.

18. Ibid., p. 288.

19. Quoted in Henry A. Kissinger, 'Coalition Diplomacy', *Foreign Affairs*, vol. 42, no. 4 (July 1964), p. 535.

20. Henry A. Kissinger, 'Problems of European Defense', *Foreign Affairs*, vol. 40, no. 4 (July 1962), p. 522.

21. Hoag, 'Nuclear Policy', p. 288.

22. Kissinger, 'Problems of European Defense', p. 521.

23. Kissinger, 'Strains on the Alliance', *Foreign Affairs*, vol. 41, no. 2 (January 1963), p. 274.

24. Ibid., p. 272.

25. Buchan, 'Partners and Allies', p. 627.

26. Robert R. Bowie, 'Tensions within the Alliance', *Foreign Affairs*, vol. 42, no. 1 (October 1963), p. 49.

27. Quoted in Robert R. Bowie, *Shaping the Future* (Columbia University Press, New York, 1964), p. 38. Professor Bowie was perhaps the most eloquent and ardent spokesman for the Grand Design and the Multilateral Force.

28. Bowie, 'Tensions within the Alliance', p. 51.

29. Excerpt from President Kennedy's Paulskirche speech (Frankfurt, June 1963) quoted in Bowie, 'Tensions within the Alliance', p. 54.

30. Kissinger, 'Coalition Diplomacy', p. 542 (emphasis in original).

31. Bowie, 'Tensions within the Alliance', p. 55.

32. Quoted in Alfred Grosser, *The Western Alliance* (Vintage Books, New York, 1982), p. 202.

33. Ibid., p. 208.

34. Bowie, 'Tensions within the Alliance', p. 66.

35. Hoag, 'Nuclear Policy and France', p. 289.

36. Ibid.

37. Perhaps the best brief account of the origins of the MLF is Alastair Buchan's *The Multilateral Force: An Historical Perspective*, Adelphi Paper no. 13 (IISS, London, 1964).

38. See, e.g., Catherine M. Kelleher, *Germany and the Politics of Nuclear Weapons* (Columbia University Press, New York, 1975); W.B. Bader, 'Nuclear Weapons and the "German Problem" ', *Foreign Affairs*, vol. 44, no. 4 (July 1966), pp. 693–700.

39. Bowie, 'Tensions within the Alliance', pp. 67–8.

40. Bader, 'Nuclear Sharing and the "German Problem" ', p. 698.

41. As Harold Wilson put it, 'If you have a boy and wish to sublimate his sex appetite, it is unwise to take him to a strip-tease show.' Quoted in Kelleher, *Germany and the Politics of Nuclear Weapons*, p. 252.

42. Grosser, *The Western Alliance*, p. 256.

43. Henry A. Kissinger, *White House Years* (Little, Brown, Boston, 1979), p. 422.

44. Ibid., pp. 87–9.

45. Ibid., p. 89.

46. Ibid., p. 423.

47. Ibid., pp. 408–12.

48. Bowie, 'Tensions within the Alliance', p. 51.

49. Kissinger, *White House Years*, p. 425.

50. Consider Kissinger's difficulties with the Year of Europe. See, e.g., Grosser, *The Western Alliance*, pp. 263–82; Kissinger, *Years of Upheaval* (Little, Brown, Boston, 1982), especially pp. 729–35.

51. It is now clear that de Gaulle had taken his decision by the time he met with Macmillan at Rambouillet and before Macmillan joined Kennedy at Nassau. See, e.g., John Newhouse, *De Gaulle and the Anglo-Saxons* (Viking Press, New York, 1970); Harold Macmillan, *At the End of the Day* (Harper and Row, New York, 1973), pp. 345–54.

52. For example, of more than thirty relatively senior American officials interviewed in the late 1970s, only one took the view that nuclear weapons were largely irrelevant to Britain's standing in the Alliance.

53. Interviews.

54. Declaration of the North Atlantic Council, Ottawa, 19 June 1974. *Department of State Bulletin*, 24 June 1974.

55. The phrase is Giscard's. See his interview with *Der Spiegel*, 1 January 1979, translated in *Foreign Broadcast Information Service* (vol. 7 — Western Europe) (hereafter *FBIS*), 3 January 1979, p. K-1.

56. See the President's press conference of 21 November 1978. *FBIS*, 22 November 1978, p. K-4.

57. Fritz Stern, 'Germany in a Semi-Gaullist Europe', *Foreign Affairs*, vol. 58, no. 4 (Spring 1980), p. 874.

58. Interview.

59. See the Chancellor's remarks in the Bundestag security policy debate of March 1979. *FBIS*, 12 March 1979, p. J-18.

60. Ibid., p. J-7.

61. Interview.

62. House of Commons, Sixth Report from the Expenditure Committee, Session 1978-9, *The Future of the United Kingdom's Nuclear Weapons Policy* (HMSO, London, 1979), p. 218.

63. Interviews. Interestingly, CDU representatives — some of whom subsequently entered the Kohl government — tended to see the political contribution of national nuclear forces in their reinforcement of the self-esteem, rather than 'objective' power, of Britain and France. The distinction is, of course, irrelevant to considerations of systemic stability.

64. Interview.

65. Interviews. It is probable that Giscard raised the matter with Callaghan at Guadeloupe in January 1979 and this may have led directly to Callaghan's observation about the effect that British abdication may have on 'others'. See Prime Minister's remarks in Parliament, *Official Report* (Commons), vol. 960, 16 January 1979, col. 1501.

66. Stern, 'Germany in a Semi-Gaullist Europe', p. 868.

67. Europeans of the leadership generation at this time had, in many cases, long regarded the United States as a model society and '[d]isappointed lovers make harsh judges'. Ibid., p. 872.

68. See Helmut Schmidt, 'The 1977 Alastair Buchan Memorial Lecture', *Survival*, vol. 20 (January/February 1978), pp. 2-10.

69. See L. Davis, *Limited Nuclear Options: Deterrence and the New American Doctrine*, Adelphi Paper no. 121 (IISS, London, 1975).

70. The United States intended to deploy GLCMs and Pershing II missiles in Europe. With warning, these forces were to disperse and once dispersed were expected to be survivable. In their bases, they appeared unavoidably vulnerable to surprise attack.

71. Interviews.

72. See, e.g., *Official Report* (Commons), vol. 977, 24 January 1981, col. 976 (Francis Pym).

73. Interview.

74. Interviews.

75. Wilfred Kohl, *French Nuclear Diplomacy* (Princeton University Press, Princeton, 1971), pp. 158-64.

76. Quoted in David S. Yost, 'The French Defense Debate', *Survival*, vol. 23 (January/February 1981), p. 20.

77. Ibid.

78. Interviews. One well placed French Socialist adviser opined that Mitterand's decision to support the independent nuclear force derived 'entirely' from his concerns about Franco–German balance.

79. *New York Times*, 10 March 1983, p. A15.

80. Stern, 'Germany in a Semi-Gaullist Europe', p. 884.

81. The SPD, for example, made favourable noises. See e.g., *FBIS*, 14 January 1983, p. J4.

82. See Defence Minister Manfred Woerner's interview in *Der Spiegel*, 24 January 1983, pp. 40–6; translated in *FBIS*, 25 January 1983, pp. J6–J12.

83. Lawrence Freedman, 'The Dilemma of Theater Nuclear Arms Control', *Survival*, vol. 23 (January/February 1981), p. 4, n. 8.

84. See discussion in Chapter 6 above.

85. Interviews.

86. Laurence Freedman, 'British Defence Policy after the Falklands', *The World Today* (September 1982), p. 336.

SELECT BIBLIOGRAPHY

Books

Armacost, Michael H. *The Politics of Weapons Innovation* (Columbia University Press, New York, 1969)

Bartlett, C.J. *The Long Retreat* (Macmillan, London, 1972)

Baxter, J.P., III *Scientists against Time* (Little, Brown, Boston, 1946)

Baylis, John (ed.) *British Defence Policy in a Changing World* (Croom Helm, London, 1978)

Bellini, James and Pattie, Geoffrey *A New World Role for the Medium Power: The British Opportunity* (Royal United Services Institute, London, 1976)

Bowie, Robert R. *Shaping the Future* (Columbia University Press, New York, 1964)

Bradley, Ian *Breaking the Mould? The Birth and Prospects of the Social Democratic Party* (Martin Robertson, London, 1982)

Brown, Neville *Nuclear War* (Pall Mall Press, London, 1964)

Bush, Vannevar *Modern Arms and Free Men* (Simon and Schuster, New York, 1949)

Chichester, Michael and Wilkinson, John *The Uncertain Ally: British Defence Policy, 1960-1990* (Gower, London, 1982)

Clark, Ronald *The Birth of the Bomb* (Horizon Press, New York, 1961)

Cline, Ray *Secrets, Spies and Scholars* (Acropolis Books, Washington DC, 1976)

de Gaulle, Charles *Memoirs of Hope* (Simon and Schuster, New York, 1971)

de Porte, Anton *Europe between the Superpowers* (Yale University Press, New Haven, 1979)

Eden, Anthony *Full Circle* (Cassels, London, 1960)

Eisenhower, Dwight D. *Waging Peace 1956-61* (Doubleday, New York, 1965)

Freedman, Lawrence *Britain and Nuclear Weapons* (Macmillan, London, 1981)

Gallois, Pierre *The Balance of Terror* (The Riverside Press, Cambridge, Mass., 1961)

Gowing, Margaret *Britain and Atomic Energy 1939-45* (St Martin's Press, New York, 1964) (Gowing I)

—— *Independence and Deterrence: Britain and Atomic Energy, 1945-52* (2 vols., St Martin's Press, New York, 1974) (*Policy Making* – Gowing II; *Policy Execution* – Gowing III)

Groom, A.J.R. *British Thinking about Nuclear Weapons* (Frances Pinter, London, 1974)

Grosser, Alfred *The Western Alliance* (Vintage Books, New York, 1982)

Groves, Leslie R. *Now It Can Be Told: The Story of the Manhattan Project* (Harper and Row, New York, 1962)

Hastings, Max and Jenkins, Simon *The Battle for the Falklands* (Michael Joseph, London, 1982)

Hewlett, Richard G. and Anderson, Oscar E. *A History of the United States Atomic Energy Commission*, vol. I, *The New World 1939-46* (Pennsylvania State University Press, University Park, 1962)

—— and Duncan, Francis *A History of the United States Atomic Energy Commission*, vol. II, *Atomic Shield 1947-52* (Pennsylvania State University Press, University Park, 1969)

Howard, Michael *The Continental Commitment* (Temple Smith, London, 1972)

Kaufman, William W. *The McNamara Strategy* (Harper and Row, New York, 1969)

Kelleher, Catherine M. *Germany and the Politics of Nuclear Weapons* (Columbia University Press, New York, 1975)

Kissinger, Henry A. *White House Years* (Little, Brown, Boston, 1979)

—— *Years of Upheaval* (Little, Brown, Boston, 1982)

Kohl, Wilfred *French Nuclear Diplomacy* (Princeton University Press, Princeton, 1971)

Leifer, M. (ed.) *Constraints and Adjustments in British Foreign Policy* (Allen and Unwin, London, 1972)

Lerner, Daniel and Aron, Raymond *France Defeats EDC* (Praeger, New York, 1957)

Lilienthal, David E. *Journals*, vol. II, *The Atomic Energy Years 1945-1950* (Harper and Row, New York, 1964)

MacDonald, Ian (ed.) *Anglo-American Relations* (St Martin's Press, New York, 1974)

Macmillan, Harold *Riding the Storm 1956-9* (Harper and Row, New York, 1971)

—— *Pointing the Way, 1959-61* (Harper and Row, New York, 1972)

—— *At the End of the Day* (Harper and Row, New York, 1973)

McNamara, Robert S. *The Essence of Strategy* (Harper and Row, New York, 1968)

Mosely, Leonard *Dulles* (Dial Press, New York, 1978)

Moss, Norman *Men Who Play God* (Victor Gollancz, London, 1968)
Murray, Thomas E. *Nuclear Policy for War and Peace* (World Publishing, Cleveland, 1960)
Neustadt, Richard *Alliance Politics* (Columbia University Press, New York, 1970)
Newhouse, John *De Gaulle and the Anglo-Saxons* (Viking Press, New York, 1970)
Olive, M.M. and Porro, J.D. (eds.) *Nuclear Weapons in Europe* (Lexington Books, Lexington, Mass., 1983)
Pierre, Andrew *Nuclear Politics: The British Experience with an Independent Strategic Force* (Oxford University Press, London, 1972)
Reuhl, Lothar *Le Politique Militaire de la Vème République* (Presses de la Fondation Nationale des Sciences Politiques, Paris, 1976)
Scheinman, Laurence *Atomic Energy Policy in France under the Fourth Republic* (Princeton University Press, Princeton, 1965)
Schlesinger, Arthur M., Jr. *A Thousand Days* (Houghton Mifflin, Boston, 1965)
Slessor, Marshall of the Royal Air Force, Sir John *What Price Co-existence?* (Praeger, New York, 1961)
Snyder, William P. *The Politics of British Defense Policy, 1945–1962* (Ohio State University Press, Columbus, 1964)
Truman, Harry S. *Years of Trial and Hope* (Signet Books, New York, 1956)

Articles

Baden, William B. 'Nuclear Weapons Sharing and the "German Problem" ', *Foreign Affairs*, vol. 44, no. 4 (July 1966), pp. 693–700
Bowie, Robert R. 'Tensions within the Alliance', *Foreign Affairs*, vol. 42, no. 1 (October 1963), pp. 49–69
Carter, M.W. and Moghissi, A.A. 'Three Decades of Nuclear Testing', *Health Physics*, no. 33 (July 1971), pp. 60–71
Chichester, Michael 'Britain and Nato: The Case for Revision', *The World Today* (December 1982), pp. 474–81
Dawson, Raymond and Rosecrance, Richard 'Theory and Reality in the Anglo–American Alliance', *World Politics*, vol. 19 (October 1966), pp. 21–5
Freedman, Lawrence 'The Dilemma of Theater Nuclear Arms Control', *Survival*, vol. 23 (January/February 1981), pp. 2–10.
—— 'British Defence Policy after the Falklands', *The World Today*

(September 1982), pp. 330-9

—— 'The War of the Falkland Islands', *Foreign Affairs*, vol. 61, no. 1 (Fall 1982), pp. 196-210

Goldberg, Alfred 'The Atomic Origins of the British Nuclear Deterrent', *International Affairs*, vol. 40, no. 3 (July 1964), pp. 409-29

—— 'The Military Origins of the British Nuclear Deterrent', *International Affairs*, vol. 40, no. 4 (October 1964), pp. 600-18

Gott, Richard 'The Evolution of the Independent British Deterrent', *International Affairs*, vol. 39, no. 2 (April 1964), pp. 238-52

Harlech, Lord 'Suez SNAFU, Skybolt SABO', *Foreign Policy*, vol. 1, no. 1 (Spring 1971), pp. 39-49

Hartley, Anthony, 'The British Bomb', *Survival*, vol. 6 (July/August 1964), pp. 170-81

Hoag, Malcolm W. 'Nuclear Policy and French Intransigence', *Foreign Affairs*, vol. 41, no. 2 (January 1963), pp. 286-98

Kissinger, Henry A. 'Problems of European Defense', *Foreign Affairs*, vol. 40, no. 4 (July 1962), pp. 515-41

—— 'Strains on the Alliance', *Foreign Affairs*, vol. 41, no. 2 (January 1963), pp. 261-85

—— 'Coalition Diplomacy', *Foreign Affairs*, vol. 42, no. 4 (July 1964), pp. 525-44

Martin, Lawrence W. 'The Market for Strategic Ideas in Britain: The "Sandys Era" ', *American Political Science Review*, vol. 61, no. 1 (Spring 1962), pp. 23-41

Schmidt, Helmut 'The 1977 Alastair Buchan Memorial Lecture', *Survival*, no. 20 (January/February 1978), pp. 2-10

Sherfield, Lord 'Britain's Nuclear Story, 1945-52', *The Round Table*, no. 258 (April 1975), pp. 193-204

Simpson, John 'The Polaris Executive: A Case Study of a Unified Hierarchy', *Public Administration*, vol. 48 (Winter 1970), pp. 372-85

Stern, Fritz 'Germany in a Semi-Gaullist Europe', *Foreign Affairs*, vol. 58, no. 4 (Spring 1980), pp. 867-86

Turner, Stansfield and Thibault, George 'Preparing for the Unexpected', *Foreign Affairs*, vol. 61, no. 1 (Fall 1982), pp. 122-35

Wohlstetter, Albert 'The Delicate Balance of Terror', *Foreign Affairs*, vol. 37, no. 2 (January 1959), pp. 211-34

—— 'Nuclear Sharing', *Foreign Affairs*, vol. 39, no. 3 (April 1961), pp. 355-87

Wood, Derek 'Reshaping the Royal Air Force', *International Defense Review*, no. 3 (1982), pp. 311-16

Woods, John E. 'The Royal Navy since World War II', *Proceedings* (March 1982), pp. 83-8

Yost, David S. 'The French Defense Debate', *Survival*, vol. 23 (January/February 1981), pp. 19-29

Monographs

Beaton, Leonard *Would Labour Give Up The Bomb?* (Daily Telegraph, London, 1964)

Buchan Alastair *The Multilateral Force: An Historical Perspective*, Adelphi Paper no. 13 (Institute for Strategic Studies, London, 1964)

David, Lynne *Limited Nuclear Options: Deterrence and the New American Doctrine*, Adelphi Paper no. 121 (International Institute for Strategic Studies, London, 1975)

Greenwood, David *Reshaping Britain's Defences*, Aberdeen Studies in Defence Economics (ASIDES) no. 19 (Aberdeen University, Aberdeen, 1981)

Kemp, Geoffrey *Nuclear Forces for Medium Powers*, Adelphi Papers nos. 106 and 107 (International Institute for Strategic Studies, London, 1974)

Martin, Laurence *British Defence Policy: The Long Recessional*, Adelphi Paper no. 61 (International Institute of Strategic Studies, London, 1969)

Smart, Ian *The Future Conditional: The Prospects for Anglo-French Nuclear Cooperation*, Adelphi Paper no. 78 (International Institute for Strategic Studies, London, 1971)

—— *The Future of the British Nuclear Deterrent: Technical, Economic and Strategic Issues* (Royal Institute for International Affairs, London, 1977)

Government Publications

Cmd. 9388 *The Supply of Military Aircraft* (HMSO, London, 1955)

Cmd. 9391 *Statement on Defence: 1955* (HMSO, London, 1955)

Cmnd. 124 *Defence: Outline of Future Policy: 1957* (HMSO, London, 1957)

Cmnd. 363 *Report on Defence: Britain's Contributions to Peace and Security, 1958* (HMSO, London, 1958)

Cmnd. 537 *Agreement between the Government of the United Kingdom of Great Britain and Northern Ireland and the Government of the United States of America for Co-operation on the Uses of Atomic Energy for Mutual Defence Purposes of July 3, 1958* (HMSO, London, 1958)

Cmnd. 859 *Amendment to the Agreement between the Government of the United Kingdom of Great Britain and Northern Ireland and the Government of the United States of America for Co-operation on the Uses of Atomic Energy for Mutual Defence of July 3, 1958* (HMSO, London, 1959)

Cmnd 1963 *Statement on Defence: 1963* (HMSO, London, 1963)

Cmnd. 2270 *Statement on Defence: 1964* (HMSO, London, 1964)

Cmnd. 4119 *Amendment to the Agreement for Co-operation on the Uses of Atomic Energy for Mutual Defence Purposes of 3 July 1958* (HMSO, London, 1969)

Cmnd. 4383 *Amendment to the Agreement for Co-operation on the Uses of Atomic Energy for Mutual Defence Purposes of 3 July 1958* (HMSO, London, 1970)

Cmnd. 8212-I *Statement on the Defence Estimates 1981* (HMSO, London, 1981)

Cmnd. 8288 *The United Kingdom Defence Programme: The Way Forward* (HMSO, London, 1981)

Cmnd. 8517 *The British Strategic Nuclear Force* (HMSO, London, 1982)

Cmnd. 8529-I *Statement on the Defence Estimates 1982* (HMSO, London, 1982)

House of Commons, Twelfth Report from the Expenditure Committee, Session 1972-3 *United Kingdom Nuclear Weapons Programme* (HMSO, London, 1973)

House of Commons, Sixth Report from the Expenditure Committee, Session 1978-9 *The Future of the United Kingdom's Nuclear Weapons Policy* (HMSO, London, 1979)

House of Commons, Fourth Report from the Defence Committee, Session 1980-1 *Strategic Nuclear Weapons Policy* (HMSO, London, 1981)

Ministry of Defence *The Future United Kingdom Strategic Nuclear Deterrent Force*, Defence Open Government Document 80/23 (HMSO, London, 1980)

Ministry of Defence *The United Kingdom Trident Programme*, Defence Open Government Document 82/1 (HMSO, London, 1982)

US Congress *Report of the Joint Committee on Atomic Energy*, HR 2299, 85th Cong., 1st Sess., 1958

INDEX